In Forsaken Hands

In Forsaken Hands

How Theory Empowers Literacy Learners

La Vergne Rosow

HEINEMANN
Portsmouth, NH

Heinemann
A division of Reed Elsevier Inc.
361 Hanover Street
Portsmouth, NH 03801-3912
Offices and agents throughout the world

Every effort has been made to contact the copyright holders for permission to reprint borrowed material where necessary. We regret any oversights that may have occurred and would be happy to rectify them in future printings of this work.

The author and publisher would like to thank those who generously granted permission to reprint or adapt borrowed material:

The California Adult Learner Progress Evaluation Process (CALPEP) is reprinted with permission of the California State Library, Sacramento, California.

"How Schools Perpetuate Illiteracy" by La Vergne Rosow from *Educational Leadership*, September 1991, 49(1). Reprinted with permission of the Association for Supervision and Curriculum Development.

"Adult Illiterates Offer Unexpected Cues into the Reading Process" by La Vergne Rosow from *Journal of Reading*, November 1988, pp. 120–24. Reprinted with permission of the International Reading Association.

"Literacy Vignette: The Story of Irma" by La Vergne Rosow from *The Reading Teacher*, March 1992, 45(7): 525. Reprinted with permission of the International Reading Association.

"Arthur: A Tale of Disempowerment" by La Vergne Rosow from *Phi Delta Kappan*, November 1989, 71(3): 120–24. Reprinted with permission of the *Phi Delta Kappan*.

"How Long Does It Take, Harry?" by La Vergne Rosow from *Phi Delta Kappan*, October 1992, 74(2): 168–71. Reprinted with permission of the *Phi Delta Kappan*.

Library of Congress Cataloging-in-Publication Data

Rosow, La Vergne.
   In forsaken hands : how theory empowers literacy learners / La
Vergne Rosow.
     p. cm.
   Includes bibliographical references and index.
   ISBN 0-435-08116-0 (acid-free paper)
   1. Literacy—United States. 2. Educational anthropology—United
States. 3. Functional literacy—United States. 4. Literacy—Social
aspects—United States. 5. Literacy programs—United States.
I. Title.
LC151.R67 1995
302.2'244—dc20   94-43727
                                           CIP

Editor: Cheryl Kimball
Copy Editor: Alan Huisman
Production: Melissa L. Inglis
Cover design: Joyce Weston
Cover illustration by Guy Lawrence

Printed in the United States of America on acid-free paper
99 98 97 96 95   VB 1 2 3 4 5 6 7 8 9

My dear Aunt Harriet Weckel

Robert S. Rosow

Freida Rosow

L. Paul Rosow II

To them I dedicate this book

Contents

Many Thanks

To my editors, Dawn Boyer, for all her cheerful encouragement, and Alan Huisman, for attention to detail and continuity; Ruth Colvin, my literacy godmother; Robert Rosow, for reducing apparent hurdles to figments of the imagination; Freida Rosow, for listening; my dear Aunt Harriet, for keeping faith; my son Paul, for involved dialogues and patient proofreading; Jim Fortune for getting me out of a computer quagmire; Neville Robertson, for sending me much needed information sometimes years before I knew I needed it; Joyce Ragsdale and Gayle Miller, for open doors and encouraging words; Bill Boaz, who taught me how to value every single student's efforts; Clare DiFelice, who agreed to support my experimentation first and digest the details later; Mike Garrett, who had a dream of a better life for ghetto dwellers; Steve Krashen, who pushed me to keep doing what had to be done; David Eskey, who helped me stay focused on the work at hand; Linda Light and Sue Berman, whose energies started a literacy movement that has served thousands of adult learners; Al Bennett, for statesmanship that encourages all levels of literacy development to bloom; Gary Strong, whose vision fostered the California Literacy Campaign and who granted permission to reproduce the early version of the alternative assessment CALPEP form; the thousands of adult learners and their volunteer tutors, whose forward thinking netted the CALPEP; Kenneth Fulk, who taught me to understand fairs as an educational resource; Al Koppenhaver, for making the connection between research and our survival on the planet; Paulo Freire, for delivering the word and the world to America—and then delivering it again; Gary Rhodes and Shalee Cunningham, for reaching back and pulling me up; Robert Mauller, for giving praise when it was needed most;

Mary Fox, Edith Schwartz, Fran Powell, Paul Brent, and Mackie Faye Hill, for being there in mind and spirit . . . for decades; Nannette Levy, for enthusiastic inquiry; Pauline Gough and Janet Binkley, for offering ideas and casting me safety nets; Edmund B. Levy, Jr., for Shakespeare . . . in process . . . early on; Karen Klammer, for understanding and making space for the nontraditional; Marta Thomas and Patty Biggerstaff, for providing countless contacts; Awatef Siam, Judy Mzinyatti, and Seraj Muhammed, for helping me compare literacy in America with literacy elsewhere; all of my adult learner/research partners, who bared their souls to make literacy more probable for all; Dick Evans and T. R. Fehrenbach for wise and thoughtful counsel; the editors of the journals who have granted me permission to use portions of previously published articles—to all of the above I extend my gratitude.

And for sharing ideas, opening doors, reviewing manuscripts, providing insights, and offering invaluable colleaguial and spiritual support, I must acknowledge Linda Weber, Terry Craig, Leo Richards, William Rideout, Jr., Nelly Stromquist, Ed Finegan, Linda Organ, Audrey Schwartz, Steve Hackbarth, Milt Goldman, Mabel Knudsen, Ann Colburn, Judy Grayson, Lowell Rose, Trudy Le Clair, Brian Hoyt, Judy Gappa, Kathy Tozzalina, Ramon Daniel, Lee Perry, Dan Towler, Carlton Blanton, George Spindler, Richard Ullrich, Mary Ahlman, Betty Harrington, Nancy Boyer, David Hudson, Rendell Drew, Greg Conner, Joni Ward, Pam Perkins, Betty Meltzer, Ann Pell, Virginia Howell, Anita Rowley, Vivian Zatto, Michael Zatto, Rocco Costanzo, Roy Skeirik, Eva Lopez, Leonard Lopez, Ruthie Jennings, Lee and Reba Stiles, Margot Burke, Jo Ann Roberts, Lee Hackney, George Turlis, Irene Stater, Ellen Bancroft, David Heinicke, Ann Tangpanit, Mimi Collins, Jerry Edwards, S'Ann Freeman, Mary Ann Ponder, Mary Miller, Cathay Reta, John Walter, Wanda Burzycki, and Anne Meek.

And to all the unnamed Kappans, literacy volunteers, editors, literacy coordinators who traded workshops, teachers who opened their classrooms, administrators who just said yes, unmet colleagues who wrote thoughtful and provocative letters of response to my articles, and to my community college and university students and colleagues who gave careful criticism to my methods and materials, I extend my deep appreciation.

La Vergne Rosow

Introduction

For anyone able to read this book, the notion of illiteracy—widespread and on the rise—in this highly literate society may seem the figment of a politically motivated imagination. I know in my case, even after witnessing blatant evidence of functional illiteracy, I didn't have a clue about the implications of such a deficit in terms of an individual's quality of life. Certainly we can hypothesize that a person who can't fill out a job application will have difficulty finding work. Surely we will all admit that kids who can't read in school will do poorly and, as a result, view themselves less mentally able than good readers. It follows, too, that kids who don't learn to read during their school years will probably enter the adult world as nonreaders. And nonreaders are likewise nonwriters. All of this might seem common sense until we are confronted with the enormity of the problem. At that point:

- We may look for machines that will fix the problem. (Computer programs are big business these days.)
- We may look for biological reasons why the problem can never be addressed. (Many labels have been devised to satisfy the learner in this regard.)
- Or we may trudge out, determined to do what we can to put a dent in this wall that divides the fortunate from the disadvantaged.

I chose the last alternative and, with many years of formal teaching under my belt, enrolled as a tutor for Literacy Volunteers of America. Lacking a personal definition of literacy, however, I was ill prepared to understand exactly what I was supposed to do. Still, the initial eighteen-hour training program had given me an awesome toteful of methods, and the freedom to do whatever worked allowed me a chance to experience some extraordinary successes. Yet I needed to understand why things were working and why people who were able to learn as adults had not been able to do so as children. That need led me back to school, where my continued literacy volunteer work and focused research gave me:

- A definition of literacy that connects text with inquiry: **Literacy is the use of text as a jumping-off point for thought.** For the literate person, form follows substance naturally. Too, literacy, the kind that yields visions from text, transfers easily from the global situation to the specific—writing a love note, for example, can make the task of filling out a marriage license application form logical and uncomplicated. *But the reverse is not true.* That is why people only trained to fill out one kind of form will likely remain unable to document ideas. Indeed, they may not even be able to fill out other kinds of forms.
- An early childhood profile of the adult illiterate (see pages 15–16).
- The concept of the disempowering significant other (DSO) (see the story of Arthur).
- The notion of placing theory directly into the hands of the learner, hands forsaken by the traditional system. My early literacy research; my dissertation case studies; my subsequent English as a Second Language (ESL) and literacy projects with community college students, gangs, grass-roots groups; and the whole language–based library literacy program I'm currently developing have given me an opportunity to experiment with the notion of giving theory to the learner, who, in turn, participates in his or her lesson design—from an informed, professional position.

This book tells, in detail, exactly how I delivered theory to a number of learners. The fact that each case is different from the others illustrates why a single program or method cannot be imposed on every student . . . not if we demand success for *every* student. Individual learners must be taught individually. And it is critical to note that the *life* of the learner and the *literacy* of the learner are inseparable. Just as the *whole* environment plays out in the classroom, so the *whole* life of each adult mandates who reads and writes and how much. Even so, I've discovered common threads. Watch for multiple illustrations of:

- The isolation factor.
- The missing-joy factor.
- The zero-privacy factor.
- The fugitive phenomenon.
- The chaos phenomenon.

This book addresses anyone involved in the study or teaching of reading and writing for critical thinking:

- To the **literacy volunteer**, I suggest reading it aloud to your adult learner, perhaps starting with the teaching papers in the appendix. Then talk about them.
- To the **teacher educator** seeking a good way of introducing the reading and writing development of a particular age group, I suggest perusing the cases and beginning with one that seems to match your needs.
- To the **student teacher** just getting acquainted with theory and to the **grass-roots designer**, I simply say, Begin at the beginning . . . and apply Post-Its as needed.
- But if you are simply **seeking more insights into the issue of illiteracy and ways to address it**, I think flipping to a chapter that looks interesting and then working backward or forward from there would be a very reasonable approach. And if in the process you get ideas that you want to share with me, I invite you to write them down and when you are ready send them to me . . . to become my literacy partner.

This book documents many journeys I've made while searching for the right answers. The truth, I've discovered, is a mobile thing that must be sought in process and again and again. Each time I've found it, it's been brand new.

One

Literacy Everywhere, But Not for All

First Light

In a huge tent, briefly stationed in the parking lot of a Southern California race course, I set up one of the most entertaining art projects of my life. In that same location, I was shocked into facing the reality of mainstream illiteracy in America. One might expect to stumble into a few "reluctant readers" in any public place; or one might imagine a problem that was in reality a matter of forgotten glasses or a headache. But the sample size of this accidental pilot study was about five thousand. My assignment had been to offer art exhibits and opportunities for artistic expression for those passing through on their way to the race track. Exhibition, expression, and education were mandates to be incorporated into all departments of this small-scale fair. The art department was included to fulfill both legal and creative requirements. I'd been called in because over a number of years I'd revamped our county fair art department from a copybook art show into an active, world-class event. Still, this new race track art project had parameters that prevented me from simply replicating the traditional show. There were two major differences. First, I didn't need to fund-raise for supplies; the racetrack would provide all the money I could spend. Secondly, there was to be *no security*, not from the elements, not from the fans. So the resulting design was one that allowed people of all ages to enter the tent, look at exhibited art, select art supplies, and then sit at long tables to make something that would, in turn, be placed on exhibit. After the races, each artist was to retrieve his or her work. The horse races were the main event; no one expected the tent to attract more than a handful of people. Participants would most likely be the children and spouses of regular track fans. Projected participation was ten to fifteen people a day. The projections were wrong. After the first few days, the tent bulged with hundreds of people, parents and children, together and independently, as the race fans sat down to make art and as busloads of school children filed in to participate in the windfall cultural event. The fair board wanted me to account for the extra supply dollars and, as is standard at fairs, I was also supposed to account for who participated. That seemed easy enough—at first.

When I set up a notebook to register participants, however, it became startlingly clear that a large percentage of the participants were unable to write down their names, much less their addresses. They were not just the children. They were also adults—thousands of them. Some were certainly at the track to spend their welfare checks. But others were well dressed . . . and well manicured. And it was not a matter of wanting to hide the fact that they had been to the races: we weren't asking for verification, so any name or address would have done. It was simply that in Southern California in the early 1980s, many people had difficulty writing down elementary information. I had to go back to the board to get funds to hire people to assist with registration. Then I had another revelation.

Because of the number of people in the tent, artist anonymity was a hazard to maintaining order. Therefore, in addition to asking everyone to sign in, we hung name tags on everyone, so we could call out a name rather than have to yell, "Hey, you, come get the glue" . . . or "don't squirt the glue" . . . or "don't drink the glue" . . . well, you get the idea. The electricity level in the tent *every day* was like any classroom on a rainy Friday afternoon before a big holiday. The name tags, which required only a first name or a nickname, were to be filled out by the artists. Again, many people needed help. Many school-aged children had no idea how to spell their own first names. They could neither write it down nor spell it out for my assistants. (Before continuing, I do want to acknowledge that many American public schools are doing an amazing job considering the lack of financial support, the enormous and still-growing class sizes, and the fact that many students once excluded from the testable system are now part of the standard classroom. What I am reporting here are simply the facts as I encountered them.) These facts clearly demonstrate that illiteracy is a widespread problem not being sufficiently addressed at the primary or secondary levels.

Post-Vietnam War immigration had not yet begun to make an impact on this particular social institution. By and large, the race fans had, in compliance with the law, attended American public schools where reading and writing were part of the elementary curriculum. So why had so many of these law-abiding citizens failed to learn what we have always called "the basics"? All of the people mentioned here were functioning successfully and independently in society. They had money to spend, knew where to go for entertainment, had solved the everpresent problem of transportation, and were able to interpret the signs of a new activity in the parking lot. This was not a formally protected group. This was *us*.

Though I'd been a schoolteacher, had worked in banks, insurance companies, medical products manufacturing firms, and real estate—all jobs that exposed me to literacy-related errors, errors that in retrospect I realize have increased dramatically over the years—it wasn't until the track experience that I saw, full blown, the widespread implications of that word *illiteracy*. And it would be much later still before I would begin to understand the mastery with which these everyday folks conceal their deficiencies, hiding the truth from families, friends, employers, and others who might judge them stupid, shun them, or fire them.

Day in and day out, they prove themselves intelligent enough to survive in highly competitive surroundings. By their

3

wits they demonstrate abilities to compensate that rival pioneers' creative skills. Yet they live in a world where cover-ups are an in-process requirement. So, though the marginal users of text come from all economic levels and fit into the full range of occupational categories, the illiterate lifestyle as it exists in today's literate world carries behaviors and attitudinal markers as distinctive as those of any cultural or religious group. But wouldn't it be easier, you might ask, for these folks to use their brains to learn to read? Well, you see, it isn't simply a matter of cognition.

Because literacy is initially a social phenomenon, practitioners of literacy must sense they have a social right to do so. Yet the poor reader or writer is excluded from what Frank Smith terms the literacy club.[1] Not one illiterate adult feels *invited* to participate in the reading and writing that is common to members of the club.

Beyond that, however, if an adult has been a nonreader for a lifetime, an invitation alone may not be enough to give him or her membership in the literacy club. That adult must be willing and able to commit to emotional change that is experienced in a hundred little ways each day. It means giving up part of one's self—a delicate matter, indeed. Supposing I aspire to function successfully and smoothly in a literacy club, the school may have a difficult time giving me insights into the sought club without insulting me for the existing memberships that make me who I am. The issues of introductions, greetings, thank-yous, memos, and the like are so ingrained in each of us that at some level we just know the right thing to do and when to do it; at another level, we feel . . . out of step. Even when we have memorized the protocols, there can be a giant gap between doing and having the right to do.

From the poor reader's or writer's perspective, for example, the gap between knowing how to address an envelope and taking the liberty of putting one's own name in the corner where only important names have gone before can be as difficult as signing a death certificate. For a death certificate it is, on a membership of long standing. It may not be time. It may never be time. Disabling though my failure to "do" envelopes may be, that failure and I have survived many treks together; we sense a comfortable familiarity in our misery. We are isolated together. We know what to expect even when it is awful; we know what we know. To set that association aside would be to turn a back on a long-established comrade. The very thought of change puts a lump in the throat and a weight in the heart. It's risky out there!

As with many social groups, membership in the illiteracy club runs in families for generations. The features are not genetic, however; the behaviors are carefully taught. How does one "teach" illiteracy? To answer that, one might begin by looking at the opposite question. How does literacy begin? Or even, what is literacy?

Serendipity Stops By

Between teaching, fair projects, commercial artwork, and attempts at "real" art, I renovated rental property and managed about a hundred homes in Orange County. One evening, as I waited for tenants to stop by my office to pay the rent, I called the newspaper to place an ad. I'd done this many times before and knew what worked. But on this particular evening, I got an operator who was determined to give me assistance. As it turned out, that operator changed my life.

After going through the preliminary rituals of name and account number, I told the woman at the *Register* what typeface I wanted and how the heading should run. Then I began reading her my copy, carefully written to get the maximum number of words per line. But she wasn't content. Repeatedly she stopped me to explain how I could shorten a word or abbreviate an entire phrase by using one of the standard acronyms she'd mastered. Each time she tried to help, I explained slightly more elaborately that I already knew what I wanted. Still, she was determined to save me money. But my purpose in running the house-for-rent ad was to rent the house as quickly as possible, not to save money on a few lines of type. Finally, I said something to the effect of people having a hard enough time reading the ads when they're fully written out without my slowing them down by abbreviating. The race track experience had continued to weigh heavily on my mind, but I'd had no idea how to address it in concrete terms.

Suddenly I heard this pushy operator saying, "Well, if you're as concerned about the problem as you say you are, you'll do what I'm doing tonight." I don't think she gave me a chance to ask exactly what it was she was doing on a Monday night in traditional, straight-laced Orange County before she informed me that she was going to an orientation meeting for Literacy Volunteers of America (LVA). The timing happened to be right; I was between volunteer commitments and a rest would have been welcome, but now this strange and unsolicited option was presenting itself. I took the information down, but because the last tenant was late, I didn't go that night or even that week. When I finally did follow up, it was months later, and I discovered there was a new program starting at a library near my home. I never met that *Register* operator but hope she can feel that she made a powerful sale that evening.

During part of the time I was running the rental business, I was also working as a high school Community Resources Coordinator. A reading teacher with whom I'd written a grant application invited me to go to the University of California, Irvine to hear a speaker. She was a little unsure what to expect and didn't really know why she was going herself, but it was very clear to her that I should go with her to hear Paulo Freire speak. We arrived at a packed house, so my colleague found the only seat in the back and I went to the front to sit in the aisle at the feet of the man from Brazil who would change the way I thought about reading and language. His sandaled feet exposed toes that had clearly been tortured. It would be much later before I realized that the torture had been because of his

literacy efforts in Brazil and later still before I could comprehend why. It is so obvious now. **Literacy is power.**

- *"Power is having the strength and ability to design questions from conventional givens and the courage to let the answers change over time."*[2]
- *Power is knowing you have both the right and the responsibility to question the unquestionable.*

The illiterate peasants, like powerless masses all over the world, were easy to oppress because they had no way of communicating their condition. For an educated, literate man to go into the fields to teach reading and writing to people who had grown up knowing they were unable to think in literate terms was an act of treason against the ruling class. The peasants knew they needed their rulers to make decisions and negotiate land contracts because these acts required a special gift inherited, perhaps, by divine right. Suddenly to start giving that gift to anyone who happened by was irresponsibly to remove the need and purpose of the ruling elite. Over time it became very easy for me to understand why Paulo Freire, having figured out a way to transfer power to the oppressed and openly acted on it, had ultimately been exiled from his homeland. He was undeniably guilty of setting the stage for social revolution.

In the UCI lecture hall where the crowd hardly stirred, Freire talked for long periods in obtuse terms, but the bits that I was able to grasp kept me rapt. He spoke of farmers who needed to think critically. He described learning situations that disempowered the learners. He explained the importance of having the right words so that one could evaluate the world, suggesting that *the world* depended on *the word* to make it real to the thinker. After emphatically stating that children and farmers needed the language of literate people, he complained that English was the most difficult language he'd ever tried to learn and that it lacked some of the words his native Portuguese provided for truly meaningful expression. I got the distinct

impression that this man believed that native users of Portuguese were born into a much richer and bigger world than the rest of us, simply because their language allowed them to think about it analytically and spiritually—thinking that was beyond the comprehension of others. There would be a question from the audience and then a monologue, interrupted only by his requests for the translation of a Portuguese word. Two, three, sometimes four people would offer possibilities. He would select one—sometimes a very useful one, sometimes one that barely got by—and then he'd continue as though in a trance. After three short hours of this, the woman who had driven me to this place of awe was ready to leave. But that wasn't the last I'd see of this great teacher.

The new LVA affiliate, when I got there, was being organized by Linda Light and Sue Berman, both of whom had gotten involved because the timing was right for them, as it finally was for me. As in many volunteer organizations, members of LVA nudged great ideas around until somebody decided to go ahead. Trios are very often two people figuring out what the third should do. We were no different. In my absence one day, Linda and Sue decided I should attend a workshop given by a literacy person who would only be in the area a short while. Having no idea I'd had an earlier encounter with him, Linda and Sue conspired to have me represent us in the company of the great Paulo Freire. I signed up for his weeklong workshop at UCI.

Followers of his had come from all over the United States and many other places around the globe. Most memorable were a rough-and-tumble-looking American who worked as a house painter in the States to fund his volunteer literacy efforts in Belize and a beautiful young East Indian woman in white who'd come to California because Paulo was here. Henry Giroux, another name I had yet to learn, was from the East Coast. There was also a priest from Central America who I was told had gotten into political trouble for his ideas about literacy. At that time I couldn't grasp why. I'd read none of Paulo's work and had no idea just how long his influence had been

modifying thinking about how people learn to read. But during that week I met with painters, artists, academics, and philosophers, all of whom made casual references to things Paulo had written. I bought what I could find at the UCI bookstore and began struggling through *the* literature by night and taking part in exhausting sessions by day. It was rather like forcing myself through a series of cult rituals.

Slowly, through lectures, group work, mural making, shadow study, message writing, storytelling, and dialogues, unconnected people whose only common interests were either Paulo or literacy—could the two be separated?—began to experience the reality that everything is connected. Literacy is art is storytelling is language is humanity. . . . It was just by chance that I had met illiteracy head-on at the track, had my consciousness raised so I was ready to hear that advertisement page operator's suggestion. It was just by chance that she knew what I needed to know and that none of my tenants had interrupted us. It was strange chance again that my colleague from the high school decided to take me to hear Paulo when she hardly understood why either of us should go. And chance again that Linda and Sue decided La Vergne should spend a week of her summer at UCI. I believe that had any of this perfect order been otherwise, the outcomes might have been too. As it stood, by the time I entered the University of Southern California's doctoral program that fall, I was a very different person from the one who'd been admitted the spring before. Ever since I learned the word, I've been seeing *serendipity*.

The Cradle's First Lesson

From my first contact, I was very active in Literacy Volunteers of America's (LVA) adult tutoring programs for both basic reading and writing and English as a Second Language. Having moved through the ranks from tutor to tutor trainer, I had enjoyed more than my share of successes. My first student had been a college graduate who needed help learning to read well enough to pass the California Basic Education Skills Test

(CBEST) reading comprehension section, so he could accept a job of high school coach and English teacher. His mom and later on his girlfriend had always provided the papers he needed to write and his coaches had helped him take exams orally. It wasn't until he was faced with the CBEST that he could no longer compensate by using his available human resources. Stopped at the door of a coveted coaching job, he decided to request help formally. Sue Berman paired us up. Within three months, he'd brought me a huge bouquet of flowers and announced he'd passed the CBEST. That was one of several impressive stories attributed to either my gift or my methods, but I had little idea of why things were working or when they might stop.

The LVA training gives the volunteer eighteen hours of initial formal education that includes a smorgasbord of methods much like those offered in many university teacher education programs. In addition, informal mentors and a broad battery of other workshops are available after the tutor has begun to work with a student. After the eighteen-hour program, matched one-on-one, the tutor and tutee figure out what works and what doesn't. The notion that each student has unique needs frees the pair from following rigid programs designed by someone who has no idea who the student is. And it allows methods that feel comfortable to the student to take precedence over something from a generic curriculum. Inherent in the program design is a basic trust in the ability of two adults to solve problems in creative ways.[3]

Considering that the LVA reading/writing tutor is usually working with an adult who has been failed by years of exposure to professional educators in the formal system, each success— and there are many—is quite remarkable. And it raises a question: *If a person can learn to read at the age of fifty with the help of a volunteer tutor, couldn't that person have learned to read as a child in school?*

There was another gnawing question that I couldn't seem to voice clearly and found little collegial support for. LVA had two distinctly different programs for two groups of adults:

basic literacy and English as a Second Language. However, from neither tutor nor trainer perspective was I able to distinguish how the methods really discriminated between native and nonnative speakers. It was several years before I realized *there is no difference. It's all language arts. It's about using language to convey ideas from one thinker to another.* In both programs we started with the language base of the learner and the interests of the learner and moved toward communication from there. Both programs were about using language, spoken and written, for communicative purposes.

Yet, some ESL groups learned to read and write the new language more quickly than others. In fact, some of the nonnative students picked up written English skills quicker than some natives. From my nontheoretical basis of literacy volunteer, it just didn't make sense. And there was the additional puzzle that some of the "fast learners" came from places where the alphabet as we write it did not exist. Why were they able to write more easily than people who'd had exposure to our writing system all their lives? One frequently voiced opinion was that some groups of people are just more intelligent than others. That didn't jibe either, considering the extraordinary survival skills all of our students exhibited. But why did a former shopkeeper fleeing Iran learn to write in English more quickly than an escaping peasant from El Salvador or a farmhand from drought-ravaged West Texas? Why did Iranians I taught later have just as much trouble learning to write English as the farmhand had? We discussed such puzzles during LVA meetings, but having no theoretical guidelines, we had no defensible assumptions. Over time, I found the key to that ability not on the map but in the cradle.

By the fall of 1986, my literacy volunteer work had caused me to go back to school, where I was just becoming acquainted with emerging literacy theories. My teaching assistantship required I place student teachers in the field and then supervise their progress. I therefore spent a great deal of time in kindergarten through twelfth-grade classrooms and in community college and university classrooms as well. Some of the master

teachers I observed in the process made indelible impressions, tempering everything I thought I knew about learning and literacy. The experience made me realize that effective teaching has certain constants, regardless of grade level or content. I was getting a crash course in the realities of classroom life in three counties, Los Angeles, Orange, and San Diego. It was so stimulating that ever since I have made it my business to get into at least fifty classrooms a year, simply so I can know what *is*. (I must add that neither observations nor their benefits run one way. I, in turn, probably have at least as many observers in my literacy, ESL, and workplace classrooms. All of them are expected to be active participants. Everyone contributes. I learn as much from my observers as they do from me. Somehow the classroom dynamics reveal information that readings don't.) I have a strong need to keep understanding what happens when. . . .

I had entered my LVA experience with one master's degree in education—instructional media and photography—and had taught at the university and community college levels and in K–12 regular and special education classrooms and had worked extensively with the gifted. I was, by many measures, an experienced and appropriately degreed teacher. But through all my formal encounters and collegial contacts, there had been little to suggest to me what Paulo Freire had demonstrated during that week at UCI—that language *arts* are essential to literacy. It took several more years of digging for me to get at what I can now see as the theoretical core of literacy development.

I had not only learned to believe but could also convincingly argue the "truth" of many popular myths that actively impede the teacher's ability to teach and the student's ability to learn. Some of those myths include:

- Readers run in families because the ability is inherited.
- After the age of six or seven the brain just can't learn to read.
- Some people arrive at school ready to learn; others never get ready.

- If the home is not fit, there's not much a school can do for the child.
- One look at the record of James Baldwin, Richard Wright, or Richard Rodriguez proves that anyone who really wants to learn will find a way.
- You have to get the letters before you can get the sounds.
- You have to be able to sound things out before you can read.
- Slow learners (the ones who enter school not knowing how to read already) need more structure and discipline to learn to read than fast learners (the ones who came to school as readers).
- Adults learn differently than children do; their brains are different.
- Standing up and reading out loud is good for the poor reader.
- It's okay to put little kids into embarrassing classroom situations because in the first place, they won't remember it anyway, and in the second place, that will help prepare them for the real world.
- It's okay to put adults into embarrassing classroom situations because they're used to it in real life, so they expect it in school.
- Students should be encouraged to get everything perfect the first time because anything worth doing is worth doing well from the start—including reading and writing.
- Good writing means beautiful penmanship.

For all my myth gathering, I failed to see what was missing. It would be a very long time before I recognized the insidious implications of *not* knowing what was so good about reading a book. Nor did I see what it would mean *not* to be able to write a little book just for my own little boy. I now call that empty space in the lives of the marginal users of text the missing-joy factor. Joy, the joy of literacy, is everpresent in literate lives.

Consistently, studies of successful students show that

- Literate parents read to their preschoolers many hours each day and almost ritualistically at bedtime.

- Literate homes are chock-full of reading materials.
- Literate people leave notes for one another on refrigerators, coffee tables, and sometimes doorsills or walls.
- Use of pencils, papers, and books is a relatively unstructured thing that just about anyone in the literate house can be expected to try.

And schools with high numbers of good readers have

- Classrooms where teachers read stories to children several times a day.
- Walls that are covered with print (much of it child generated).
- Books that are within easy access of any would-be reader.

We can conclude that if being read to just for the fun of it and having good books around in case somebody needs one are not the main ingredients for learning to read, they are at least essential ingredients.

Before the elementary school can engage in theoretically sound practice, schools of education must model it. By the fall of 1987, I had whiled away countless hours listening to lectures about creative curriculum models, platitudes about test stress, and more lectures on the advantages of whole-to-parts over parts-to-whole reading lessons (even as the material presented came in small snippets!). The theoretical support for student-centered lessons and teaching that started at the learner's level or that built on the learner's background knowledge seemed to cry out for the teacher to find out who the student was. Yet, even in relatively small university classes, the teacher might learn the names of only half the students—the favored half? Such was the dichotomy between what was said and what was done. So, I "learned" the theoretical concepts without feeling them and I designed my pilot questionnaire for adult literacy students from a cognitive perspective, knowing what my outcomes should yield and why:

- I wanted to know what techniques had caused the new readers to succeed. (Thereby locating *the best methods*.)
- I wanted to know what people knew as readers that they hadn't known as nonreaders. (Identifying *the right content*.)
- I wanted a dollar value that I could place on LVA tutoring. (Justifying continued programming.)

Such information could be fed neatly into bar graphs and possibly result in a workbook for volunteers. The plan would have worked, too, if I'd just stuck with the questionnaire, maybe restricting the answer choices to three or five cognitively oriented multiple choices and perhaps hiring an impartial person to administer it for me, preferably one with no background knowledge in literacy. But, lacking funds and foresight, I administered the questionnaire myself using many open-ended questions and letting my tape recorder do the note taking. As a result I discovered a mushrooming set of data that wouldn't fit neatly into a bubble on a scantron form. Not knowing the term "affective domain," I called it "feelings" and related it to self-esteem. That was the only way I could package it. But packaged that way, there was an awesome 100 percent problem.

While grappling with the conflicts between my precious myths and my developing theoretical awareness, I attended a national literacy volunteers convention in New York where tutors and students from all over the country had gathered to discuss issues and acknowledge successes. During that time I began a series of interviews that established the early childhood profile of the adult illiterate.[4] When I returned to California, my ongoing interviews with students and tutors continued to support two staggering percentages:

- **One hundred percent of the adult poor readers or non-readers experienced child abuse — either profound neglect or physical violence or both — during the years when they should have been learning to read.**
- **One hundred percent of the adult poor readers or non-readers report no memory of being read to for pleasure**

either at home during the preschool years or in school during the early years.

Isn't that interesting? The literature suggests again and again that being read to is the first step toward loving books and learning to read.[5] And here we see that the person who was not read *to* as a child has no cause to pursue books as an adult. This is the missing-joy factor.

Further, the little boy whose mommy was holding him close, thus causing him to connect a loving voice, a safe place, and literacy in his mind for all time, loves books. While the little boy who was being beaten or locked away by his caretaker has made no bonds with books.

Literacy starts in the cradle. For the blessed it begins at home and is supported by bedtime stories and trips to the library for story hour. It is a birthright in a literate society, one that is passed on without question from parent to child. The specific language is unimportant. Children who love books love them all their lives, even when they move to a new land. Literacy transfers across languages. That is why the shopkeeper who loved his Persian folktales picked up Aesop's fables with delight, enthusiasm, and comprehension. It is also why the refugee who could not read in his native land continued to fail to understand the importance of text in America. Literacy is a value system that once set in motion cannot be changed. Far from being a sterile activity in which marks are decoded and sounds are barked, literacy is emotionally charged. As the shopkeeper touched a book, distant memories of wonderful stories and fantastic ideas recalled the babe in his mother's lap, saying, "Remember me? We met long ago in a happy time. We're old friends." Just marking a page or coming to the end of a good read may trigger forgotten sounds and smells that cause the eyes to blur and the heart to stir. But sometimes it doesn't happen that way. Sometimes it is up to the school to begin that first association that will lead to a love of print.

The Power of Truth

When I explained to one professor that my new readers had attributed a quagmire of feelings-related issues to their literacy development, I met a look of disbelief and the suggestion that the connections were spurious. How could literacy have anything to do with a woman's ability to grow long fingernails after a lifetime of biting? How could *literacy development* be related to a man's campaign to get *oral driving tests* in his state? How could learning to read cause a person to divorce? And how could I, as a would-be researcher, take all those unrelated leaps of the imagination and group them under self-esteem? This academic problem caused my work to be called garbage by a real authority, and there was nothing I could conjure that would cognitively defend what was on my tapes and in my conclusions. It felt as if I held a bagful of kittens that might either land in the river or grow up to catch field mice. But I needed help finding the formula to get them started.

That same semester I was taking my first language acquisition class from Stephen Krashen, a world-class researcher and theorist who practiced the theory he preached. His classes were huge and filled with a grand mix of international students, local teachers, and school administrators, many of whom themselves gave testimony to the frequency of the biased and humiliating educational sorting that had delayed their own progress by decades or had even rerouted their entire lives. Many had faced, failed under, and, until this class, forgotten tricky teachers toting terrible instructions designed more to entrap than inform. Interestingly, regardless of the country of origin, these educators by and large had not experienced school as a place of comfort and joy. So, how was it possible, one might rightfully ask, for *them* to convey comfort and joy to *their* students? Though you have to be nurtured in order to pass nurturing on, rarely would a teacher go to graduate school to learn how to look after her sheep. Nor would she expect a language acquisition theory class to teach such a skill. But for many that was the most valuable lesson language acquisition theory had to offer.

Krashen had begun the semester—in what I later realized was his traditional empowering style—by telling us that there were no deadlines, no tests, and that we could write on any subject we thought was important. If we were already involved in a paper of consequence, he was willing to help with that. And we could start turning papers in the next week or any time thereafter. "When's the other shoe going to drop?" whispered one high school principal dubiously. Further, Krashen assured us there was enough power in our classroom to change the world, that not one of us could have gotten where we sat without incredible aptitude. Everyone was expected to have something of importance to share sooner or later. That was his expectation, his presumption. It had nothing to do with knowing isolated trivia for a standardized exam. Therefore, in this elementary language acquisition class, bits of research were presented, modified, re-presented, and then polished as a result of collegial interaction. This very serious work was a game we played together; this game was the most critical work a scholar could undertake.

Though the class was officially attended by those interested in second language acquisition, many of his lectures dealt with literacy. I use the term "lecture" loosely. The organization of the class varied from meeting to meeting. He might, for example, begin chatting informally, engaging the early birds in discussions of their teaching, research, or even scheduling problems, allowing the latecomers to enter without blushing. On the other hand, he might enter the classroom after student dialogue had fired itself up and join in with an anecdote that had just happened at the copy shop down the street. Then he might mention that he was delivering a speech somewhere that weekend and wanted us to help him with any rough edges. During the speech—which became his lecture—he would make spontaneous references to the input he'd just gotten from his informal conversations with the early students, asking their confirmation of the powerful connections he was designing. Or his opening anecdote would reappear. On occasion there would be handouts, or references to things in our class notes. Or he might draw elaborate diagrams on the chalkboard, simplifying them before our eyes, based on feedback from the class *in process*—always *in process*. This class was a day-to-day demonstration of that term. After the lecture, he would open the floor to almost totally student-centered dialogues, much like the kinds I'd experienced with Freire some years before. (Indeed, Krashen had considerable familiarity with Freire's work.) After class, there were often long lines of students waiting to give individual input, to set up research presentation appointments, or to make an appointment for feedback on work in process. Need I point out that this man was showing us how to build a common base of background knowledge so we would be able to comprehend what was coming next? During his "lectures," Stephen Krashen taught us and taught us to teach.

In a lecture designed to promote reading as a way of learning vocabulary, Krashen seemed to make the presumption that most students could read in some language and, that reading was therefore a reasonable avenue for advanced language acquisition. I can still feel my discomfort at hearing him say that there weren't as many nonreaders in America as the media would have us believe. "Note that (basic) literacy is in general on the rise in the U.S.: there are fewer nonreaders than there were a hundred years ago. The problem is that the demands for literacy have risen faster than the literacy of the population. It's not that people can't read, it's just that they don't read well enough to handle the demands of our more technological society" (Krashen FAX, January 11, 1993). Though it had been many years since my race track experience, those huge numbers remained real to me. Luckily, during class Krashen had let it slip that he valued data gathered by his own teenagers. He also had suggested more than once that comic books can lead to literacy, a suggestion that extracted all manner of confessions, including some from the most stoic administrators in the room. So it seemed likely that he could tolerate an off-the-wall kind of data base. After class I told him my race track story, expecting him to offer some foolishly obvious resolution to the conflict between his observation and mine. Instead, he remarked that that was an extraordinary way to collect information "without bothering anybody." I knew some of my colleagues had begun to contemplate giving up on their degrees because the process of getting permission to gather the data they needed for their dissertations had become more time consuming than their studies would be. Informal, noninvasive ways of gathering useful information were not understood by many academics stuck in the traditional large-sample/ statistical mind-set. It was my good fortune, however, to discover over time that one of this great teacher's gifts was his ability to push his students into doing research that had a purpose and could be handled within a reasonable amount of time. In his classes, people who had come in just for the credit were often suddenly caught up in the most important work of their lives.

Time and again he talked about the affective filter,[6] that wall of stressful feelings that prohibits learning, and said we must find ways of lowering it if we expect to teach effectively. We were not to try writing down everything he said while he was talking. To do so might make his filter go up. He was interested in our reactions and suggested we jot them down. It was not enough that he toss his gems of humor and wisdom into the air, he needed to connect with his audience. But it was impossible for him to tell if we understood when we were staring down, writing. Besides that, he was convinced that most of us, brilliant as he claimed we were, could not write notes about what he'd finished saying while listening to and contemplating what he was saying in the moment. Further, he suspected that if his lectures were interesting (as rumor confirmed to him they were) and if we were busy thinking (as he suspected we would be), our thoughts would take their own paths. This famous researcher was telling us point-blank that he knew that during his lectures, we would daydream from time to time! When we did rejoin the crowd, he wanted it to be possible for us to catch up as quickly as possible. To that end, he delivered huge stacks of class notes with related readings collated in. That made it possible for a person to read ahead when he or she had time, or to catch up when necessary. Krashen's purpose was to teach us language acquisition theory in such a way that we could make the world a better place for students; his purpose was not to test us on our study habits.

Too often school is a test, he told us. Students are tested on what they already know and what they learn on their own, but seldom on what they are taught *in* school. Krashen not only had faith that teaching could be done in school, he felt *he* could do it. He didn't just lecture about lowering the affective filter, he let us find out what a low filter felt like. That lesson was so well received that many of us discussed ways we could get other professors to follow suit. And I, for one, promised myself to make this part of my future teaching. Indeed, during interviews with volunteer literacy students, I documented huge amounts of frustration over being tested on things presumed taught elsewhere.

Though cooperative learning was being mentioned in many classrooms, Krashen showed us how to combine the cooperative concepts with notions of student empowerment. He surveyed his classes for interests and then grouped us to do research, allowing us to coauthor papers or just serve as support teams.

As a computer and statistics enthusiast, Krashen felt true sympathy for all the people who failed to know the joys of statistical results dancing across their screens. He posited that statistical appreciation should be a basic human right. To that end, he decided to offer minicourses in statistics five minutes before each class. He would zero in on research problems addressed in studies that were on tap for the day, studies we had had time to read because they were collated in with our class notes, the ones typed up by the professor himself. Again, the process of getting new information in a comprehensible context demonstrated to us how as teachers we might strive to connect the known with the interesting and useful unknown. Comprehensible input, as Krashen put it so succinctly, was not only a theoretical term, it had very practical applications. Comprehensible input meant new information that could be understood because it connected with something you already knew and might want to discuss further or write about. Ministat class attendance was voluntary, and little by little math anxiety yielded to comprehension as Krashen, like Freire, began at the level of his learners and worked up from there. It made so much sense that some previously discouraged students decided they might not have to drop the program and a few actually started to enjoy statistics. Having grown up with the notion that all of the females in my mother's family had a genetic deficiency for math, I settled for just understanding that I *could* understand.

He never took roll but seemed to find ways of learning the names, countries of origin, and places of employment of his students, thereby setting the stage for a show of comprehensible input, information that is delivered at the learner's level and in a way that it connects with the learner. When I tried to puzzle out the difference between how comprehensible input works with native and nonnative speakers, he seemed willing to let me think there was no difference. It was as though I had a right to draw my own conclusions. This was a radical departure from the lecture/test method being offered in some of my other classes.

Holding little regard for artificial motivators himself, Krashen tried to accommodate those whose self-perceptions were externally controlled. By midsemester, having demonstrated that he really would take papers from us at any time and that he would meet with us as much as necessary individually or in our groups to discuss our work, Krashen had given grades to anyone who wanted grades and had offered to let us keep working on whatever papers we wanted. If we'd earned a B and were content with a B (or had too many other classes to care about this one), that would be the grade on record. But if we wanted to try again, we had the security of knowing that a B was the lowest grade that could show up on the transcript, no matter how badly the next draft turned out or whether we ever came to class again or not. We were adults and he knew we had other classes and other lives. Yet even if we'd gotten an A at any point, we were still free work on the project with his help or to start something entirely new. The presumption was that we were there to learn and he was there to teach. Grades were an inconvenience, perhaps designed to give record keepers something to do in their spare time, but not anything Krashen wanted his students dwelling on. Again, I promised my future students similar treatment.

I don't know of any students who actually stopped coming to class; each session was like attending a keynote address at a conference, a standing-ovation-type show. To miss one was to rob yourself. But removal of the stress related to end-of-the-semester deadlines and grades made the room seem less packed. So it was that I had finished the requirements for my Krashen A when I showed up with my ill-received bits of illiterate data, wondering if there was any hope for me as a scholar.

After explaining that I'd done nothing to coax my subjects into giving the information they did—it was all on tape and I was prepared to play back many hours of interviews almost monologues, during which time I'd done little more than raise an eyebrow, nod my head, or say, "Really?" to let the informant know I was paying attention—I showed Krashen my findings, suddenly realizing as I spoke that the affective filter also comprised bitten nails and self-esteem. But at that point I still had a very small sample size (about fifty, including those interviewed in New York and those from a variety of programs in California) and not all interviewees had responded to every question on my list. "Just tell the truth," he advised. "Point out your shortcomings yourself and then let others value your research if they wish." There were also those embarrassing

100 percent recurrences. I'd been reading enough research studies to know that 98 percent of anything would cause question; 90 percent looked a bit like an unfortunate coincidence; and 89 percent began to reach the hearty and humble category. Still, I couldn't see any way of reorganizing my data to get a more presentable percentage. I had to know, so I simply asked if I'd wasted my time: What did the 100 percent mean? This mathematician with a Hercule Poirot twinkle answered, "It means you're onto something." Then he reiterated, "Just tell the truth. You don't have to defend the truth." When I finally understood that he meant exactly what he was saying, nothing between the lines, no double-talk, I also understood that this was advice I could work with. It was so liberating not to have to see one thing and talk about another. "Now, you need to do another study," he advised. I didn't argue . . . after all, there were *weeks* left until the end of the semester. As it turned out, the new study, one looking at successful-reader international students, further clarified data gathered in New York. Rewritten, it was something Krashen thought should be submitted for publication. *Empowerment is the process of learning that text is generated by mortals for mortals' use. It occurs when the individual views herself or himself as both a consumer and creator of text. And it happens again and again, throughout the literate life, regardless of when the process begins. Effective teachers empower their students.* Within the year that little bag of castaway kittens appeared in print . . . in *The Journal of Reading.* My affective filter lowered.

When the Torch Is Passed from Home to School

Notions of the self-fulfilling prophecy[7] are so commonplace, they are often deleted from teacher education classes now. After all, everyone knows that if the teacher expects success, the child will be much more likely to deliver success. So, the child who is expected to love books will be much more likely to enjoy them than the one whose test scores alert the teacher that this one suffers from . . . A READING DISABILITY. The person with a reading disability fulfills that prophecy for all time.

Richard Allington has shown us that children who enter school as readers get very different treatment from those who don't—even in the same classroom. The readers are given books to read silently. The nonreaders are given worksheets and commands to stand and recite. So, in school, the child who loves reading is called smart and is rewarded with beautiful books, while the child who knows nothing about them is made miserable at reading time. One adult after another has recounted to me tales of being forced to read aloud in front of the whole class when they simply could not. Memories of teachers' corrections and classmates' jeers bring tears to the eyes of even the oldest and the strongest survivors of this subtly administered classroom abuse committed in the name of literacy. But the school's role in child abuse is often blatantly overt for the children of illiterates and the very poor.

A Plague Without Boundaries

While the highly visible evidence of low literacy suggests that it is the exclusive domain of the poor and unemployed, in truth it is a plague without boundaries, infesting every level of society, the employed as well as the unemployed. This plague is at epidemic proportions, affecting, according to Kozol, one of every three American adults.[8] Still, in every case that I studied, there remained certain consistent features suggesting that educators had failed to understand or apply the learning, reading, literacy, and language theory that would support a better educational system than the one we have. Collectively, as educators we do know better. And we are paid to do better. But we have clearly failed to serve our students the best we know how.

- We know that humiliation limits learning.
- We know that being read to is an essential first ingredient for learning to read.
- We know that the interest of the learner is the place to start in lesson design.

We have at our disposal the power of theory that has come from study after study, generation after generation, clearly pointing the way to effective pedagogy across age groups and economic levels. Even so, for every adult poor reader who has passed through our publicly funded elementary school system, we haven't chosen to use it. In fact, in too many cases, our schools of education have not even passed the power of theory on to their students through word or practice. While issuing assignments in modern lesson planning, and parroting names like Dewey, Vygotsky, and even Eisner, many teacher education classes continue to model the outdated lecture/text/test approach, still having students sit row upon row, in uncomfortable desks, sometimes in assigned seats! Often the pressures of deadlines and product outweigh the values of process and discovery. The time required to do critical thinking is a moot issue as the excuses used for employing excruciatingly unreliable multiple choice exams "in this special case" demonstrate the real value system of the university. And much too often new teachers are simply sent out into the field to copy the old or to blindly repeat what was done unto them, without any guidance in how to evaluate what they've experienced.

So, if professional educators (for whom reams of journals and weeks of conferences each year supply findings about such things as the affective domain, self-esteem, and the power of prophecies) have had theoretical support and have failed to use it (whether knowingly or through oversight), then they have forsaken the hands that reach out to them. **What would happen, I wondered, if the power of theory were placed directly into those forsaken hands?** If understanding why people learn to read helps the parent or teacher foster reading, wouldn't that information have a value to an adult who had *not* been taught to read? And if somehow false messages have taught you you cannot read, wouldn't you just not try? But what if you learned that this was a false message and that in fact you were born to read? Wouldn't that give you power? Just knowing you had the brain to do it would not in and of itself be enough for you to begin reading any more than knowing you can learn to cook will enable you to follow a recipe. But, what if you also had the same information that parents and teachers of young readers have? **And *then*, what if you were given the foundation that you'd originally missed?** Only, *this* time, you knew more than you had as a little child and could direct the activity to suit your needs. And what if you understood that taking that control was a normal and natural part of the process? What if you were suddenly informed, as though you were a professional educator, so that you understood that student-centered learning was the most effective kind known? Mightn't the understanding, the control, and the courage to try, combined with the assumption that you could address this information as professionally as any other educator . . . mightn't all of that give you power you have never had before? Mightn't you use that power to serve yourself well? And mightn't you deal with your children differently? It seemed to me that it was worth a try.

In the case of an illiterate adult, all else had already failed, making time the only thing left to lose, and time was passing anyway. I wanted to try teaching adult nonreaders about theory as part of their reading lessons. I wanted to share what Krashen had to say about the affective filter and what Frank Smith said about boredom. I wanted them to know how Paulo Freire, Sylvia Ashton Warner, and Septima Clark had all used key words to provide literacy in the interest area and at the level of the learner. I wanted them to know about power and disempowerment and how a significant other might really be a disempowering significant other whose real agenda was to keep the nonreading adult at bay.

I wanted them to understand the language of writers and how it was a language any reader could learn to use. But *in*

*order for them to begin learning the language of writers, they first
needed to be read to.* I could do that. And in order for them to
begin using the language of writers, they needed help getting
ideas from the head into text. I could help there, too.

And *I wanted them to understand the joy* a child gets reading a
card from grandma or that a teenager gets starting a Stephen
King novel. I wanted to eradicate the missing-joy factor by
sharing the joy of literacy. *For that they first needed to be read to.*

The approach was simply to put all these complex theories
at the disposal of the learner and then to offer guidance in
their use. It was a not a notion that I'd found in the literature,
and so I could only hypothesize about it. My work with LVA
and other grass-roots groups gave me a positive track record
for working with adults on a "whatever works" basis. And,
in retrospect, I realized that much of what had worked with
my literacy volunteer students had followed empowering theory. For example, I was miserable trying to use phonics and
word pattern practice and my adult students were equally
opposed to those "literacy tools" so we just didn't use them.
That such decision making was empowering to student or
tutor, that the illogical phonics and boring pattern practice
were parts-to-whole time killers, and that the time saved by
not doing them was then time available for me to read more
to my students did not occur to me as theoretically sound
because I had no theoretical background. Like many other
teachers, I had viewed my successes as luck. I was fortunate
indeed to be in a setting of academic freedom where I could
experiment, having admitted to my students that we were
going to have to find the answers as we went along. Or as
Krashen had advised: just telling the truth. I had pledged to
do my best, but there can be no real guarantees in human
learning. However, now I understood that understanding the
theory was empowering because it enabled wild guesses to
become educated ones.

It was in the spirit of experimentation based on educated
guesses that I decided to try teaching my newly discovered
theory to people who had previously failed to enjoy its fruits.

The Search for Subjects

Because I have been active in several professional associations for a number of years and, in addition to my Literacy Volunteers of America work, I regularly help grass-roots literacy and language programs organize through churches, schools, or community associations, it seemed that finding subjects would be relatively simple. I was, after all, willing to take research cooperation in trade for experimental literacy instruction. There were only four requirements:

1. The subject had to have been a student in the formal education system, where reading and writing were presumed to be taught and used.
2. The student had to be willing to stay with the experiment for three months, working as my research partner, sharing findings and taking responsibility for decision making. This may seem minimal enough, but there is a very high dropout rate among those who show up for literacy tutoring. I will talk more about the "fugitive phenomenon" later on.
3. The subject had to have suffered profound life problems as the result of poor reading ability. Many who show up for volunteer literacy programs need very little help to move on into formal adult education programs. And there are others who are able to suffer along through text, eventually figuring out how to follow a recipe or fill out a job application and, in so doing, are able to "get by." There are many who can bark words fairly accurately, giving a reasonable show of ability. These people often call themselves poor readers and writers. They may become frozen if someone is watching them read or write, but, alone, they can manage to do something, albeit less than they believe is the minimum. However, I needed those whose pursuit of *happiness* had been restricted by literacy. Such people might have failed to apply for a job advancement because they would be discovered in a higher-profile position. In fact, they may have been fired either because they had

done literacy-related assignments inadequately or because an employer who'd found them out thought they might. I needed people who had documented either no or very low literacy, in spite of the exposure they had gotten in school. I did not want there to be any question that it was the power of theory that had made the difference.

4. The subject had to agree to my publishing the results of our sessions. I would not use real names of people, places, or employers. I would not publish any specific information that would allow the casual observer to identify my research partners/subjects, though, of course, because of anecdotal material, they would probably be able to recognize themselves.

So, the search was on for adults whose literacy problems had crippled their abilities to function with confidence in the things they considered normal activities. Recommendations came from colleagues, former students, LVA, grass-roots groups, my university professors, family friends, and others who got word that I might possibly help someone they knew. *Everybody knows somebody.*

Over time, I met a rich cross section of people who contributed new data and supported familiar hypotheses. Each of the cases presented here offers a unique view of emerging literacy and the reasons it has repeatedly failed to flourish. Because I was conducting the entire experiment alone, I began working with the subjects as I found them. As a result, you will notice I refer to one study within another from time to time. And although the target population was initially adults, there are children who presented examples of the root causes that are sometimes buried over time.

Those included here—and those not included—all contributed insights only an insider knows. Obviously, to have attempted such a task without my subjects' encouragement, understanding, and support would have yielded an anemic, one-dimensional report with little to say and even less to think about. To my students/subjects/research partners, I am indebted beyond words.

Meet My Partners

For all my aggressive pursuit of subjects, occasionally someone passed my way simply through fortuitous timing. That was the case with Farra, a child no one would have brought forward for special attention. I believe her story and those of the people around her shed light on the complexity of the cycles of poverty and illiteracy and how the gang has become a magnet for those who have little hope of escaping either. Consider, if you will, that a person who loves to read and has a safe, quiet place in which to do so has a different way of seeing the world than the person who cannot and does not.

Henry, who had spent his short-lived childhood attending schools for the children of migrant workers in the Midwest, came to California with the family of an uncle who was active in NAACP (National Association for the Advancement of Colored People) school integration efforts. Though he didn't graduate, he did learn a lot about racism and poverty, some of which he tells here. He also successfully completed many government-sponsored job training programs, none of which provided the basics for successful employment. If he'd had the power of theory from the first grade on, he would not have had any more food in his stomach, but he might have saved himself some of the misery associated with feeling stupid and worthless. Had any of the multitude of government workers involved in his training understood the very basic premises on which education must rest to be effective, he never would have entered any of the extraordinarily expensive programs he did.

The product of an upper-middle-class home in a closed community, nine-year-old Arthur gives an inside look at how family illiteracy works to maintain itself. Arthur's story led me to the concept of the disempowering significant other (DSO). Although she understood the theoretical implications of the methods used to teach her son to read, his mother did many things that undermined the process, demonstrating that theory in and of itself is neither good nor evil. But it is powerful. And once the young child began to grasp the language of theory, he had the power to analyze events in his world in new ways.

Madonna, as a young teen in a Southern California public school, was placed in a class for the retarded because she couldn't read. Mitzi, the child whose birth allowed Madonna to drop out of that humiliating situation, failed the first grade because of reading difficulties. What may be most interesting about their story is that both did start reading and writing within a short time of at-home intervention. (With five children and no car, Madonna observed that this may have been the only way she could get help.)

Danny was a middle-aged high school graduate who, when we first spoke, claimed he couldn't read a stop sign. Yet he became a prolific writer within a few months' time. And his son, Charlie, also a high school graduate, had spent a number of semesters following teacher-centered instructions on how to design computer pictures without making mistakes and how to avoid such things as electrical fires in a high-tech learning lab but had never learned that he could use the computer to produce his text. (He was the servant of technology.)

I worked with three high school boys at the same time—their choice, not mine! Jonathan, whose reading deficiencies were impeding his ability to succeed in his academic classes, had tested at the fifth-grade level in reading when he entered high school. Records indicated he had "plateaued," meaning he could not be expected to rise above that score. Midway through our work, he tested at above the seventh-grade reading level. But more reliable than standardized test scores was his behavioral change. Not only did he begin reading for pleasure, he was able critically to compare sustained silent reading programs under his old and new principals. Beau, actually a dropout who "could not benefit from further schooling" when we

met, began to contemplate reentry when he started to comprehend the roots of his reading problems. Reynaldo was so
frightened by social encounters he could hardly speak. Though
he did seem to appreciate the sessions he was able to attend,
he lacked support from home or school and by all appearances
found a more secure source of self-esteem in an emerging gang.

There is an elusive population whose common denominator
is terror over the threat of exposure to literacy. That terror is
school generated. I very lightly touch on the story of Zintozonke, a South African woman who had tried to go through
an adult education program in the United States. And, finally,
Harry and Maureen give you a glimpse of what it is like in
this literate world to be "the fugitives."

1. Frank Smith uses this powerful metaphor in much of his
   work. To read one salient chapter on club membership, see
   his *Insult to Intelligence: the Bureaucratic Invasion of American
   Schools* (Portsmouth, N.H.: Heinemann, 1988).
2. La Vergne Rosow, "Consumer Advocacy, Empowerment,
   and Adult Literacy," *Journal of Reading* 34(4) (December
   1990): 261.
3. Sue Berman says it is the well meaning volunteer spirit that
   is responsible for many of Literacy Volunteers of America's
   successes: "The one-on-one approach gives the adult
   learner something she or he may never have gotten before—
   a literate human who believes in them and is willing to
   give them very specific attention. The caring person can
   use awful methods and still get really remarkable results."
4. La Vergne Rosow, "Adult Illiterates Offer Unexpected
   Cues into the Reading Process," *Journal of Reading*, 32(2)
   (November 1988): 120–24.
5. In his study *The Meaning Makers: Children Learning Language
   and Using Language to Learn* (Portmouth, N.H.: Heinemann, 1986), Gordon Wells tells of two children, Jonathan,
   the top student in his class of thirty, and Rosie, the bottom
   student. During three years of observation, neither child

changed rank. The big difference? Before entering school Jonathan had heard over five thousand stories; Rosie had heard none.

6. Stephen Krashen, *Fundamentals of Language Education* (Torrance, Calif.: Laredo, 1988). Also see Appendix A.

7. Robert Rosenthal and Lenore Jacobson, *Pygmalion in the Classroom: Teacher Expectations and Pupil Intellectual Development* (New York: Holt, Rinehart and Winston, 1968). Ray C. Rist, "Student Social Class and Teacher Expectations: The Self-Fulfilling Prophecy in Ghetto Education," *Harvard Educational Review*, 40(3) (August 1970): 411-51. Rist found that teacher expectations led teachers to treat expected low achievers differently and that this behavior set up a classroom pecking order that was never reversed. Also see Appendix B.

8. Jonathan Kozol, *Illiterate America* (New York: Anchor Press/Doubleday, 1985). And the National Adult Literacy Survey (NALS) (Washington, D.C.: United States Department of Education, 1993) reports that over 40 percent of the adult population falls short of the literacy skills needed to succeed on a day-to-day basis.

Two

The Roots of Disempowerment

Literacy is a value system that most often begins in the cradle. Though there may be enormous blocks to obtaining books and other literacy materials, once begun, the literate lifestyle is unlikely to stop. A person who associates good times with books will find them and read them, even if it means reading in a foreign tongue, even when the cover price is very high, even when the hour is late and the eyes are tired. For the literate person, living in a literate world means having a wealth of text available for whatever purposes the user may have in mind and possessing the skill to create text for whatever purpose. Indeed, having the right to make decisions about text means having power. It is a birthright.

But not all members of this society have that birthright. For some, the illiterate way of life evolves over years of exposure to a complex formula of aliterate events. Just the right things must occur at just the right times to stifle an intelligent human being's right to read and need to write. The evolution of illiteracy begins in a million cradles each day. And over time it is fostered by a terrible conspiracy, one that typically engages the family, the educational system, and society. These systems are interdependent, each sending the same message and threats to the illiterate who sees the world as a place where she can only get those parts of the picture she deserves. Her mother called her irresponsible, her school called her stupid, and her society calls her worthless, so she doesn't deserve much, does she? Together the home, school, and society feed the roots of disempowerment.

Within our "mainstream" social system are many subsystems that exist apart. Much of the disempowerment exerted in schools serves to exclude members of these subsystems from participation in that "mainstream." Though the background of each protagonist in the case studies in this book is quite different from the others, I want to use one social system close-up to introduce some of the circumstances that support the cycle of disempowerment.

Through my work in a publicly supported housing project, you will see how the home, the school, and society work in unison to perpetuate illiteracy and the related behavior patterns that, in turn, keep the cycle going. Then you will meet one child, Farra, who is just learning what it means to be a victim of that terrible conspiracy. As we go, I ask you to think about how different life would be for all of us if all the players arrived at the field fully equipped. That is, *what if* the teachers, administrators, parents, children, police, and politicians *all knew that they all knew the theoretical implications of every event?* What if everyone understood the long-term effects of calling names, hitting children and adults, and setting up requirements that cannot be met? What if everyone understood that hurt feelings and a sense of foreboding are natural and normal signals that something is awry? *What if everyone had the power of theory?*

My literacy work with gang members and their families and friends in the project gymnasium gave me a crash course in the effects of illiteracy and disempowerment across generations.[1] The residents, many whose parents and grandparents had been born there, had barely a clue about what it could mean to live independently outside the project—in a place where one of your own is on the school board or someone you know is attending college. Still, some of them managed to express a sense of being trapped in their public holding tank— more like pets than people. They knew life had to offer something beyond what they had. Just living in the project gave a person at once an unshakable identity and a feeling of being less powerful than those on the outside. While some were mute—lacking the *word*—others expressed a strong need to be recognized as valuable and a wish to shine at something. This was a place where the school could have a profound impact. As I learned from one story after another, it did . . . an incredibly negative impact. This was also a place where low self-esteem could be used to make people do most anything. As one person after another explained, that was why gang membership was so important to him or to her; it filled a void . . . gave a sense of belonging . . . a sense of worth. Gang membership was one thing a person could get very good at, though often at extremely high personal sacrifice.

Consider that physical jeopardy and long hours—well beyond anything a person would expect to give to an employer—are automatically assumed with membership. And once you're in, you can't get out—you have no freedom of choice. Hair style, clothing, tattoos, manner of speech, posture, and gait mark you, not just to the members within, but to society without. And so marked, there is no secret about where you belong. The other gang members work to keep you in while the mainstream works to keep you out. Joining a gang makes you a prisoner for life—physically and mentally.

Yet, well before the gang has made permanent its claim, the school has an opportunity to effect change. But the message that you don't belong starts very young in that institution of socialization. The process of being pushed from school to gang may begin with the first few school performance failures or even before you are born.

One teen mother who'd discovered in the gym that she really could read and could even foster literacy in her daughter, tearfully confessed staking out her first-grade child's school yard. The teacher, having seen school records on the mother's insubordinate behavior, was restricting the child's recess movements, a kind of punishment-in-advance program. By preconceiving the child's future misbehavior, the school was proving she didn't fit into the educational system. What's more, the little girl was not learning to read there. By the time her daughter reached the third grade, the mother told me, the decision to join the gang would be made. Unable to see what her mother was only just beginning to observe but dared not express openly—that gang membership did not really safeguard kids against abusive teachers—child, like mother, would spend her early elementary school years looking forward to the day or night when she would get "jumped in," proving her acceptance to some society and fortifying her with the power to avenge herself. Of course it is a false promise, based on doublethink. "Gang" and "safe" have been so tightly packaged, the child cannot be expected to think of them separately. Her revenge against the system that failed to welcome her may manifest itself short-term in broken car windows or arson at the school—ultimately self-destructive actions if they lead to an arrest record, jail time, or even just demands from the gang that she outdo her most recent destructive act. And though her revenge will no doubt prove expensive in terms of tax dollars, it will do little to improve the way she lives. As a gang member she will remain powerless. You may think to yourself that the child need only look at her mother to see the world as it truly is. Well, in the first place, the child believes that the world she knows *is* the way the world is—the way it is supposed to be. But even if she could work through this emotional puzzle on a cognitive level, the gang offers something she needs very much: hope.

So the promise of gang membership fosters costuming and behaviors that lead to unsuccessful school experiences. The unsuccessful experiences there create a need to shine elsewhere, which means nights become filled with activity that leaves school children sleepy, a condition circling back to more unsuccessful school experiences. Failure in a place where you are mandated to be day in and day out may cause severe resentment to build.

My purpose in going to the project was to foster a love of reading and the power of writing in gang members and their families and friends. I set up shop in the project gymnasium where, on the battered Ping-Pong table next to the boxing ring, I spread out books, magazines, hand puppets, art supplies, song sheets, and other bait in hopes of attracting those who had been so burned in the formal system that direct approaches were out of the question. Using carefully selected parts of my children's book collection, on each visit I would unveil some notable feature that would help explain the theory behind reading development. For example, one feature I particularly enjoy is having the same story told in different ways, like the folktale *Stone Soup*. This introduces the notion that retellings belong to the storyteller. It also opens discussion of background knowledge, showing how new vocabulary can be built during the use of familiar subject matter and that familiar stories are easier to read than unfamiliar ones, even when the vocabulary is more sophisticated and the sentences are longer. Multiple servings of stone soup were easy to digest after Eric Carle's *Caterpillar*. The same ideas were illustrated via ample helpings of my collection of Aesop's fables, which ranges from small paperbacks to huge, beautifully illustrated hardbound copies. Because the stories of Aesop were originally delivered orally and because they were first designed for adults and later interpreted for children, they fit particularly well into this setting. I gave away countless *Stone Soup*s and *Aesop's Fables*.

Though many residents never got beyond peeking around the corner of the gym door, representatives of all generations began to ease into sessions where I read stories aloud from both new and traditional books, leaving them open and within easy reach of adults, teens, and children, many of whom had never seen "good" books up close, let alone touched them. Some of the books were bilingual, shocking to those who had been taught to shun all words not English. That I am not bilingual both added to the confusion of and supported confidence in one gang member, who began to help me read the unfamiliar text. Jonsey was a big man who had grown very fond of the alliteration and musical qualities of nursery rhymes. He was attending my sessions to "maintain order" and to follow up on more serious literacy work he was attempting. But hearing nursery rhymes had been the real hook for him. As he'd see me enter the gym, he'd drop his basketball and walk over to greet me, draping a heavy arm around my shoulders more often than offering to carry my load of books. His sweet nothings promptly segued into questions about which of his favorite poems I would read that day.

During the early stages of my involvement, I'd struggled to get him to use the services of the bookmobile that made biweekly stops right outside the gym. Telling him outright that his participation in that literacy event would have a profound influence on the other members of the community, I gave him step-by-step instructions on library use. I assured him that he had the right to get a card and order any books that weren't in stock on a given day. Seeing him emerge triumphant would boost everyone's interest in books and library use. This was modeling and we talked at length about club membership and the power of modeling literate behaviors so that the children and less notable gang members would feel safe trying out the system. From the start I'd made it very clear that my presence was temporary, that I was *not* setting up a teacher-dependent system. So the bookmobile appeared a very easy and appropriate step toward getting folks from the books on the Ping-Pong table to the collection shared by the literate thousands in the community beyond the gym. Still, Jonsey, squinting more than usual, told me, "La Vergne . . . you just gotta understand . . . you . . . ." He got so choked up, he couldn't finish his argument. It wasn't until later that I learned that many members of the Ping-Pong crowd had entered and been humiliated in that vehicle from the outside world. So it was that I lugged in different parts of my youth and children's book collection, serving as a different kind of bookmobile for a very different kind of population. And so it was that after hearing me read and act out hundreds of stories and poems, Jonsey had begun to read aloud the nursery rhymes he'd missed as a child.

One day my spread was largely a mix of bilingual and Spanish texts. Earlier I'd brought in a copy of Eric Carle's *The Very Hungry Caterpillar*, which I'd read, much to the delight of everyone who got to participate in the predictable text, supported by ideal illustrations and a good story line. This time, I had a Spanish version, *La Oruga Muy Hambrienta*, one I'd never tried to read before. I had only planned to show it that day, sticking firm to my rule that you don't read for show until you've practiced and feel very comfortable with the text. In the first place, it needs to sound good, and in the second, I always tried to read the large texts upside down so that I could quickly pan the pictures for the audience as I moved along. This day, however, Jonsey was sitting beside me and decided I should read the new Spanish Carle. My Spanish is limited to what I learned as a resident of San Antonio, Texas—it is, at best, a mix of words, phrases and a few idioms I picked up when trading ballet lessons for Spanish dancing lessons many years before. It would be an understatement to say my accent far outweighs my vocabulary. But Jonsey wasn't buying excuses. He *liked* to hear me read and, besides, if I'd bought the book, I must know how to read it. The audience, a mix of kids, teens, and "older" citizens were anxious for the show to start, so I revved up for a disaster. After a few failed attempts to get me to do the first page right, Jonsey took over the book, forgetting that anyone other than himself needed to see the pictures. He struggled through one page, the next, and the next, until there were no more pages.

He was breathing hard and sweat was streaming down his forehead into eyes that badly needed reading glasses. (He owned some, but had quietly explained to me that the homeboys didn't respect a man who wore glasses. There was no way he was going to enter the gym with glasses even in his pocket.) I had to assume that he'd missed some words, and I was expecting someone to complain. It didn't happen. Instead, he was, for that moment, a literacy leader. Children were squirming under his arms to get a closer look at the book and several adults were asking me questions all at once. What followed was a book-handling frenzy the likes of which had never occurred before. Indeed, the pattern had usually been one of adults snapping at children who dared too near the untouchable "sacred" texts I'd brought to lure in readers.

Through smoothly delivered tales, I'd planned to show how good authentic literature could be. Now, in an unexpected moment, a fumbled reading usurped by a complete novice had done the deed. Seeing a respected community member engaged in text use—and perhaps encouraged by the fact that there was obviously no teacher around to correct them—several people very quickly began to read from the first printed Spanish they had ever seen. Though none of the Ping-Pong-table set had ever contemplated issues surrounding the bilingual education controversy before, the political concepts discussed in Jim Crawford's book on bilingual education, Krashen and Biber's *On Course*, and Jim Cummin's ideas for empowering minority students provided stimulating dialogue on many subsequent Sunday afternoons. And as they, at first timidly, then more assertively, began to note when the wrong Spanish words had been selected for some of the translated books, we were able to slip into discussions of literacy and empowerment.

Can you see how the transfer of power occurred? The learners were the exclusive authorities on Spanish, so only they had the power to evaluate word choice. Giving them the freedom to question printed text opened the door to more empowering dialogue involving other kinds of evaluation on other topics.

Consider this: If I think of you as my superior, I will be absolutely unable to imitate you over an extensive period of time, even if I sense that my life would be better with your speech patterns. But if, for whatever reason, I suddenly see us engaged in an intellectual balance of power, we are free to exchange the best each has to offer. I can look at you objectively and decide this is good—I'll take it, that is absurd—I'll leave it. So if I'm externally motivated to bark sounds like yours in school, you must plan to be around all the time to act as watchdog. On the other hand, if I have the right and responsibility to make changes at will and the basic understanding of why things do or don't work, I have power—over my speech, over my literacy, over my life.

My presence at the Ping-Pong table was the only consistent feature in the Sunday afternoon sessions.[2] The roll call of attendees changed weekly. So materials I would bring in for follow-up on a particular story or question would go untouched week in and week out. Then, when I would opt to leave them at home, the target person or persons would show up again. This see-saw of progress proved very frustrating. It was not at all like having a classroom where you know the students and can expect a certain percentage of them to show up each day. It took some time for me to understand that I would see some of the people only once, some of the people every three months, and that others would pop in and out all afternoon almost every Sunday.

I began to realize that if there was to be any kind of continued dialogue when I was out of the system, I needed to provide a kind of communal wisdom about language acquisition and learning theory. It was slow work. Not everyone adopts new words and the accompanying concepts at the same pace or with the same number of exposures. But little by little, bits of dialogue began to show that there was an increasing level of consciousness. For example, after several discussions of the esteem/learning connection following readings of my affective filter teaching paper (Appendix A) to different members of the Ping-Pong club, a hurtful remark would be met with something like, "Don't bother my filter" instead of the traditional elbow jab in the stomach or back. For some, the language of theory carried a bigger punch than a fast-flung limb.

Chaos Time

Common among the adults with whom I have worked is a prevailing element of turmoil—I call it the chaos phenomenon. When things are naturally calm for a period of time, the adults themselves do something to stir the stew. Perhaps it is a sub-conscious need to repeat history or perhaps it provides a reason not to focus on solving problems that are too many and too huge. But whatever the reason, self-inflicted chaos shows up to end many a tranquil interlude. For the gangs, obviously, one traditional avenue to chaos is a rumble. I made a point of making myself very predictable. I always said when I'd be back, called to say I was on my way, parked as closely as possible to the same spot, and left as scheduled. Sometimes when I called ahead, I'd be told not to come. I never had to ask why but would think, "Oh, God, it's chaos time."

Chaos arrived in a very unexpected vehicle one night. There had been such a period of calm that some of the local people had spent considerable energy planting grass on a playing field outside the gym. They had carefully roped it off, too. Several shifts of partially enthusiastic volunteers tended the watering and, in spite of a severe heat wave, the grass had actually sprouted. Yet, when I arrived one Sunday, there was a pall over the gym. Huge tire tracks ran from the street all across the wet playing field, leaving deep permanent scars in the turf. It couldn't have been an accident because of the prominently placed barricades. Who would do such a thing? Had a rival gang gotten so daring? No, there hadn't been any trouble in the project for weeks. Maybe that was the problem. The tracks were left by a police car. No apology was issued. A certain amount of unrest is expected from the project. That is how it becomes clear who's in charge. It is a matter of control—of power. It is difficult to describe the sense of helplessness and frustration that emanated through the community over this. The following Sunday, I was told not to come.

Slowly, various participants of different ages began to try out more elaborate language to express ideas—not just theoretical jargon but other words, too. And in so doing these players made conscious or subconscious announcements of internalizing change. When language changes, behaviors change as well. Or, perhaps it works both ways.

I was not the only one to see and understand the implications of change. Though there were truly altruistic citizens involved in the process, some members of the community began to see literacy as a new source of power, not one to be handed out to just anyone who wandered into the gym. You see, there is a kind of hierarchy within the gang-oriented social system that is intolerant of tampering—from without or within. One senior gang member who had begun to engage in text, perhaps more enthusiastically than he was engaged in the serious business of maintaining chaos, vanished for several weeks because he was embarrassed to tell me that the little story book I'd loaned him had disappeared—stolen?!

For him it was not just the loss of a prized book belonging to a person he'd officially claimed as a friend, it was also an indication that he did not completely control his environment. And being able to show physical control of the environment was how power was manifested in this social system. Shortly after he was again visible at the Ping-Pong table, he was targeted by a rival gang, one that had not expressed an interest in him for years. He'd missed getting shot this time, but the business of rolling over a car hood and under a dumpster had left this very big man an aching mound of flesh. Coincidence? Perhaps. But change is resisted, even by those officially complaining about the status quo.

Part and parcel with the well-publicized chaos within the housing project, there was a certain kind of predictability. For example, whenever residents called up to complain about services or living conditions, the simple command "Put it in writing," directed against a person who could not write, had always put an end to the complaint. You want toilet paper in the gym restrooms? Put it in writing! This tossed the ball back into the court of the complainer, who would predictably fail to comply. Participants in the Sunday dialogues explained with disgust that the purpose of such manipulation was to take pressure off the political controllers, who could point to the unwillingness of residents to take even minimal steps to "help themselves." They had participated in such scenarios so often they could predict the timing from complaint to squelch.

Meanwhile, however, discussions of Allington's research on the difference in school treatment of poor readers and good readers (in which good readers get to read good books and poor readers do skill tasks)[3] and the Ray Rist studies involving the self-fulfilling prophecies in ghetto classrooms (see the summaries in Appendix B), caused these adults and teenagers to understand their own history in a different light. Little by little they taught me the reasons why the people who went to the ghetto school—only to learn that they could not read and could not write—began to seek other sources of power. Within the project, an aliterate subculture had to develop. An invisible wall kept the residents in their place. By the time I arrived, ghetto contact with the outside world was limited to those paid to come in to manage the project; the brief treks some residents made into the world of temporary employment (leaving the participants older and poorer than when they began); and the sojourns through the penal systems, from which some participants emerged folk heros wielding agendas for turf wars, high-visibility events that for brief moments afforded diversion from the issues of powerlessness. But these contacts do little to disturb the balance of power between the literate and nonliterate societies.

Over time, frustrations regarding subhuman living conditions have erupted into the destruction of property and even open warfare against representatives of small political empires. Certainly, it is possible quite literally to kill off opponents; gang violence is a totally aliterate activity. And it serves both to diffuse tensions and provide a sense of accomplishment. But once the funerals and police activity have ended, there remains written documentation of all service requests . . . made only by those responsible citizens who really want service. For the rest, there's not even a letter on file.

When an oral culture and literate culture are butted head to head, the literate culture will be able to document anything and the oral culture will have nothing more than words in the wind. Literacy designs history. Literacy is power.

Eventually, some of the gang leaders began to discover that with form and spelling help they could communicate in writing with the political figures beyond their oral community. After considerable effort, one man attempted, for the first time in his life, to work within the system to get special consideration regarding living conditions in the project. Perhaps wanting to make his literacy volunteers feel more at home, he made written requests for paper towels, toilet paper, and light bulbs in the gym restrooms. That is to say, he dared to usurp the power held by those who had a vested interest in his illiteracy. Those small slips of paper may have forewarned a fundamental change in the social system.

Juanita Remembers

In the gym a cross-sectional study emerged, supported by grandfathers, uncles, nephews, sons, cousins, aunts. . . . Inspired by a sudden comprehension of theory, people would unload tales of horror, describing the ways in which a small child can learn to dread the thought of going to school. Though physical punishment of children is not allowed in California schools (as it is in some states[4]), solitary confinement, slapping, punching, and other forms of violence are routine educational treatments for the ghetto children of East L.A.

Though she was a grandmother by the time we met, Juanita's eyes swelled with tears and her voice cracked as she recalled misspelling a word in first grade. The teacher had taken a metal-edged ruler and whacked the child across the fingers. This happened often enough that Juanita still gets a lump in her throat when she sees a ruler and an absolute sense of terror if the edge glistens gold. But it wasn't until I read her my little teaching paper on the affective filter (see Appendix A) and the *Journal of Reading* article in which I detail my discovery of the early childhood profile of the adult illiterate that she realized she had experienced child abuse. What was worse, she in turn, had supported the school's like treatment of her son, a young man now in the penitentiary for murder. She told me she had believed that beatings taught good behavior and that name calling would help "straighten kids out." She had aggressively abused her children and grand-children in a effort to make things better.[5] Not only that, but when the children had entered school, she had made a point of going in to tell the teachers to do anything they needed to keep her youngsters in line—including hitting them.

Then, after minimal exposure to theory, Juanita experienced a cognitive leap. Suddenly she saw that what she'd done was just the opposite of nurturing, that the school had joined her in the conspiracy against her children and later so did the police! This assimilation and application occurred not after many semesters in graduate school but within a matter of minutes. For the luxury of control with a gilt-edged ruler what had society lost?

I must add that later Juanita began taking the parent/child reading lessons I taught in the gym into a project counseling class for parents whose children had been removed from their homes because of the parents' drug or physical abuse. I would write and rewrite little lessons so that she would be able to read the notes in front of an audience. Then I would supply her with appropriate book samples (e.g., predictable text, beautiful pictures, one author). She became the abusive parents' reading teacher, explaining the value of holding the little child safe in your lap as they hear your voice, the voice they will always connect with good stories. Tears always streaked her face as she practiced reading to whatever little child passed by. I have no idea how she survived in front of an audience of her peers. But she kept reporting progress, personally and professionally, and she kept coming back for more individually designed lessons. Of course, Juanita was in a unique situation. She could tell them that she knew how terrible they had been, but that she understood exactly how they'd come to be that way. She could tell them that she'd been there, too. But she could also explain that there were theoretically sound reasons for how things had been and how they could change. There was no way I (or any regular teacher) could have gotten into those rehabilitation sessions. And to be sure, none of those parents ever ventured into the gym on Sundays. They were an officially untouchable population. But as an "insider" Juanita was able and eager to help put back into her community some of what she'd gotten, albeit very late, from me. Her need to give back the gift of literacy illustrates not only a behavioral change, confronting the enemy head on, but also demonstrates how much a new reader must value literacy. She was ready to transfer the power of theory into the most forsaken hands.

In all the time I spent in the ghetto community, I never met one high school graduate. An entire social system devoid of successful educational experiences gives bleak testimony about what has gone on in the public schools serving it. Beyond that, however, are the statistics that contrast the prognosis of the haves against the have nots. According to the National Center for Education Statistics (*Digest of Education Statistics 1992*), for the last two decades the proportion of seventeen- and eighteen-year-olds graduating from high school has remained relatively stable. In fact, 78 percent of the population over twenty-five years of age has either graduated or has completed the GED exam. And 21 percent of the over-twenty-five set has completed four or more years of college. Both high school and college completion rates have risen since the 1980 census. But what that means for the person who has not completed high school is that the bottom is lower than it used to be. Further, it was reported that people with one to three years of high school were twice as likely as graduates to be unemployed. Unemployment for the one-to-three-years group was 14.8 percent. But to qualify for the unemployment statistics, you had to have been actively looking for work. This means that the unemployment rate in the ghetto is much higher than reported and, for those at the bottom, times are worse than ever. Dropping out of school has unmeasured consequences.

Trapped in the cycle of illiteracy generation after generation, these housing project residents have experienced such profound frustrations both at home and in the formal school setting that they rarely graduate and often turn to gang membership in search of recognition. How might it be otherwise? Consider the story of the child Farra.

Farra of the Ghetto

Though six-year-old Farra officially lived with her twenty-two-year-old mother and four younger siblings, the child was sporadically the charge of her grandmother, Jesse, age thirty-four, one of my children's book enthusiasts. So I had heard a lot about Farra long before we met. As a third-generation housing project child, she was known by just about everyone as sweet, but lazy. "She's a sexy little kid," one of the men had commented without stirring any reaction from the women. When Farra finally did arrive at the Ping-Pong table, conversation about her continued as though she wasn't there. Adults talked *about* Farra, not *to* her. Once, when a little boy came up to show Farra that he'd finished the eyes on her hand puppet, a woman laughingly said, "Farra can always get somebody else to do her work. She won't sew her puppet and she won't look after the kids." There was a kind of communal ownership of children in the project, so any adult was at liberty to offer such "character building" opinions. But I was concerned with the indirect suggestion that Farra's gender gave her an instinct to mother her younger siblings. Since she apparently lacked this instinct, the message she received was that she was deviant. For most of the women in the project— women who too often, like Farra, had been neither loved nor wanted by their mothers—such early programming oriented them into saying they "loved" and "wanted" children long before they had any experience with decision making.

The quality of life for any child born to a child is going to be limited. In the environment in which Farra lived, however, there was less need to think ahead about the physical well-being of the child than there might be in the case of a lower-middle-class baby born to a young teen mother who would be forced to work at a minimal job. For families with children, survival-level financial support through welfare and food stamps is automatic in the ghetto. So the dollar cost of children was not a factor to be thought through by anyone of any age, unless there was a struggle between custodians over rights to benefits. Therefore, for most, the production of babies was automatic and often relentless, even when the mother and other "loved ones" were inclined toward profound emotional and physical abuse of the babies after birth. During pregnancy, limited prenatal care, chronic anemia, smoking (in the environment and by the mother), alcohol and drug abuse, and insufficient rest for the mother also served to lower the present and future quality of life. The programming of girls to expect to be mothers was so much a part of the social system, no one questioned whether it was beneficial to the participants. For Farra, the unsubtle hints were dropped by anyone who might wish to extend power over her.

I moved away from the conversation area to open a large picture book in front of Farra. She lay her head down on her arm and began slowly turning the pages as the woman and Jesse continued to degrade her for being a very unreliable baby-sitter, one who goes to sleep when she's on duty. I eased around the Ping-Pong table to work with other children, but as the remarks grew increasingly cutting, I decided to go over and start reading the book aloud to Farra. It was too late; despite the melee in the gym, Farra had fallen asleep.

"I was thirteen when Farra's mother was born," Jesse later explained, "what could I say when my daughter wanted to marry at fifteen?" Though this very young grandmother can now see that having a series of babies so quickly keeps each child from getting quality time, there seems no way of breaking the pattern. Kids just have to grow up a little faster when the mother is busy. So, as an old kid in terms of her family,

Farra is expected to look after herself. That includes getting herself to bed at night, getting herself up in the morning, finding something to eat if she expects to eat (but she often chooses not to), and getting herself dressed and transported to school—a hazardous trek even for big kids.

During Farra's first week in first grade, her grandmother informed me, Farra checked out two school library books, the first books she'd ever touched in her life. They were apparently sent home with her to be read. But, having a mother who couldn't read and a grandmother who was only beginning to understand the reading process, neither Farra nor her siblings had ever heard a nursery rhyme or story. "Storytelling is not part of the culture around here," explained Jesse, after only just learning that it was part of the culture in literate homes. There were no books at all in Farra's home, Jesse volunteered, not a surprising situation in a home where Farra didn't even have a regular sleeping area. Before she could locate a place to lie down, Farra had to wait until visitors, relatives, babies, and television noise (and we're talking about wrestling, videos, and *The Simpsons*, not *Sesame Street* or *Mr. Rogers' Neighborhood*) had stopped. The idea of educational television didn't fit in with what people liked, Jesse told me. An enthusiastic researcher, she had done an informal survey but was able to locate no one in the project who had ever even seen one of the PBS children's programs.

On those occasions when Farra's young mother, again pregnant, couldn't handle so many children, Jesse would take Farra and the baby, an infant who seemed to have great difficulty breathing and who never cried. But Jesse had teenage and adult children still living with her, all of whom, she pointed out, had multiple friends in at all hours of the day and night. So Farra learned to crawl into any available lap just to rest. Quiet time continued to be out of the question—chaos followed the sleepy child from one home to the next.

At her age, she was expected to make life easier for her mother, not add to the burdens. So when she was at school, she was supposed to do what she was told and not do anything that would make the school torment her family. Her mother never asked Farra what went on in school, and if the child volunteered anything, no one remembered hearing it. Listening was not the mother's forte, Jesse explained, and there was no way to get a young mother, stressed by the needs of howling babies with loaded diapers, interested in providing a special place for school library books.

With no history of book handling before entering school and apparently having received no basic library-use instructions in the first grade, Farra didn't understand what was expected of her. The books disappeared. Midyear, when she had repeatedly failed to return them, a note to her mother was pinned to her shirt. It reportedly had advised that the child was about to lose her library privileges. But the note to the nonreading mom who herself had never had library privileges failed to recover the books or collect the fines. However, school notes to gang-related families are often assumed to mean that the child is exhibiting inappropriate behavior in school. Ghetto parents, many of whom have been beaten at home for having trouble at school, are often sensitized to official looking papers. It doesn't take long before young children learn not to deliver messages from the school to the home. So it's impossible to say whether follow-up communications were actually delivered. But it is certain that her mother was not aware of the book problem. It is also clear that Farra spent her first year in school without books.

In the gym one Sunday, when Farra had seemed particularly interested in a book, I'd asked her if she'd seen it at school. "No," she said, looking like a little animal about to be trapped. I didn't want to frighten her away from the Ping-Pong table, but I did want to know if her teacher ever read to her. She shook her head no. I thought perhaps I wasn't asking the right questions. If an aid or parent volunteer came in to tell stories, I wanted to know about that. Did anyone at school read to her? But, consistent with the stories of everyone else in the gym, Farra reported that she had never heard stories at school, much less seen beautiful children's books.

This suggested that a basic introduction to literacy was not part of her curriculum. She had no one to read to her at home and she obviously had no hope of reading to herself. Her grandmother had heard me do these interrogations before and she was well into the idea of triangulation—the process of verifying information by getting several different people to give the same information through different stories. She knew what I was wanting to verify, but had a question of her own: "If the school knows my daughter can't read . . . because they had her, too, and if the school knows Farra can't read . . . they say they know that, and if the school thinks those books are so important, why did they send them home with her?"

I wanted to answer, "You *know* this is catch 22—an exercise in disempowerment! It is designed to make your grandchild fear school and hate reading!" But, Jesse didn't need any answer from me. She had begun to understand learning theory. She understood behaviorism in the very concrete terms of ghetto life. And she had begun to observe the cycle of disempowerment as it applied to her daughter and her granddaughter. Farra obviously knew there was something horribly wrong in the library and that everyone at school was mad at her. But she had no way of understanding her crime.

Without her mother's knowing it, Farra was eventually identified as a nonreader who was not doing her assigned work. In the last week of school, when she was back with her grandmother, who would not allow her to walk to school alone, Jesse was advised that Farra was about to fail the first grade and that she could not expect to get any more books the next year until she took care of her obligations. The $8 fine was a staggering sum for this impoverished family and served to increase stress in all matters related to school and Farra.

This little girl is very bright. Like many other gym participants, she quickly connects the abstractions of learning theory with the very real events in school. She has learned her school lessons well. They are:

- Books cause people trouble.
- She is stupid.
- She is not a reader.
- Reading is a secret thing that smart people do.
- Reading causes stress and humiliation to herself and her family.
- School is a place where people feel miserable.
- School is a place where she fails.
- She should drop out as soon as possible.
- She will have to find another way of looking good to the world.

What are her choices? Drug abuse? Prostitution? Gang membership? What if she just marries young and begins having children as her mother and grandmother did?

Not knowing how to read, let alone having books to enjoy, Farra has little hope of pulling against the downward spiral of minimum wage and cyclical work. Given her history of self-care, she certainly faces poor nutrition, inappropriate health care, and unsophisticated legal awareness. And considering her patterns of literacy and schooling, how can she hope to improve her life or the lives of the children she quite probably will soon begin to mother? She faces limited survival in the project, if she is lucky. If she accidentally breaks a law and handles the results inappropriately, she may end up in jail or on the street. But for today, Farra is a child of disempowerment, a victim of the terrible conspiracy.

Might it be different for her in this generation? We have little reason to expect that her mother could suddenly change, so to belabor the inadequacies of her home would be a waste of energy. We also know that by the time she is old enough to venture into mainstream society, she will have so many markers—speech, dress, tattoos, hair style, gang membership, and quite probably one or more children—that she will not be capable of blending in and finding a way to effect change. That leaves only the school and only if it acts very quickly.

The school has, as we've been advised, until the third grade to make Farra decide to stay with positive social goals.

Still, can you imagine how it might be if, when she next appears at the school, someone called her aside and advised her, either in sheltered English or very carefully phrased Spanish (remember, she hasn't been talked to much in either language and won't benefit from anyone's giving her input she can't comprehend), that there has been a change of program at the school? For starters, someone now understands that little kids don't always take good care of books, but that they still need them; therefore, her $8 fine is forgiven and she has a clean slate. And then, it is understood that the school is about five thousand stories behind in its work with Farra, so she is to join a breakfast/lunch/after-school storytellers club where real teachers and librarians will provide everything a little kid could need to love books and stories. And all this extra work will take extra energy, so snacks will be part of the story times and naps will be allowed during the afternoon. And Farra will be told, point blank, that it is important to feel proud in school. To that end, if she wants to bring a friend along to the storytellers club, she may do so. Eventually, when she is ready, Farra will be allowed to dress up in costume and present stories, too. She'll want to do that because storytellers get free books, beautiful ones, that they can keep for all time. Attempts will be made to engage caretaker members of Farra's family in the process, but it will be the school's responsibility to make those contacts, not Farra's. Certainly there are many writing projects and other speaking events, too, that could come from the special focus on language arts. But just knowing that the school is a place where people really care about her and where she will learn to read this year may be enough to cause her to delay a deadly decision about gang membership or drug use. Needless to say, the school must keep checking with Farra to assure her needs are being met. And needless to say, the effort must be concerted and consistent, not a quick-fix program tacked on to diffuse one crisis. The threats to Farra's academic achievement will go on for many years. But every minute spent making her school life worthwhile may represent another minute she won't spend living the traditional life of the ghetto school child. That should be enough, shouldn't it? In addition, however, she not only will prove that the society that takes care of its children is a society its children will respect, but also, such focused TLC may break her family's cycle of illiteracy. If Farra loves to read and understands why being held makes literacy likely for little kids, her own children will have a much greater chance of entering school advantaged. Considering that, the project more than pays for itself. And we haven't even talked about Farra's future self-esteem and quality of life. She may do a study of those benefits when she goes to college.

1. I had just spent between six and eighteen hours each week for the better part of a year working with the inhabitants of this ghetto housing project when the Rodney King verdict came in, so I was not at all surprised at the L.A. riots. That civil unrest had less to do with one jury verdict than with generations of oppression. Indeed, I wonder why there hasn't been more frustration vented on the streets. After all, where people have no voice, they must *act* out their feelings. As a society, we could decide to end the terrible conspiracy. As educators we could refuse to groom the criminals of the next generation. Allotted even half the funds used for incarcerations, the schools could do an extraordinary job of giving the children of poverty a voice.

2. Sundays I offered drop-in literacy to anyone. Other days I attended community meetings and worked with individuals who were too busy or too shy to be seen at the Ping-Pong table.

3. Richard Allington, "The Reading Instruction Provided Readers of Differing Reading Abilities," *Elementary School Journal* (May 1983): 548–59.

4. Some states actively protect the rights of school authorities who use sticks or boards to beat the children under their care. In Florida, for example, teachers and administrators are allowed by state policy to hit students. Though beating

students to the extent that the bruises last for extensive numbers of days may result in the name of the offending teacher or administrator being put in the State's Child Abuser Registry, abuse cases (there were 208 investigations during the 1988–1989 school year) can muster strong sympathy for the accused. One judge suggested that an arbitrary number of days a child remains bruised from being hit with a wooden weapon in school could lead to "capricious" interpretation of the law. He questioned whether a bruised child had been beaten "in anger or with ill will or intent to injure" (Peggy Zirkel "De Jure, You Bruise, You Lose," *Phi Delta Kappan* 71[5] [January 1990]: 410–11). Isn't the slamming of a wooden board or stick against a human body intended to inflict pain? Doesn't the public humiliation of a human being constitute ill will? Is it remotely possible this judge believed such behavior would foster a love of math or science or reading? The violence done against these children by their "professional" caretakers is trivialized by the use of words like "paddle" and "paddling" and made to sound conventional in a militaristic sense by calling it corporal punishment. The reality is that the people who are hitting them with sticks or boards are modeling child abuse and the solution of problems through the use of force. Some children pay close attention to these lessons and save them for applications in society. Violence is a taught behavior.

5. Juanita had worked at one company at minimum wage for a quarter of a century, only to be told one day that the company was closing, taking with it the retirement she had imagined she'd earned. Much older and having nontransferable skills, she was unfit for further use in industry. Gone were her dreams of one day moving to a little place of her own, out of the ghetto.

▰ *Three*

Henry:
The Training Program Pro

Not part of the ghetto but having grown up at least as poverty stricken, Henry was a man with the inside skinny on many of our nation's leading job training programs. A forty-nine-year-old part-time high school custodian, Henry was unable to do the paper work and take the proficiency exam necessary to apply for full-time employment. He was so afraid of failure that he preferred to delay any attempt until he had improved his chances. And he was quick to admit that in spite of many years of schooling, he had profound problems related to reading and writing. For example, in the self-reporting California Literacy Campaign (CLC) adult learner inventory (see Appendix C), Henry indicated that the only regular reading he did was street and traffic signs, not particularly demanding for a man who didn't drive. He read menus occasionally, notes from school once a week or so, newspapers—which he found "very hard"—once a month, and church Sunday school lessons and other religious materials—which were "a little hard"—about once a week. He did find labels and instructions easy to read, but said he only read them "about once a year." He never read comics, TV guides, or magazines because they weren't good material. (This judgmental attitude toward the functional value of reading materials is one I've encountered frequently among parents and other early teachers of poor readers and nonreaders. Reading for the fun of it is an almost blasphemous idea to them, and they pass a fear of text down to the children in their care. The joy is missing.)

"I can read, but I can't understand" and "I can read, but not under pressure," he'd checked off on the inventory, as well as "I can write, but I can't spell." (To be clear: Henry didn't actually put any check marks down or read any of the choices.) The CLC inventory is designed for the literacy tutor to read aloud to the student, who then makes the choices verbally. It is an extremely well-designed tool and allows even the new tutor to get a comprehensive survey of the learner's self-perceptions. This self-reporting begins a process of learner empowerment because it is the learner, not the traditional teacher/authority figure, who is judging the learner's ability. It also minimizes the stress that literacy evaluations can engender. Though there are some reporting flaws, the errors are decidedly less dramatic than those inherent in a teacher test or a test designed by someone who does not know the learner at all. The only writing Henry indicated he could do were notes, forms/applications, and letters, all of which he categorized as "very hard" to write. And although he claimed to be able to fill out forms, one of his primary reasons for seeking help was his inability to negotiate the school employment forms.

After we finished the self-report, he said that he was participating in the high school's sustained silent reading (SSR) program that called for the entire campus to read for fifteen minutes each day. This reading had inspired him to think he might be able to survive an adult basic education class. So two months earlier he had signed up for one and was told he would be called. He was still waiting. His stated reasons for wanting to learn to read were (1) to help his five-year-old son, who could not read at all by the end of the first grade, and (2) job improvement—he needed to pass a written test to get full-time custodial work. Earlier in our discussion, Henry had said his son was "doing real good" in school. This deliberate misrepresentation is part of the low-achieving adult's profile. Time and again the parents of unsuccessful children say that the children are doing well, that they like school, and that they have lots of friends, when this is simply not the case. Later on, you will see that the mother of nine-year-old Arthur even taught the boy to lie about his status. And you'll meet Madonna, mother of six, whose sister claimed her own children were very successful even as she pulled the report cards of failure from her purse. So much emphasis has been put on grades and other nonlearning issues that people seem to feel the cover-up is more important than the cure. This is one more way in which the terrible conspiracy of home, school, and society is perpetuated: We cannot solve problems we deny exist.

Migrant Worker Roots

As the oldest son of a military family, Henry, who said he had eighteen sisters and nine brothers, complained that his mother didn't give him any attention and his father was never there for him. While Dad moved around, Mom kept the kids in Oklahoma, where they worked the cotton fields and pecan groves. Henry didn't actually pick cotton; his job was to jump down in the long burlap bags and stomp it down as his mother and older sisters picked. He was also responsible for tossing his younger sisters up into pecan trees to shake the harvest loose and get stung by bees in the process. It was not a happy childhood.

At an unclear time, his mother, deciding she had too many kids to look after, gave Henry and one of his sisters to an uncle who was a schoolteacher and who became Henry's schoolteacher and principal for grades one through six. The uncle, who did not believe in wasting time on storytelling or reading to kids, did, however, demand perfect penmanship. As a result, Henry has a distinctive, elegant handwriting that he combines with very creative spelling and almost no punctuation. This harks back to the issue of teaching that focuses on surface not substance. In the next chapter you'll meet Arthur's mother, whose beautiful penmanship reflected countless hours of thought-free cursive copywork. One of the critical points to be made here is that *the adult illiterate always confuses penmanship with writing.* Whether he or she can actually do nice calligraphy or not, there is a long and painful history of trying. Poor pedagogy has consistently promoted surface over substance. You saw it with Juanita in the ghetto. You see it with Henry. And you will see it again and again—every time you see a person who was not taught that writing is about making marks that speak.

Even as you read these lines, a child somewhere is spending creative writing time copying and recopying some meaningless passage in an effort to make it *look* right when it has no voice at all. Then, during reading time, you can bet your boots that same child will be obliged to bark sounds—the right ones, perfectly—instead of seeking meaning from the text. The curriculum says "reading time" and "writing time," but that child is spending hours each week learning the wrong definitions. That is what happened to Henry.

Race Relations

His education started in an all-black school in Oklahoma. Then he spent a year in Texas, where he "didn't like the system. I had to walk seven miles in the snow—in Waco. They had no program there for [migrant children]. It was a good school in the summer 'cause there was not snow, but we had to go out for the harvest. I picked cotton most of my life and chopped wheat and baled hay." Finally, because of his uncle's work with the NAACP, Henry ended up in Southern California in the eleventh grade.

"Did anyone recognize you weren't reading?" I asked.

"They probably did, but at the time for me, I was the only black in the whole school . . . my uncle was heading up the NAACP and I lived in an area that was white and . . . Spanish . . . whatever.[1] It took me about five years to get in there because my uncle had to fight [for] it. . . . That must have been about 1960 something. It was real hard I tell you."

Time and again I've observed a severe sense of isolation among nonreading adults. Even when, like Henry, they've come from large families and even when they've been in very crowded social systems like the prisons, they harbor the notion that they are alone in the world with unique troubles and circumstances that no one else could comprehend or care about. I call this the isolation factor. During one of his bouts of self-pity, Henry described it this way: "I was always taking care of somebody else's kids. And I need someone to be there for me, too, and they wasn't. It hurt. Sometimes I put myself into a shell and I didn't want to come out . . . because I was tired of being hurt by people . . . I lost my ability to do anything for myself, because I feel 'Why talk about it? Nobody wants to help me nohow.' And everybody down on you because of your color." He complained that those around him have always had many material goods he has been unable to buy. At fifteen, he'd left home. "I couldn't accept going to bed hungry, didn't have no clothes, you know, decent stuff like that. I've never had, let's put it this way, 'good money.' "

He claimed to have been around the world nineteen times, but the time had apparently all been spent in the galley of a ship where he worked as cook. He talked of no off-ship adventures and had essentially no awareness of other cultures. In addition, because of battles brought by unions in which he had no membership and perhaps because of simple exploitation or not understanding his contracts, he had never made any money during his seagoing time. Though many of the details in his stories didn't match up, the inconsistencies seemed to me to stem from an inability to document dates and facts rather than from an intent to give misinformation. Indeed, he was so open about issues that he might have wanted to keep secret, it seemed there was little left to hide.

He had encountered the law in many negative ways, the most recent of which was a stint in jail. "I had a big fight with my son—*her* son. I went to jail for six months because of it," he said, insisting that the teenager had always been unruly. He felt trapped in the marriage that had brought with it two stepchildren. "I needed someone to talk to . . . [and so] got married to a young lady that had two kids . . . it was hard for me to raise them cause they were both white. . . ." He regularly complained that he didn't like what they were "turning out to be," reflecting an attitude that predestiny, more than environment, determined such things. He was also very unhappy that his wife refused to discard the teenagers when they proved "bad seeds." His very rigid attitudes about children and their rights were plainly seated in his own experience. For all his talk of his undeserved suffering and his religiously instilled "goodwill toward men," he seemed to have done little reflecting. The way things were was the way they were supposed to be, God's will, even when he could see he wasn't getting a fair return on his efforts. For Henry life was simple. Mothers were good, all mothers, even the one he complained gave him no time but did give him away. His uncle was good for taking him in, even though the life had been horrid for little children and he had been used as a servant for his adoptive family. Things were right or they were wrong. He also had a blind faithfulness for "loved ones" even when he hated them. When he was unable to support the rituals of gift giving, for example, he devoted energy to worrying about it.

He frequently brought up the fact that he had never gone out with a black woman, and was confused at my failure to understand that without explanation. "They has a attitude. They don't appreciate nothin' you do . . . ." He'd never needed to contemplate it; it was just a fact. He seemed to be in permanent turmoil over issues of race, sometimes justifiably but just as often on the basis of manifestations of his own imagination. He felt he'd been punished unjustly for beating up the incorrigible stepson. "The law told me I couldn't do this and I couldn't do that. . . ." The things "the law" had told him were in stark violation of the blind obedience required of him as a child and promised him in his fundamentalist religion. Having known only a rigid, inflexible lifestyle, he was having great difficulty with a world that was changing the rules just as he reached what he had assumed would be a position of power. As a nonreader, he had no opportunity to tune in to what the world was writing about other realities. Henry was trapped by his illiteracy.

Meanwhile, his five-year-old was being taught that it was wrong to be black, as though the mixed-race child could make a decision in the matter. When Henry brought in an expensive studio portrait of his son, I said, "What a beautiful little boy!"

"Yeah, he's almost white, ain't he."

Chaos from Within

Self-generated chaos was very much a part of Henry's life. He was regularly planning to divorce his wife and take his son, an impractical move for a man who could neither support himself nor write his own checks. He did, however, take his child to stay in a motel for a couple of weekends during our sessions. The expense, coupled with the inconvenience of having to maintain the child in such circumstances, brought that crisis to a close.

It was replaced, however, by a sudden need to rush to Texas to introduce his son to his long estranged uncle (the one his mother gave him to), who was in a coma. My reminder that the uncle would not understand what was going on dissuaded him temporarily. But when the uncle died, Henry felt he should attend the funeral and help pay for it. The fact that he did not have the money for transportation, let alone a funeral, was less important than the fact that finally helped him decide to skip the event—he couldn't stand the relatives who would be there.

Perhaps because he had never gotten along with any of his siblings or cousins, he seemed to feel he needed to do something dramatic. Then he did. He wrote a poem for his widowed aunt. But consistent with his concern over surface issues, he wanted the writing on the card to be perfect, so he asked me to print his poem on my computer. I took in several printouts of it, allowing him to select the one to be folded into a card. Then this man who had a natural flair for drawing flowers laboriously worked on designing the "right" kind of design to go on it. Since I was trying to discover topics we could expand on, topics that would be of vital interest to him, I brought in postage stamps that featured historical events and people. When he selected an Ida B. Wells Black Heritage stamp from my commemoratives, I hoped there would be a history connection—but there wasn't. Later, he decided, he might make a donation to the NAACP in his uncle's name.

Job Corps Galore

His troubles with the law and frequent bouts of unemployment qualified Henry for a multitude of job training programs, all verified by completion certificates that he kept in a three-ring binder with his letters of recommendation. "I've been in about twelve Job Corps skills. They learn you a skill or a trade, something like that," but as for literacy, "it's not on a one-on-one basis," he said, reflecting an awareness of a study we'd just read. "They have so many guys in the Corps; they have about fifteen hundred people in the Corps and they don't have the proper instructors to come in and help you with it." He described a shotgun approach to teaching . . . those who caught on, caught on; those who didn't, didn't. And the instruction focused on entry-level skills, with no hint of what went on at higher levels of a trade.

This is another manifestation of the parts-to-whole philosophy. There is a remarkable similarity between learning a lot of letter sounds and letter combinations and learning isolated job skills. In neither case is the learner given the meaning or purpose of the "whole." The focus is on the "basics."

People who landed in such training were already identified as losers, according to Henry. He claimed to have had no peers who were "any count." And there was no individual counseling or follow-up. The Job Corps not only failed to help with Henry's literacy but also never trained him in a field that interested him.[2] One such failure was a cooking program. Though he claims to be a good cook, he hates cooking. (And during the CLC interview, he initially claimed to have never used a recipe.)

Nevertheless his certificates and letters of recommendation reflect years of entrepreneurial effort. He had a shoe-shine business, but, he complained, people wear tennies now. He had a wash-and-fold service out of a laundromat, but when the business sold, he was not part of the package. He has worked hard all his life and feels very cheated by never having anything to show for it. A major factor has been not having the literacy skills to negotiate effective contracts.

Theory Agrees with Experience but Not Practice

The ideas I presented in our sessions made sense right from the start to this man with a gift of gab. My teaching paper on the affective filter was right on target, he claimed. And Rist's ghetto classroom observations might have been made in Henry's classrooms. For every study, he had supporting anecdotes. But putting the theory into practice as we continued to meet was quite another matter.

There were flickers of very literate behavior in his nonreading, nonwriting habits. When I first read an Aesop fable to him, he studied it carefully, then dated and numbered it. We discussed which words were difficult. Then he announced that he would like to have one of these little stories each time. An expressly stated moral seemed to make the difference in whether he could allow himself the privilege of enjoying the text. I delivered a steady stream of Aesop to an eager audience. But he wouldn't attempt to read even very short fables on his own. He was a willing passenger, but that was as far as he would go.

Convincing him to transfer his own delight in storytelling to his son proved initially impossible. I relentlessly explained that both father and son would benefit from the reading of good children's books, books on Henry's level. Henry could first read the books to himself, silently, developing his vocabulary as he read; seeing this, his son would get a positive impression about literate behavior. Then once he felt secure, Henry could read the books aloud to his son. Henry understood the idea behind studies showing that children who are read to become book lovers. And, I explained, Frank Smith says being read to, seeing their parents read for pleasure, and observing parents involved in other literacy-related events teaches children that the big people in their families are automatically users of text. Smith calls that club membership. We discussed club membership, and Henry fully agreed with the passages I read him from *Insult to Intelligence*. But the idea of just running around loving books was repugnant to this man for whom functional literacy was the only kind of literacy worth pursuing.

Henry wanted only books that had useful information. If it wasn't a "school" book, he'd learned long ago, it had no place in a good person's hands. But, even the elementary-level history books I had were beyond him and when I read them to him, he lost interest. In other words, what he believed he *should* want, he *didn't*. Put still another way, this is one more illustration of how surface (or appearance) is more important than substance (or what a person really thinks and feels.) But falling asleep during "real" history stories and getting involved during "fluff" fables was not proof enough to Henry that he should do what came naturally and help his son do the same.

And at first he insisted on blaming his wife for not taking care of the child's story times. This, it turned out, stemmed from his belief that child care is women's work. (Rigidly assigned gender roles is another consistent feature among nonreading adults. In the ghetto, it was Farra's duty to love child care. In Henry's home, child care was the woman's work.) He also refused to ask his wife to read to him ten minutes a day. He flatly stated that he didn't want his wife to read to him, (1) because his problem was that people had been reading to him all his life and, (2) because she had scoffed at him when he first announced he wanted to go back to school. She said he couldn't hack it. Eager to find avenues for self-pity, Henry complained bitterly that he was always working and so couldn't be expected to read to his son. The fact that he was also complaining that he only had a part-time job—not enough hours to get the money to buy the material goods he longed to own—did not interfere with this logic in the least.

Children's Literature Is Strong Stuff

I hauled in a vast assortment of books each session, in an effort to get his attention, and always left price stickers in place to let him know where the items had been purchased and for how much. Henry did pay attention to this information, but didn't think I should leave the stickers on the covers once he'd registered it. Biographies of Martin Luther King, Jr., and Harriet Tubman made an impression, but they were too difficult. Of a book called *Jamaica's Find*, he said his son wouldn't want to hear about a little girl. But finally I read him the humorous Robert Munsch book *Something Good*, a story about a little black girl who responds so literally to her white father's command to behave and be still when she goes shopping with him that she is mistaken for a doll and she is given a price tag. As a result he has to pay to get her out of the store. Henry agreed that the father had finally gotten something good. He took it home to read to his son, and I scrambled to find other light fiction with black characters. A beautifully illustrated *A Whistle for Willie* by Ezra Jack Keats, a whimsical storybook *The Stories Julian Tells*, and most of all the folk legend *John Henry* finally managed to push Henry into the world of pleasure print.

Father and son began enjoying books together. And at one point he told me his son was as black as he was, indicating a shift in his own self-perception. When neighbor kids began to come in to listen, Henry reported his wife had started to get interested too. But he didn't want her butting in. (You'll see more of this partner exclusion in Madonna's chapter and again in Danny's. And you may recall that some gang members had to have private sessions during the week. Emerging literacy is a very private affair.)

About that time, however, Henry's hours were increased for the summer, making further work impossible. And, although buying books of his own was still beyond his imagination, he did get very enthusiastic about the possibility of finding more books he could share with his son and show off to his neighbors' kids. To that end, this man who had no car or phone made a plan to take his son to the public library after work on the Saturday following our last session. It would have been a major trip involving a long walk to and from the bus on both ends, more than an hour on the bus, and the time spent in the library—possibly more than a three-hour commitment at the end of a very physical work day. He chose Saturday because it was the only workday he got off early enough to use the bus before it stopped running for the day. Still, this plan, he understood, would begin a process of teacher-free literacy, essential to his continued success and the only way to get through the summer. If father and son had a positive experience, they might make a regular thing of it.

Fortunately, he disclosed his plan to me. Otherwise I could not have made the necessary phone call and he would have shown up with his son at the doors of a library that closes at 5 P.M. on Saturdays, placing access to literacy on hold until Monday. In this service area of the working poor, the hours exclude them. Shouldn't it be the other way around? Shouldn't the library also be open for people who can't come in at midday? Shouldn't the libraries be open at least as many hours as pool halls and shopping malls? What does this say about our values as a society? Doesn't Henry have as much right to take his child to the children's book section of the library as parents who can afford good books for their home libraries? What did Henry's little boy lose that day? And what did society lose?

Reading for Fun Fosters Writing for Meaning

During his sessions with me, Henry began to write his life story. He would dictate ideas on tape, which I transcribed and printed out for him to read and approve. He took the triple-spaced copy home and wrote in more ideas. The process was working, but the meter was running too fast. Henry would not have time to work with me during the summer and he was not yet prepared to take independent action for himself or his son. I had another three months to give him, and he knew he needed more help, but he couldn't give up the chance to earn full wages. Henry and I had met at the high school where he worked; we had permission to use an office there during his nonworking time. He was always punctual and always brought in information related to whatever we were working on at the time. I worked with him on his résumé, giving him progressively more complete copies to work on. As a result, he did develop a full and interesting résumé before our work together ended. But emerging literacy at any age must have continued support over several years. Henry still needed formal assistance. Even a program where he could have gotten more reading materials from a librarian familiar with his situation or regular writing help from a literacy office might have been enough. But Henry's library door was locked.

Over the summer he wrote me two letters of appreciation. In one he said he'd taken a trip to Disneyland with his little boy, no doubt spending enough money to have stocked a small personal library. His literacy attitudes, were, as might have been predicted, moving backward.

Though I'm sure he had initially understood that my commitment was individual, experimental, and limited, when I went back to do some paperwork at the school the following fall, Henry spotted me coming across the parking lot, rushed out to meet me, and inquired into my schedule. Seeming to believe that need qualified him for help, he ran through his standard litany of qualifications—low-level employment, a family to support, even his belief in God. Society had taught him a powerful set of rules about being eligible for aid and he either didn't remember or didn't want to believe that my criteria were different and that I simply couldn't come back again. While at the school, I spoke with the administrator who had set us up; he said that Henry wanted to know what the school was doing to get someone else like me to come in. That's how it had been all of his adult life, hadn't it? Education was just a set of rubber stamps and if you stood in line and got stamped enough times, sooner or later one of the stamps would be right—right? Having gone through formal processes all his life, Henry didn't seem ready to believe that what he'd participated in was unique. If history always repeats itself, then didn't Henry have the right to believe that the months of individualized instruction had really just been one more training program?

Is there any point in teaching Henry to read at fifty? Well, humanistically there are certainly arguments suggesting he deserves a better quality of life during his twilight years than he had during his youth. But it seems pragmatists are running the agencies in charge of funds. So, pragmatically speaking, we can expect Henry to live another twenty to forty years. We also know there is a strong correlation between illiteracy and incarceration, and Henry's track record supports that correlation. So, at fifty, Henry may voluntarily work part-time for ten years more, or he may settle for unemployment, or . . .

But, if given careful support over the next three to five years, we know he'll at least be able to fill out the application form for the job he wants. He might get the job; he might stay out of jail; and he might make an incalculable difference to the life his young son leads . . . and his son . . . and his son. . . . Can we afford not to give Henry a chance?

1. Like others who seem excessively concerned about race, Henry had adopted his opinions by proxy, assuming that the ideas of people he admired were good enough for him. Upon close examination, Henry proved to think that anyone who spoke Spanish was Mexican and all Asians, including the Vietnamese students at the high school where he worked, were Chinese.

2. Student interest in the subject or level of training and follow-up regarding the success of the training are not concerns for many programs reported to me by participants. One woman in the gang literacy project, who had been "sentenced" to training as a condition of her parole, was put through a lengthy and strenuous firefighter training program, a career in which she had absolutely no interest. That didn't seem to matter to any of the players. And upon her release, the issue of getting a job in firefighting was dropped by trainers, trainee, and all other disinterested parties. She immediately went back on welfare and currently supports herself on Aid for Dependent Children.

Four

Arthur:
Disempowered in the Extreme

At the opposite end of the economic scale from Henry, Arthur was a nine-year-old boy from an upper-middle-class home, where he lived with his original parents, close to doting grandparents, and within walking distance of his cousins. Common knowledge, the media, and popular movies suggest that illiteracy is the special domain of the poor. Certainly attention is drawn to the destitute person who is unable to read or write "functionally" enough to do what employers want done. However, it is the *failure to function for others' purposes* that causes the brouhaha, *not the root of the failure*. So if the victim of poor pedagogy can learn to keep the failure under wraps by concealing the symptoms, the family, the school, and society can contentedly perpetuate the conspiracy of disempowerment unfettered. As hiding the symptoms is paramount, there is no limit to which the creative family of means will not go to keep illiteracy in the closet. Such was the case with Arthur.[1]

In this study you will easily identify how surface-over-substance issues are reflected in far more than reading and writing. You will also see how the isolation factor encompasses both mother and child. But, most intriguing, Arthur's story is a dramatic illustration of how disempowering significant others operate to give the illusion of tender loving care, perhaps even literacy assistance, while actually working to prevent the development of literacy. Intuitively seeing literacy as power, the DSO, though often little more proficient than the victim, works surreptitiously, creatively, even violently to maintain control over the nonreader. DSOs are common to the stories of poor readers and nonreading adults. However, in Arthur's case, you will see DSOs pressing in from all directions.

Arthur Bonadventure almost gave the game away when, after being a "model" student in the school since kindergarten, his end-of-third-grade test scores in reading, writing, and spelling indicated he should be held back the next year. But his mother, a dedicated and regular volunteer at the school, insisted this would be much too difficult to explain to the family, so the school authorities, unaware of Mrs. B's own literacy problems, told her that if she would either help him or get him help over the summer, he would be fine.

The suggestion sounded easy enough. Mrs. B would get help for herself and then pass that help on to Arthur. Midsummer she did sign up for a tutor, but couldn't follow through because her schedule was on overload. Suddenly it was two weeks before the opening of school, and she realized she no longer had time for her own lessons. Deciding she'd better get Arthur some help quickly, she connected with me through a literacy program that knew of my interest in working with a child whose parent was also learning to read.

They were an hour and a half late for the first meeting. During our initial interview, Mrs. B seemed eager to impress me with how important she was, how good-looking her family members were, how community-oriented they were, and what an impressive circle of friends she had, even though her husband didn't really fit into her class. Arthur was agreeable and friendly. His biggest impact on the interview was to position himself in such a way that his mother could just see him out of the corner of her eye. With a slow movement like a frog up to a fly, he would move his index finger toward his face. Then . . . zap! His finger was in his nose. "Arthur, don't pick your nose," she'd bark, midsentence, whereupon he would go limp for about twenty-five seconds. During the interview, I began to make little tick marks on my note pad; there were over thirty Arthur-don't-pick-your-noses in as many minutes. This was the primary contact between mother and son. Most conversation concerning him was conducted as if he weren't there, just as adults in the ghetto gymnasium had talked about Farra.

I explained to Mrs. B that my work involved using learning theory to help the learner understand how reading developed. But with a young child like Arthur, I wanted to be able to give the insights to his mother so that she could facilitate his reading at home. Also, I wanted her to give me feedback on her discoveries. Though she was welcome to observe any time her schedule permitted, our formal plan would be to talk on the phone after my sessions with her son, so I could update her on his needs and she could keep me posted on her own reading progress. She thought that was just great. She loved to talk on the phone.

Though during the interview Arthur had been allowed to recite the family's huge inventory of electronic toys, memory telephones, and televisions for every room, he had never seen children's programs on public television. I also learned that Arthur didn't have a favorite book; in fact, he didn't own any books at all. Knowing that Mrs. B's own test results indicated she could handle only very basic text, I introduced the importance of reading things that are both very interesting and very easy, so that frustration wouldn't interfere with the joy of reading. She understood immediately. Then, in keeping with her expressed interest in helping her son herself, I explained the value of being read to and how she might use very simple bedtime stories to foster her own reading ability while sharing them with Arthur. She seemed to understand this too. I showed her some of the children's books in my tote, pointing out why some were more appropriate than others for Arthur. Again, there was complete comprehension on her part.[2]

I then suggested that when they left the interview they stop by a local market and pick up some books for Arthur that were within her reading ability. She could use them to get in her ten minutes a day of practice reading and have something available for her son at the same time. Mrs. B looked as though I'd hit her. She said she'd have to "rob a bank" to get enough money to do that. This came only minutes after she'd drawn attention to her own designer clothes and then to the expensive costumes that Arthur wore, feigning complaint about the speed with which he ran through them. The issue was not money; it was money to buy books. Books ranked very low on the family's priority list.

Surface Surface

The Bonadventure home was in one of those gated communities entered by way of a complicated set of codes. Once inside the main entrance, however, I discovered another hurdle. Unlike most other homes in the complex, theirs had no address posted, so it was somewhat by luck that I wandered up an unmarked path to an unmarked door. As it opened, Mrs. B gave me a thousand-watt smile and took a movie-star stance in front of a giant poster with the single word LOVE blasting out many times in many colors. Then she led me to her elegantly furnished living room where Arthur sat like a little wax doll, his double-breasted designer jacket all buttoned up and his wavy hair all slicked down as though it was supposed to be straight. On command from his mother, he stood up, gave a little bow, and smiled, showing scummy, unbrushed teeth. As I joined him on the huge pastel sofa, I noticed walls of books, all of which seemed to be color-coordinated with the couch, the carpet, or the prominently exhibited and costly-looking art. Near a fireplace was a large armchair (Mr. B's chair I later learned) surrounded with books on Hollywood. Across from it were a set of video recorder/players and a television.

What showed at first glance was a well-dressed young man who lived with his biological parents and near many members of his extended family, in a home where books were on display. It would have been impossible to tell how a child could be a poor reader in these circumstances. I could see how the principal, who had been a guest in the home numerous times over the years, had been taken in. What's more, when asked about how he was doing in school, Arthur had been taught to lie, even to me, who needed the truth in order to help him. Well aware of the need to keep up appearances, Arthur told people that he was making good grades and that school was fun even when he was failing and hated it. Setting kids up with profiles of humiliation is disempowering. So is telling them it is bad to lie and then that their truths are unspeakable.

Once Arthur and I were seated on the couch, in front of a coffee table bearing huge conversation-type travel books, I looked around for a reading lamp. There was none. As I reached into my tote for some storybooks, Mrs. B asked Arthur if he wanted anything to eat. Since Mrs. B and I had discussed the need to be physically comfortable while reading, I presumed this sudden offer of food was an effort to show she'd understood. There was really no need for this very bright woman to prove anything—she clearly caught on to theoretical concepts and theory-to-practice ideas with the same speed as the ghetto grandmother who turned teacher. The puzzle remains to this day. Time and again there was terrible evidence that Mrs. B's understanding wasn't working to her son's advantage. On this day, for example, though it was 2:00 P.M., he hadn't yet eaten.

I asked him which book he would like me to read and he quickly latched on to *The Cat in The Hat*. But his mother intervened. She wanted me to read an autographed children's book she'd gotten at a lecture by a famous psychologist. Mrs. B and I had already talked about the many facets of decision making in literacy development and how this decision making could be observed transferring to other areas of a person's life. For example, the simple matter of guessing at an unfamiliar word or just skipping it is something the good reader does automatically and the poor reader interprets as inappropriate. And the idea that text is here to serve, not dominate, the reader allows the good reader several options: to start a story, to continue it, to put it down before it's over. The poor reader generally expects that once something is begun he or she must tunnel through. Mrs. B and I had also discussed the powerful decision about what text to choose in the first place. When I reminded her about the decision-making issues connected with literacy, she simply redirected her attention to her son, trying to get him to select her book.[3] However, Arthur held firm, and soon I began reading Dr. Seuss's poetic tale of two children, left without a mother to guide them.

At first Arthur just listened, then he chimed in, and finally he eased the book away from me and took over the reading himself, though with great difficulty, missing some words important to comprehension but never going back to correct for meaning. My process as I read to students is over time to call attention to when I am going back (regressing), thus letting them know that good readers do this all the time; eventually, and almost imperceptibly, the students begin to acquire both the theory and the strategy. But in this first encounter with Arthur, he had taken over the reading, preventing that kind of demonstration teaching. Slowly, I began asking him questions using words he'd missed, trying to give him context cues without direct correction. After several seemingly strange errors, I realized that he had made no connection between the pictures and the text. Here he was, nine years old, and he did not know that you look at the pictures to find out more about the story. With a younger child I might automatically have done some of the prereading things like look through the book and discuss what it might be about. I had let Arthur's age temper my approach, even though I was already convinced that learning to read is learning to read, regardless of age, language, or culture and even though I do use prereading activities with adults. So Arthur was already in (forgive me) the swim of things when, as I asked him why the fish in the pot was unhappy, I pointed to it. (He'd missed the word *pot* and the meaning that depended on it.) After a few such efforts, a light went on. He looked away from the book to give me a genuine smile. Then he began looking at the pictures as he went.

Over time, I met numerous aunts, cousins, and a great uncle, all of whom avoided literacy-related activities as much as possible. No one in Arthur's extended family had any time at all to look at books with him. And over time, there were far more missed lessons than meetings. Countless other things had priority, and there were many cancelations and reschedulings. And in spite of our frequent phone conversations, sometimes Mrs. B simply forgot that a session had been scheduled, taking Arthur off somewhere or sending him to a friend's house. As a result, instead of weekly, we met only on an average of about once every five or six weeks.[4]

Finally, when Mrs. B told me not to come one day because Arthur's grandmother had decided that Arthur's lesson hour would be the perfect time to take all the grandkids to a movie, I refused to reschedule. "Your family does not value literacy and Arthur doesn't stand a chance of learning to read with all of you working against him. We are just wasting our time," I blurted. When Mrs. B realized that I really wasn't interested in rescheduling, she put her little boy on the phone. He pleaded for me to come that day, saying that he could go to a movie any time and that reading was important to him. That got me. He gave up the movie and I gave up the point I was trying to make. Three weeks later Grandma set up a contest between a seldom-seen visiting cousin and me. Arrangements had been made for me to pick up both boys that day so that Arthur would have the best of both worlds. Meanwhile, I'd conjured a lesson plan that I hoped would lead to the boys' becoming pen pals, because according to Mrs. B, this was the "smart" cousin, the one who could read. But when I showed up to collect them, Mrs. B was gone and Grandma was in charge. She'd ever so slightly changed the plan: only Arthur could go. That meant a very lonely little boy had to choose between literacy and company his own age. Literacy lost.

Arthur tried to tell me so many things each time we met that ideas tumbled out like marbles from a broken bag, but getting anything into the writing ring was quite another matter. So, early on we agreed that his standing homework assignment would be to draw pictures of anything he thought about. However, he had had no drawing materials before I gave him some. And although Mrs. B claimed to be an artist herself and exhibited art in her home, she hadn't time even to look at Arthur's work.

After a session one day, I explained to Mrs. B that I've been in classrooms where the children are rushed through frustrating media-use frenzies in the name of art time, netting neither relaxed abstractions nor rich detail. Yet art, when allowed to expand naturally, cracks open fossilized cocoons of boredom and inhibition and sets loose incredible intellectual butterflies. But thinking takes time. And the art process is more successful when it is allowed to progress uninterrupted. The point of Arthur's artwork was that it would provide the foundation for a language experience activity in which he wrote about the pictures he'd had time to think through. I told her that it would be important to make sure that Arthur's art supplies could be spread out in his own room and left undisturbed. She worriedly led me there, explaining that a teenage cousin was visiting for an undetermined period and had to use Arthur's room. A frilly dress was strewn across his bed and his little-boy artifacts had been pushed to the rear of his dressing table to make room for lipsticks, makeup, perfumes, hair gel, and a variety of other teenage-girl stuff.[5] Arthur had been temporarily assigned to a couch facing a TV in a high-traffic den, making his life not much different from Farra's in the ghetto.

For the present, any art he was able to do needed to be put away immediately. When I reminded Mrs. B that Arthur needed positive reinforcement, she did agree to praise whatever drawings he came up with. But when I offered her some magnets so she could post her favorites on the refrigerator door, she told me that, quite honestly, she really didn't expect much to come of all this. He'd brought home stuff from school before and, unlike the children of her friends, Arthur had never done anything worth displaying. And from her perspective, to praise imperfect products was to encourage mediocrity. By the time he and I next met, Arthur had one drawing, of a smoking, whiskey-drinking, cussing monster on a motorcycle (clearly altered by an adult to look more angelic). Several other pieces he'd enthusiastically described over the phone had inadvertently been thrown away.

Though I did phone Mrs. B regularly and though true to her claim she did love to talk, Arthur's reading was by no means her favorite subject. Nonetheless, I did keep feeding her the theoretical underpinnings for our work. At one point I discovered that Arthur knew neither his unlisted phone number nor his address. Mrs. B understood that since their address was not posted outside the house, Arthur hadn't been exposed to those numbers; she didn't understand my concern that should Arthur get lost, he would have no way of telling anyone where he belonged and couldn't phone home. "He has no reason to get lost," she assured me. "He's never far away unless he's at his cousin's house, where they have the information." It was true, Arthur was generally confined to his gated community, in someplace he'd been officially transported, or at school. This is the isolation factor concretely demonstrated. At any rate I was embarking on a language experience lesson designed to overcome a problem only I perceived as real.

Nevertheless, I told Mrs. B that to teach Arthur his address in a meaning-filled way, I would have him self-address envelopes into which I would later put a personalized message (a joke using his name, a funny poem written about something he'd done, a secret clue about something he had to read) and some lightweight trinkets (stickers, stars, play money) and then mail to him. Or I might take him to a post office of his choice to put his own mail into the slot and generate that specific post mark. Either way, he would see his address when he wrote it on the envelope and would get a reminder when he actually received the mail. This was authentic use for an address and wouldn't require memorization. The collection of self-addressed envelopes would also serve as a low-key self-evaluation tool over time. Mrs. B thought this a novel idea. However, because of the infrequency of our sessions, the envelopes were only addressed every few weeks. Still, he then had the mail to keep and peruse at will. Arthur was a very bright child who loved riddles and mind games, and his memory for details of events over the months was very keen. So I was a little concerned when he answered the phone one evening, several months into the process and gave me a really vague answer about what I'd mailed to him . . . as though he couldn't remember clearly. Then I discovered that Mrs. B was bringing in the mail and delivering the contents to her son without the envelopes.

Process . . . Found Out

To accommodate the chaos of the Bonadventure home, I took Arthur to a stationery store to buy some brightly colored oversized envelopes in which to store his photocopies of poems (mostly Shel Silverstein's), short stories, and writings. The business of keeping children's books handy for him had proven impossible, and this seemed the only way to give Arthur access to the essential reading ingredient: something to read. In his best handwriting, he'd proudly written his name on magenta and chartreuse envelopes, chosen, I suspect, as much for the strange sounds of the names as for the actual colors. It had amused him that I couldn't spell those words and had to find a dictionary right there in the stationery store to look them up. He wanted to know what I'd do if I were in a coffee shop! I had trouble spelling coffee, too. We talked about the problem of knowing whether it started with a "k" or not. Arthur had taken care of the problem by going up to a teenager with purple hair and asking him for help. The startled young man had actually come over to the dictionary with Arthur and after a long discussion about the sounds, this newfound teacher remembered that coffee starts with a "c." I didn't try to explain to Arthur that he'd programmed the young man's schema to look for the wrong letter first, but I'll bet he would have understood. We did talk about the problems a person can have relying just on phonics and that tapping into the available human resources was an excellent way of solving a problem. He understood that. And that wasn't all he understood. He suddenly looked at me incredulously and said, "You knew how to spell coffee all the time! You were just *teaching* me!" I felt embarrassed. It had been a cheap trick. So, I'd been caught twice that day. (I really wasn't sure about the spelling of chartreuse.)

There was a lot of meaning attached to those brilliantly colored envelopes that held his prized poems, short stories, and personal writings. And their vibrant colors guaranteed they would be visible, regardless of where in that chaotic house they got stashed. But each, in turn, disappeared . . . contents and all.

Law of the Jungle

I was very surprised to be greeted by a rumpled and distraught Mrs. B one afternoon. She never ventured out of the house looking less than a Vogue model. But on this particular day she didn't even seem to notice how she looked—or so I thought. Within a few minutes, though, I learned that this was again part of the drama that made up the Bonadventure household.

At Grandma's invitation, Grandma's brother was coming to town and Mrs. B and her sisters were extremely upset about it. She wasn't really clear about how this man managed to dominate the entire family, but there was no doubt that their uncle had been chasing after his little nieces all their lives. Now, Grandma had suddenly decided that she couldn't have him staying in her home, so it was up to the "girls" to look after him. It was almost nauseating to hear her point out that he was "family." (There it was again, that false assumption that qualifying as a relative gives someone the right to destroy you. Henry had expressed this sentiment, and you'll hear it again when you read about Madonna.) Mrs. B had deliberately made herself look unlovely to discourage the man.

That night I tuned into a local public television station just as a dramatization of C. S. Lewis's story *The Lion, the Witch and the Wardrobe* was about to begin. It struck me that this could make a beautiful connection between TV, which Arthur's family clearly revered, and literature, so I called Mrs. B, who immediately had Arthur tune in. (It was incredible how this woman was able to grasp theoretical connections. Yet she still hadn't managed to meet with her tutor.) Then I settled down to watch the film myself.

The next day, armed with notes and my son's copy of the book, I was eager to see Arthur for what I hoped would be a benchmark lesson. My enthusiasm was premature. Arthur had been able to watch only a few minutes of the program. You see, his great-uncle was visiting and "he brings lots of presents and stuff, but he's really not a very nice person to argue with." So, when Arthur had acted silly about the name of the movie, the man had told him he was just as bad as his mom. Then this unwelcome guest decided to watch a different program and had insisted on using the only TV that received the PBS station. The law of the jungle had prevailed.

Spells

I had been told at the start that Arthur occasionally had "spells," periods when he became absolutely unruly. One of his teachers had even suggested he be tested for hyperactivity. One day when I drove by to pick him up, he was in a snarly mood. First he couldn't close the car door. It was too heavy. Then he slammed it so hard I thought our brains would pop through the roof. He had nothing to report, no papers to show, and certainly no flicker of the sunny smile that usually kept me going. We went to a malt shop, one of our usual hangouts, where he shouted at the waitress who months before had graciously allowed him to coax her into reciting almost everything on the menu. This was the kind of spell I'd been warned about! Once his belly was full, however, he settled down, smiled sweetly, put his little head on his arm, and asked, "Would you read me a story?"

I learned that not only had he consumed nothing except a Coke since dinner the night before (it was then 2 P. M.), he'd been up most of the night baby-sitting his aunt's crying infant. Arthur's extended family included two infants, belonging to Mrs. B's two sisters, each of whom also lived in the complex, within walking distance of the Bonadventures' and the grandmother. Though neither aunt had time to read anything to any of the children, they frequently used Arthur (who barely knew how to handle himself in an emergency) as a schoolnight baby-sitter. What's more, Arthur was often sent to school unfed. The riddle was solved! But when I called his mom to let her know that Arthur's "spells" were not hyperactivity or any other bizarre problem, that he just got rude and antsy when he was tired and hungry, she grew defensive. Arthur could control his behavior if he wanted to and it was about time he did.

Environmental Car Print

Ken Goodman has suggested that the average American kid has encountered so much environmental print by the time he or she enters school, reading is old hat.[6] Through Arthur, I discovered that isn't always true. One afternoon, as we drove through a shopping center parking lot, an unusual car caught Arthur's attention. He asked me what kind it was, but I had no idea and started to drive toward it, saying, "Let's go see." "I can see it all right. I just don't know what it is," he argued, and he became increasingly concerned that I hadn't understood as I drove closer to the car. I parked and we got out. On the trunk was a brand name. Here he was, nine years old, and he didn't know you could go up to a car and read what it was. Arthur loved cars and had memorized all kinds of them. He was genuinely appreciative to learn about this new way of solving some very important puzzles. He gave me such a fine smile, I thought he was going to adopt me. Indeed, he needed to adopt somebody. During the same outing he told me that his two school friends—little Mexican boys his mother would not even allow in her house—had been abruptly transferred to another class, leaving him friendless. He said he was *very* lonely.

The IEP

Out of the blue one day, Mrs. B frantically called to ask me to attend an Individual Education Plan (IEP) meeting at Arthur's school. IEPs are a very serious process in which an individual plan is worked out to help an unsuccessful student improve. The parents, the student, and a team of school experts familiar with the child's performance and history come together to discuss the alternatives and to design a plan. Though someone from the outside, like myself, is not a standard participant, I have been asked to attend a number of them. What was unusual here was that Mrs. B wanted me there to support her, not to explain Arthur's reading needs. She was nervous and wanted me there to interpret things she and Mr. B might not understand about the school system. When I asked her if Arthur fully understood the purpose of the meeting, she said he had not been told that it was scheduled and he was certainly not invited. *Excluding children from their life decisions disempowers them.* But of course I agreed to go and was sworn to secrecy about her reading problem.

As the Bonadventures and I waited in the school lobby, Mrs. B began trying to read some children's posters displayed there. She had such difficulty calling out the words, I wondered how any of the office personnel could possibly have overlooked it. It was and still is not clear to me if Mr. B knew the extent of her reading problem or even if he was fully aware that Arthur had one. Like a silent movie extra, he seemed to play the tall, silent onlooker in his wife's flamboyant scenes.

The principal came out to greet us and ushered us to the meeting room. He cheerfully praised Mrs. B on her work with a special program the school had undertaken to increase student self-esteem. The principal had personally appointed Mrs. B to be in charge of her son's unit, where he knew she had logged many volunteer hours. But the principal was a little vague about the year Arthur had first enrolled in the school or exactly what the meeting would entail. He assured us, however, that he was very familiar with the case. Then, without even sitting down, he explained he was doublebooked and so would be in and out of Arthur's IEP meeting. That was the last we saw of him. In addition to the Bonadventures and me, seated at the table were Arthur's regular classroom teacher, the school psychologist, and a special education teacher who had an opening in her class.

As the meeting began, the psychologist and the special ed teacher seemed to zero in on some specific difficulties Arthur was having remembering long series of numbers and his inability to recite them backwards. They also reported he was unable to remember his "math facts," a new term for multiplication tables. They asked Mrs. B (not Mr. B!) if she'd ever had such problems; yes, she had. I asked how other kids learn their "math facts" and was told that they do it at home but that Arthur had refused to learn a great deal of what normal kids learn at home. Not wanting to betray Mrs. B's trust, I pointedly asked both parents if Arthur had worked on math facts at home. Mrs. B said, "Not as far as I know." Mr. B had never seen him working on math facts either. I asked how Arthur could be expected to compete with kids who were doing different things at home than he was. In response, the authorities again asked Mrs. B if she had ever had such problems. Oh, yes, she had had problems with math, spelling, homework and all kinds of reading. Before long, it was clear that Arthur was the victim of genetic deficiencies that show up in families generation after generation. Having established the problem as genetic, everyone was in the clear. No one was at fault; no one was responsible.

When his regular teacher reported that Arthur's performance had gotten radically worse just within the last month,
I suggested that the loss of his friends might have something
to do with it. Then I asked why two Mexican children, with
whom he'd had lasting friendships, had been transferred out
of the class and said that Arthur had said he missed them very
much. (I knew that Mrs. B didn't want Arthur associating
with them and that she had warned Arthur's teacher she would
no longer volunteer and might even withdraw Arthur from
the school if the Mexican children weren't kept away from
him. This was the first time Mr. B gave any flicker of emotion.
He apparently hadn't known about this and paid close attention as the regular teacher and Mrs. B exchanged glances,
perhaps realizing that his wife had had something to do with
solving the ethnic problem she'd openly complained about.)
Could Arthur's lack of performance be related to grief or depression? I asked. The psychologist quickly assured me that
Arthur's test results showed no signs of loss. And the special
ed teacher chimed in with the reassurance that Arthur would
find lots of nice new kids in her program. As Mr. B offered
no comment, that was the end of the depression and grief
discussion. Choosing to be silent during his child's time of
need, Mr. Bonadventure also chose to disempower him.

Results of a variety of tests were distributed, showing,
among things, a very low IQ score. However, having worked
a great deal with the gifted, I said I was quite sure that there
was nothing lacking in Aurthur's ability to learn; I suggested
that he just hadn't the necessary input to do well on the tests.
Besides, during the meeting we'd established that he was read
to neither at home nor at school. Never being read to and
being a nonreader, he had not had an opportunity to acquire
the broad information and vocabulary base that are needed
for test performance. The special ed teacher conceded that
Arthur "quite frankly is baffling us." He didn't fit the profile
of the usual child who was having learning disabilities. She
could only suggest that he spend a few hours each week on

phonics. Asked what I thought of that approach, I said that he seemed to have had so much phonics that he tended to cover parts of words with his finger while trying to read them, a process that caused him to lose track of the story. He put "sounding out" unknown words ahead of meaning. My suggestion that language experience be used was met with a quick explanation that that doesn't work with special ed kids and takes way too much time anyway.

Arthur was then praised for his beautiful smile and handwriting, both of which Mrs. B took as direct reflections of herself. Then a number of other parent-centered homework failures were recited, including worksheets on the Olympics (Arthur didn't even know the Olympics were going on; his parents didn't think the Olympics were important). It was abundantly clear that Arthur had failed to do the things that presupposed someone would read to him and listen to him read.

He was expected to have a quiet study area that included not only a study surface and good lighting, but also a dictionary and thesaurus. Each of these items was spelled out during this conference. While I challenged each item and Arthur's parents freely reported to the school authorities that his home environment was deficient in them, Arthur was blamed for his noncooperation. You see, Arthur was not performing to the expectations of a child of his background. His background was presumed to be upper-middle class and, therefore, literate.

Pointing out that Arthur was as quick to learn as any other gifted child I've worked with, I again suggested that his test scores and his inability to do the parent-centered current events homework might depend on vocabulary he didn't have because he couldn't read and had never been read to. Yes. But by the time a child is nine, they explained, *that is a learning disability*. Arthur was being held responsible for not knowing things that had not been taught to him, and no one seemed to understand that that didn't make sense.

When the issue of his not knowing his address came up, I explained the envelope process (this was back when I still thought he was receiving them). His regular teacher advised me of a quicker way. He could just write it over and over, thereby practicing his penmanship at the same time. The psychologist pointed out that when all else was failing, doing well in penmanship would be good for his self-esteem. The special ed teacher quickly said Arthur would get lots of handwriting practice in her class. Little did I realize that this same woman would soon be giving Arthur countless D's and F's on compositions graded for form but not content or how true her words were when she said, "We work on self-esteem."

Apparently, well before the formality of the meeting, a plan had been made to enroll Arthur in a program Arthur would learn about on the day he was transferred into it. The school's commitment: Arthur should make one year's progress in one year's time. Forms that had already been filled out to that effect were passed around for everyone's signatures. Everyone's, that is, except the principal's. On that multitude of forms designed to alter the course of Arthur's academic life, the principal's signature had been affixed ahead of time. Had the man made time to sit through the meeting, he might have learned a great deal about what was and what was not taught in his school. He might have discovered that abuse of power was, in fact, disrupting learning. He might also have gotten to know something very unusual and important about one of his students. As it stood, this powerful man, by his inattention, disempowered the little boy who'd been the topic of the day.

Special handwriting

To make sure they "really knew the basics," Arthur's special ed teacher used lockstep work sheets, regardless of student interest or prior knowledge. Arthur, who could write his name in print and cursive, reported excruciating boredom over having to write page upon page of the capital letter *A* in preparation for a big handwriting test. When I shared the problem of boredom with his mother, who had beautiful penmanship, she expressed pride at how well her son had filled those pages. As for boredom, she said Arthur had to learn that that's how school is.

The address

At our malt shop one evening, as I got out the envelopes and colored markers, Arthur complained that he was never going to learn his address. "You already know your address," I answered. "You know it perfectly and you can address this envelope without a copy." His facial expression made me want to punch his little lights out, but I knew he needed them to write. He picked up his pencil and slowly he got through the first line and then the second. Then he went blank. Just look right over there, I told him as I pointed to a blank wall. You can see your address on that wall. He squinted, he stared, he wrote it down. "You taught me my address!" he beamed, never willing to take credit for his accomplishments.

"You learned it yourself. You are in charge of your wonderful brain," I assured him. And it had taken fewer than twelve exposures.

Consider the Disempowering Significant Others

At first blush it is impossible to distinguish a genuine caretaker from a disempowering significant other. Indeed, the same kinds of activities can be used to liberate or to disempower. What may be liberating in one instance may be disempowering in another. It is important to distinguish the kind of support that provides a safety net for risk takers from a system that limits access to risk taking. For example, the mother who jumps in at midnight to type a paper her son has gotten only as far as a handwritten draft gives him the fuel to keep going. He may overload his schedule again, write too many drafts again, but he won't be afraid to try. But the mother who prints her first-grade child's homework because his work looks too messy is teaching him that his efforts are not presentable; he may always need his mama to do his school work for him. And when she's no longer around, he'll find a replacement, or two or three—willing to pay any price not to have to risk the writing he couldn't even do in the first grade. The DSO, while going through the motions of caring, takes every precaution to prevent the victim from gaining independence.

But enough of the hypothetical. For Arthur a host of DSOs gathered to foster his dependence on them, preventing his ability to stand alone. What is interesting is that the disempowering gestures made at home might just as easily have happened at school. And the school disempowerment was mirrored in much that happened at home.

Grandma's time-honored position was to serve as the hub of the family wheel, as grandmas have traditionally done. She had earned the right to love and to spoil the offspring of her offspring and then send the little problems home to their parents. But Arthur's grandma did both less and more. This Grandma's favors were Grandma-centered events, set up to disrupt rather than nurture. Recall the movie trip scheduled for a lesson time? Had she planned the movie for a time when no reading lesson was scheduled, she'd have gotten far less attention but could have given him some. She also belonged to a number of cultural organizations whose events a polite youngster like Arthur might well have benefitted from attending, but she never offered to take him to those. And though sibling rivalry can occur among cousins, great friendships extending into adulthood can also be fostered. In this story, Grandma set up an atmosphere of competition rather than camaraderie. Remember Grandma's forcing Arthur into a choice between playing with his cousin at home or going for a reading lesson? Either way, Arthur was a loser. Consider how different that day might have been had Grandma taken the boys to the La Brea Tar Pits or some other location where young imaginations are compelled to soar.

Then there was Grandma's brother, a man who'd wielded a sinister power over two generations. There was no way of knowing whether what Mrs. B said about his behavior during *The Lion, the Witch and the Wardrobe* was connected with Arthur's reading lesson, but it hardly matters, since the home had another TV he could have watched and Arthur had been set up with the program by his mother.

Mrs. B clearly made an open display of helping her son. But although she gave the appearance of taking action, she made results almost impossible. Was she afraid of having her son pass her up intellectually? Was she afraid of losing control over the one person who was completely dependent on her? Was she so terribly burned by her own past experiences that she feared getting too close to reading or writing? Consider the following conflicting signals:

- Arthur was a beloved child who hadn't been taught his address or telephone number.
- The living room was filled with books that had never been read.
- Valuable art was exhibited but the artist in Arthur was not valued.
- There was money for the child's designer clothes but children's books cost too much.
- Arthur was expected to make a good impression at the school where he was sent tired and hungry.
- His hair was always combed but his teeth were never brushed.
- His books, his art, his writing, and his little envelopes of readings vanished in the name of order.

In Mrs. B's home the quality of looks was much more important than the quality of life. Or, to put it in literacy terms, the surface—how things looked—outweighed the substance.

Arthur's aunts, too, served to disempower him, not just by keeping him up on school nights but by putting his emotional health on the line as they left him with the responsibility of their children. In almost every newspaper . . . but one must read for that to matter . . . in almost every news broadcast, then, there is mention of some small tragedy . . . fire, fall, drowning, suffocation . . . that befell a child in adult care. How would Arthur have responded to such a mark on his record?

Arthur's dad did know how to read to a limited extent, but chose not to do it. He understood that just reading to his son for ten minutes a day could make a long-term difference. The week before that ill-fated IEP meeting, Arthur had shown me a library book his father had begun reading to him two months before. There was no placemarker . . . no need for one, Arthur had memorized the spot where his father had left off. Mr. B did not continue reading to Arthur even after I mentioned this to him, and he said nothing about the transfer of Arthur's school friends.

Arthur's principal had been at that school since the child's first day. He was responsible for the supervision of every teacher Arthur ever had. Yet, somehow, he let a little boy move from grade to grade to grade without any teacher at any level taking time to teach him to read. What is more, Arthur was at the end of the third grade before a problem was even identified. This principal had time to be entertained in Arthur's home, but he didn't have time for the meeting about permanently labeling Arthur as deficient.

The school psychologist gave a battery of tests to Arthur, but failed to learn that Arthur was missing his friends. From a professional trained to look after the emotional health of children, Arthur had received something akin to the services of a word processor.

Arthur's regular teacher had never read to her fourth graders and didn't understand the connection between letter writing and address learning. She had Mrs. B as a volunteer in her room several times a week and still didn't know that the woman couldn't read. Not paying attention to signs right under her nose, she felt free to give Arthur parent-centered assignments, and when he failed to do them, she challenged Arthur, not his parents.

The special education teacher, although she worked with fewer students and had more funds than the regular teachers, still claimed that language experience took too much time. Not knowing what else to do, she gave more isolated phonics[7] in the name of reading. Then, rather than acknowledging what each child could already do, she failed to allow that Arthur, who could write his name very well, had already "mastered" the capital *A*, and had him practice it for page upon page upon page. Failing to understand the importance of self-esteem, she worked on Arthur's by marking his papers with D's and F's.

Instead of working to liberate this bright little boy, helping him figure out how best he could walk into the adult world, each of these significant others used and disempowered him. *What if one, just one, had decided not to?*

Emerging Literacy

Constantly curious about details of my school life and general activities, Arthur had begun to turn the tables on my question, "What's happened in school lately?" He seemed to want to know how other lives worked and proved such a good audience that I had to guard against spending our entire time together just discussing my projects. One day he began to ask questions about an article I'd just shown him. I'd actually only wanted him to see my name in print, a way of giving him the literacy club membership Frank Smith talks about. By knowing that he had a friend in the literacy club, especially a person who wrote things that others wanted to read, I figured he would be more inclined to accept membership for himself. But he wasn't satisfied just unraveling my name. He wanted to know what I'd written. It's a study of adult illiterates, I told him. I then left the article in the car and we went in for our malts. If I could play the scene again, I would make a copy for him, take it into the coffee shop, and read it to him. Looking back, I have no doubt that Arthur would have appreciated that material and might have tried rereading it to himself later. But that was then and all we had was a very long walk across a parking lot.

"What's an adult illiterate?" he asked. Something in his tone suddenly made me think he'd begun to discover his mother's secret.

"It's a person who grew up not knowing how to enjoy reading and writing. I've discovered that they all seem to have the same kinds of childhoods."

"Oh," he paused in thought for a long time. "What kinds of childhoods?"

"Well, for one thing, none of them had anyone to read stories to them when they were growing up."

"That's right!" he responded, stopping to point his finger in the air. "I wish we could have reading at school every day."

"I thought you did."

"No, I mean *real* reading. We just have *real* reading about two times a week. The rest of the time we just fill out forms when we're supposed to be having reading. I wish we had real reading every day . . . What else about childhoods?"

"The biggest problem the adult illiterates have is over low self-esteem."

"You mean like the project at my school? That's for self-esteem."

"I'm not sure. What happens in it?"

"Oh, we do jumping jacks and breathe a lot."

"Does that make you feel better?"

"Yeah, sometimes, if the teacher stops yelling at the kids."

"Does your teacher yell at you?"

"No, not at me; I don't do anything. But she yells at some of them when they are bad."

"What do they do to be bad?"

"Oh, I don't know. I think looking out the window is bad . . . and making the lines crooked."

"Lines? You mean in art?"

"No, at recess. You have to keep your lines straight or they yell at you."

"What do they yell at you, Arthur?"

"Well, they don't yell at *me*, but they yell 'Behave! You're old enough to know how to act! Are you trying to be a little girl?' She said that to my friend and everybody laughed. . . . It made my friend cry. He doesn't look like a girl, but it made him cry." He fell silent, remembering.

"What do you think about that, Arthur?"

"I think that's self-esteem. . . . What else about child-hoods?"

"Well, every single adult illiterate I've talked to has experienced terrible pain over feeling stupid in school. Most of them still remember being in low reading groups."

"I know about that pain," he said honestly. "I'm in the seventh reading group. There's a special room for the seventh reading group. They watch us go in there and they laugh at us. They all know I'm stupid." His sad little face glassed over. "What else?"

"The adult illiterates don't feel as if they have any power over their lives."

"What do you mean, power?"

How could I describe the power to think independently to a helpless child whose life was out of his control? "Well, they don't seem to know that they can decide what is good to read and what is dull. They seem to think other people can figure that out better than they can."

"You mean, like wanting to read *The Cat in the Hat*?" It had been months since he'd made that choice. He'd wanted me to read *The Cat in the Hat* instead of the book his mother had selected. How interesting that he was still impressed by the stand he had taken and that he understood it as power. "What else?"

"Every adult illiterate I know was abused as a child."

"What do you mean, abused?"

"Either they were neglected by their parents . . ."

"What is neglected?" I really wished I could run away. This sweet, fragile little boy was grabbing onto key words and demanding meaning. That is what literacy development was about—using language to evaluate and change one's universe—but here and now, one mental tidal wave atop another, was simply more than I'd planned on.

"Neglect is not taking care of little kids. Not making sure they have clothes to wear . . ."

"Not giving them breakfast?" he interrupted, not looking like a nine-year-old at all. His voice sounded innocent enough, but his face looked a thousand years old.

"Another kind of abuse is physical violence."

"You mean like hitting little kids and yelling at little kids?" Before I could respond, he said, "I think I know someone who does that . . . a man in my neighborhood. He yells and always says he's gonna hit kids. He drinks whiskey and smokes a cigar and sometimes he rides a motorcycle."

Enough Is Enough

The week after this conversation, Arthur's mother dropped him at a friend's house one hour before lesson time. He did not have the means to call and cancel or to get home in time for his lesson. That is to say, he was powerless. A few months later, after numerous cancellations, I offered to find him a tutor who could meet at a more convenient time. Mrs. B wouldn't hear of it. Arthur had been missing me, she reported. It wouldn't do to have anyone else. So, at 11 A.M. on the day of our next appointment, I called to confirm, but only reached the answering machine, not an unusual thing in itself as the whole family often goes out for lunch. However, at 11:30, 12:00, 12:30, 1:00, and 1:30 I called with the same result. Knowing that Arthur was sometimes out at the gated community's entrance, where he couldn't hear the phone, I decided to drive over. He wasn't there. From the gate phone I again reached the machine. Then I phoned his grandmother. She couldn't understand why I was calling her. Arthur was playing next door and I could call them, but she wasn't sure of the spelling of the neighbor's name. When I asked her to give me the number, the phone was disconnected. My patience was exhausted. I got back in my car and went shopping. I never called again and have not heard from them since.

I do feel some guilt over deserting this child when I was, perhaps, his only hope of escaping the illiterate minority. In spite of our limited lessons, progress was being made, progress that Arthur could see and verbalize. Many times he had openly expressed appreciation of my teaching in the moment. He actually pointed out the value of getting reading he could put to use. Though he'd been as good at it as any adult when I first took him to a restaurant, he no longer had to bluff a waitress into reciting a menu for him; he had learned to rely on pictures that accompanied text; he was starting to expect environmental print to be around to assist him. In short, he was beginning to develop the skills that preschoolers pick up automatically and painlessly in loving, literate families.

But, enough was enough. Many more lessons had been thoughtfully designed and discarded than had been successfully delivered. Dependent as I was on this enormous system of disempowering significant others for simple access, the task was overwhelming. Arthur's disempowerment training was thorough. By the age of nine, he had already learned:

• Literacy has a low priority among all adults in his family.
• Canceling and forgetting literacy lessons is expected behavior.
• No one has ten minutes a day to read to him.
• Books for Arthur are too expensive.
• A vast accumulation of TVs and other electronic entertainment equipment is important.
• Having expensive art and books on display demonstrates class.
• Designer clothing demonstrates class.
• In his home, he has no power to get mail, food, sleep, or attention.
• Visitors have the right to sleep in his bed and interrupt his TV viewing.
• His art is not good enough to display in his own home.
• His writing is trash and will be thrown out.
• The poems he appreciates are trash and will be thrown out.

- When he is tired and hungry, he is supposed to behave as though he is rested and fed.
- The friends he values are worthless.
- Ethnic minorities are below his class and are to blame for his academic disfunction.
- His feelings don't count at home or in school.
- His grandmother does not want him to have reading lessons.
- He must make a choice between learning and fun.
- His school does not evaluate individual needs; groups are expected to arrive uniformly packaged according to socioeconomic status.
- School authorities expect him to have literate parents and he is expected to behave accordingly.
- His principal doesn't have time to deal with his needs.
- His psychologist produces findings that agree with current expectations.
- His teacher sees his nonperformance as his failure to cooperate.
- His special ed teacher is interested in form over substance.
- Writing means penmanship, not making meaning in print.
- Anything worth writing is worth writing right—the first time.
- How papers look is much more important than what they say.
- School is a place where kids get yelled at and called names by teachers.
- School is a place where teachers and parents work together to control kids' feelings and behavior.
- School is a place that bores people.
- School is not a place where good books are read.
- His input is not important in the decision-making processes about his life.
- He is stupid.

School Could Compensate and Empower

In a situation like Arthur's, the school can compensate for much of the disempowerment at home.

First, however, the demand that the child act like the product of an advantaged home must be dropped. It is both unrealistic and unfair to require a child to demonstrate evidence of support that does not exist. With no external expectations about its students and with a plan to provide equitable treatment to each child, the school, presuming nothing, can provide food, comfortable study areas, resource books, technology, tutors, storytellers, pleasurable reading materials, and even a comfortable and safe rest area. These minimal provisions, available to all students, would eliminate the need for disabling labels and would allow each student to perform in an advantaged and empowered way.

The Status Quo Does Disempower

Without these provisions, this intelligent, sensitive boy was taught that he must yield to bigoted and illiterate values. In his world without equity, he has learned that adults disregard the feelings and needs of children in their care. He has learned to deal with the mixed messages that he is both incompetent to make decisions and responsible for the outcomes in his life. And he was capable of assimilating all of this input. As a disempowered adult and an illiterate in a literate world, he may emerge a very creative and angry member of society, prepared to fill the role that has been modeled so well for him, the role of a disempowering significant other.

1. Arthur's extraordinary situation, I've learned, is not an isolated incident. My widespread call for family literacy cases netted me another mother and nine-year-old son team at the same time, with different details but identical profiles. And when I shared early drafts of the manuscript with four colleagues from different school districts, each believed he or she had worked in Arthur's school. This is consistent with Kozol's claim that one out of three Americans is functionally illiterate, and it is consistent with my race track experience detailed in Chapter I. It is

also consistent with the findings of the National Adult Literacy Survey of the U. S. Department of Education (1993).

2. People frequently suggest that nonreaders are stupid or at least not at all clever. Mrs. B is a classic example of how wrong that perception can be. Though the nonreader lacks the sophisticated vocabulary of an avid reader, the ability to comprehend spoken ideas is no less likely, and the ways that some nonreaders compensate for their inability is quite remarkable. While Henry had an entrepreneurial inclination, Mrs. B quite quickly responded to social requirements; each gave rise to the notion that this population, like the population in general, has its stars.

3. My interpretation was that Mrs. B was either trying to disrupt her son's storytime or was focusing on the surface advantage of having him read a prestigious author, albeit one she couldn't read and he'd never heard of. However, my colleague Trudy Le Clair has suggested that Mrs. B may simply have been longing to be read to herself. These points are not mutually exclusive and the reality may have included all three.

4. One may wonder why the school didn't follow up on Arthur's summer school. I can only speculate that having contacted me, Mrs. B was able to give the illusion that a tremendous amount of her time and energy had been spent on Arthur's reading that summer. And the principal, having been a visitor in that book-filled living room, no doubt believed that Arthur had avid readers for parents. It is difficult to overstate the power that Mrs. B, a constant volunteer and contributor to whatever cause, wielded in the school. On top of that, her theatrics made everyone, including Mr. B, reluctant to question or challenge her actions. The school personnel saw these facts: She had agreed either to have Arthur tutored or to tutor him herself over the summer. He had gotten a tutor in the summer.

5. Always on the lookout for new blood, I managed to meet this cousin. She was very willing to talk about movies, music, and new clothes, but as soon as I mentioned reading to Arthur for just ten minutes a day, I hit a stone wall.

6. Ken Goodman, *What's Whole in Whole Language?* (Portsmouth, N.H.: Heinemann, 1986).

7. From time to time I'm accused of not teaching phonics when, indeed, I teach phonics all the time . . . in process. When I read poems that rhymed to Arthur, for example, I was teaching phonics, the sound symbol relationships that may not be logical in English. Consider, for example, the phonetic puzzles posed by words like *floor*, *store*, *lore*, *pour*, *flour*, and *flower*. Words like these can be taught much more effectively as the teacher is reading aloud from an entertaining story or a wonderful poem than in a meaningless list of words. Phonics must be taught, but *in process*.

Five

Madonna: In Search of a Childhood

Sexy, sassy, twenty-four-year-old Madonna (a pseudonym I chose because she was at once a mother figure and a sex symbol) was expecting her sixth child when we met. Although Madonna had not participated in any traditional testing, her oldest child's second-grade teacher had confirmed that Madonna did not read or write at the second-grade level. Indeed, whenever a note had to be sent home, the teacher first read it over and over to the child to ensure that the daughter could help her mother decode it. Less than a dozen years ago Madonna had been enrolled in a Southern California school where she had been placed in a class for the retarded because she couldn't read. She had begged her mother to get her out of the class but had been ignored. The process had been so humiliating that when, at the age of fifteen, she got pregnant with the now nine-year-old Mitzi, she was delighted to have an excuse to drop out of school. She had been pregnant every other year since.

Never having been read to herself, Madonna did not know how to do that for her children. None, she said, could read. Knowing that her illiteracy was preventing her from helping her daughter who had already failed first grade, Madonna had called her child's school in search of reading help.

By coincidence, I was looking for another research subject, an adult at a very low level of literacy development, and was willing to trade reading lessons for research cooperation. My preliminary screening showed that she was unable even to fill out minimal forms for school, read simple, printed notes, or write in such a way that her messages could be understood. The school psychologist, district and site secretaries, and her daughter's teacher agreed that Madonna's literacy level was "very low." Since it is generally agreed that empowering pedagogy will benefit higher-level students, I wanted to be absolutely certain that my subjects had profound literacy problems. Any one of the professionals involved might have been tempted to overstate the problem in order to get help for this very personable, desperate young woman who did not fit into the public system and who did not have the funds, transportation, or baby-sitters necessary for her to find help in the private sector. However, all of them agreed about the extent of her inability to read and write. Then, during our California Literacy Campaign interview, Madonna herself denied ability in every reading and writing task except the *Recycler*, a weekly advertising publication she found "very hard" to read, and forms or applications, which she found "very hard" to write.

Our initial encounter began at 2:00 P.M. in the living room of her small house, which was only four blocks from her daughter's elementary school. There, with regular interruptions by the one-year-old, Madonna took up her tragic story of disempowerment. Finally, she asked if there was anything I wanted to know. I began by explaining what my research was about and telling her that I would be using a tape recorder and that she was at liberty to have the recorder turned off or the tapes erased at will. Also, I was only available for three months, but that would be enough time if we could meet at regular intervals. For the first month we were able to meet twice a week in her home. After that, my schedule necessitated once-a-week meetings.

Madonna had had very unfortunate school experiences. Clearly, she was not retarded, but that had not saved her from a label that left permanent scars on her self-esteem. We talked about Ray Rist's studies of the self-fulfilling prophecy and about the affective filter. Yes, all that made sense; even though the misdiagnosis had made her feel terrible, she'd known that not knowing how to read was not the same as being retarded.

I told her about my research on adult nonreaders and about the history of child abuse—either profound neglect, physical violence, or both—that occurred in every case I'd encountered. In many cases, I explained, the nonreading adults did not consider their treatment as abuse; rather, they often thought they deserved the treatment they got. And very often, they continued to seek out situations that would perpetuate their tragic situation.

Although Madonna had spilled out a tirade of complaints about her mother, who used to beat her with fiberglass fishing rods, and her father, who would force all of his kids into gunny sacks and hang them on the garage wall to keep them from running off when the mother was gone, she also said that she had always been a "big problem" to her mother and stated emphatically that she had *never* been abused.

When I explained that her story might help set things straight for others, the young woman was eager for me to get her *whole* story. Even before she had any idea whether she would benefit from my intervention or not, she seemed to want to do what she could to see that her kind of suffering was understood and eradicated. Very early on Madonna caught onto my habit of asking, "Does that make sense?" She would explain some event in great detail and then ask, "Did yuh get all that?" Frequently she had me replay parts of a tape to make sure I had what she thought the world should know. And she would patiently repeat herself if I suddenly realized that she was giving testimony that I needed to record. For her lessons in spunk, spontaneity, family literacy, and the power of theory, I acknowledge Madonna as one of the greatest teachers I've ever had.

Chaos Caused by Mother, Mates, and Medical Merchants

Neither the young father of Madonna's first child nor his parents were willing to acknowledge Mitzi's existence. When

Madonna had first realized she was pregnant, her mother had said she would take care of the baby, that the young teen still needed a childhood. Madonna, hating both the physical discomfort of pregnancy and the accompanying humiliation, had asked that her tubes be tied after the birth, but the doctors couldn't follow the instructions of a minor and her mother couldn't believe that Madonna would never want another baby. At the birth, Madonna signed over the welfare benefits to her mother. Three months later she was informed that her childhood had ended. You see, Mitzi proved too much for a grandmother to handle, yet if Madonna wanted to get her benefits back, the sixteen-year-old would have to move out on her own, something she was too insecure to try.

A year and a half later, Madonna had another daughter by a man she says she was really in love with. Had he been ready for an exclusive relationship, she believes she would have been happy ever after. (This daughter, Amy, remains her favorite child.) Again she begged for sterilization, but the welfare doctors said she was too young to make such a decision. And again her mother wouldn't agree. Then, while she was on birth control pills, she had two girls fathered by a man she did marry and divorce. Twice her husband was supposed to have signed the sterilization authorization at the hospital, but twice he didn't get around to it. Madonna had a nervous breakdown at the birth of her fourth child. But when she sought a separate sterilization surgery, the welfare doctors consoled her with a movie about entire families of young children being killed in tragic accidents, leaving their sterile mothers childless. Though the scare-tactic film did make an indelible impression on her, Madonna maintained that she hated being pregnant and had no interest in looking after more kids. By the time her one-year-old, little Josephina, was born, Madonna had moved away from home and was supporting all of her children on welfare. Her current boyfriend, Joseph, lived with his parents, not Madonna, because his parents' religion did not approve of living in sin!

When Josephina, her fifth child (who was a year old when we met), was born Madonna's mother had come out to help, but when Madonna started to have another nervous breakdown, her mother left. Joseph then got the two known fathers to claim their children, thus clearing the home of all but his own new baby and the one little girl, Mitzi, who had no participating father. Subsequently, the second daughter, Amy, was returned to Madonna and then (apparently because of a battle over child support) kidnapped back by her father. So, on my first visit, Madonna had only two of her children living with her, her oldest and her youngest, and was expecting another at some unclear time in the future (Madonna had not gotten in to see a doctor yet). I began to understand why the school record keepers had no idea how many children were in the family. Even if the young woman could have read without a problem, she might have had a problem giving accurate names, dates and ID numbers for children who were in an ownership blender. Nevertheless, the case of Madonna is impossible to separate from her daughter Mitzi and begins with a spelling lesson.

The Speln Lesn: How the Poor Get Poorer

When Mitzi came in from school, she barely glanced in my direction. While her mother was spunky and talkative, Mitzi was serene and aloof. She had an almost defiant attitude about . . . what? When Madonna turned her attention to her daughter without introducing me, I thought perhaps she was embarrassed that the child had discovered us. We hadn't discussed whether Mitzi knew about her mom's reading problem, and the next few minutes only added to my confusion.

Mitzi slammed a packet of papers down on the coffee table in front of Madonna and then plopped down on the floor opposite. "What's this word?" she asked.

"What word?"

"This one," she said as she jabbed her finger down on the first of ten words she had to do for homework.

"Uh, well, you know you're supposed to sound it out. Now sound it out."

"I did! Do or. Do or. Do or!"

She'd learned her phonics perfectly. *D o* spells *do* and *o r* spells *or*. Both child and mother knew how to sound out a word they couldn't read, and Mitzi was skillful at finding the little words in the big words as well.

"How do I make a sentence with *do-or*?" she asked as she turned the packet of papers over.

"Um, well, I can think of it, but when I try to tell you it, it don't come out right. Just do the best you can. I'm not supposed to tell you *everything*," the young mother said, trying to maintain some semblance of dignity before her child.

The little girl turned the packet over again to try the next word. She was supposed to write a sentence with each of the ten words on the mimeographed list. By Friday, having done each of four activities with the words, she was expected to be able to spell all ten words on a test. This was only day two of a four-day homework assignment. Later Madonna explained that figuring out what the words on the list were was only part of the problem. Then they had to construct sentences using only words they could already spell. The proposed sentences grew shorter and shorter as the struggle progressed. Focusing on spelling, paragraph construction, format, and other surface issues consistently limits the quality of student writing, netting safe, simple, unimaginative products designed to meet the requirements of the assignment rather than express the ideas of the author. Ten minutes had passed and Mitzi still hadn't gotten the first sentence written. Mitzi, like Arthur, couldn't do her homework without help from her mother and couldn't get that help because her mother was illiterate. She was trapped.

Suddenly she said "Is it *door*?" and then turned the packet over to start writing.

"Um, no, I don't think so. I think that's spelled another way," her mother answered thoughtfully.

"Well, then, how do you spell *door*?"

"I think it's *d o r e*, you know, dore."

Mitzi seemed to be trying to take in the logic of her mother's phonetic performance. I leaned forward, hoping to be invited into the dialogue, my mind echoing with a Krashen lecture on how the rich get richer. The literacy rich, he'd said, fortify their children with good stories and beautiful books long before they enter school; poor readers don't understand that process and so perpetuate illiteracy from generation to generation. Having no invitation to intervene, I was forced to witness a true-life example of what Krashen calls how "the poor get poorer."

After half an hour or so of guesswork, Mitzi ran out to play, knowing that her faithful mother would be waiting to help her with another hour and a half of homework when she came back in. Neither mother nor child could know that production of sentences is a *test*, a call for *output* that shows what the reader already knows. Presented as a spelling *lesson*, it purported to be *input* designed to give the new reader or nonreader information. Only in homes with literate parents did children have a prayer of getting useful input from such an assignment. It called for home teaching of school subject matter, a major problem for the child of an illiterate environment, a child like Mitzi. Determined that her daughter was not going to suffer the way she had in school, Madonna was putting them both through the agonizing ritual of trying to do an assignment that was skillfully designed to prove they were failures; it was a classic illustration of formal disempowerment. Madonna also showed me the spelling test from the week before. It was a fragile slip of paper with words written on both sides. There were big red-pen circles all over it, no comments, not even the correct spellings, just big, misshapen zeros. What was this supposed to teach? She was determined that they would do better this week. She held the false belief that if they tried "hard" enough, they would prevail; it was a belief that would lead them into the self-condemnation that has disabled generations of those our schools have failed to teach.

Although there wasn't time to go into all of this with Madonna right then, I did try to share with her the notion that reading would cause spelling development to happen effortlessly. Hearing that the more you see the words in meaningful print, like good stories, the more you will be able to both read and write them, Madonna was justifiably sure that since they couldn't read, they wouldn't be able to learn by reading. I made another plug for being read *to* before I left.

The following day when I talked with Mitzi's teacher, I was told that Mitzi does absurd spelling all the time. And that her homework from yesterday was expected to take only fifteen minutes. Remember catch-22? If you don't do your homework you are failing to follow orders. If you do the homework but need more than fifteen minutes, you are violating the time limit. If you don't have a teacher in the house, you are bound to break some rule and deserve to fail.

When I met with my USC advisor, David Eskey, and explained my frustration, he came up with a very simple temporary fix: give them a children's picture dictionary. I did so the same week, selecting one for its large print and wide margins and because each word was presented in a full sentence. Madonna was so thrilled with the book she could hardly wait for her daughter to come home from school. To facilitate the process, we put yellow Post-its on the pages containing homework words. When I showed her how the alphabetical listings worked, she said, "Oh, kind of like a phone book!" It was clear that the week's homework would go very quickly. The following week, she showed me the dictionary. All of the Post-its had been moved to the new set of words, *even though she couldn't read all of them* and, because there was one less word, the spare Post-it had been carefully stuck inside the front cover for future use. What might have happened, I wondered, if ten years before instead of a class for the retarded, Madonna had been placed in a highly stimulating environment, one loaded with wonderful books and staffed with people who liked to talk about them?

Reading and Language Experience Work, But . . .

Madonna quickly grasped the notion that starting at the level of the learner is a major challenge when the adult can read hardly anything, but the technique of transcribing her taped monologues into little meaning-filled readings was something she'd have to see. I explained that this was my interpretation of the theory behind *language experience*, a term that refers to a range of reading/writing/language-learning processes that use *the language and the experiences **of the learner** to produce text*. For example, the adult learner may tell a story about a problem at work or a child may tell about getting stung by a bee; in either case the topic has come up as natural conversation and is fully told to the teacher, who draws out details—perhaps details that call for more vocabulary than required by ordinary oral reporting. And in either case, the experience and all the words come from the storyteller, not the teacher. One way to obtain the text is for it to be written down either by the learner using invented spelling or by the teacher acting as secretary. (When I, as secretary, get to a word I'm not sure I'm spelling correctly, I underline it and explain that it is more important to get the ideas down first than to worry about surface issues, thus showing the learner that the mighty teacher can also be unsure of spellings.) Once the learner's entire story is written down, the teacher reads through the text aloud, asking the learner if there should be any modifications. (I follow along in the margin with my finger to help the learner get the idea that there is a physical way to locate specific ideas.) The learner may recall details that need to be added or may want to make other changes. This gives a perfect opening to talk about how writing helps you clarify your thoughts. It is important for the developing writer to understand that the first draft may be very different from the final one. It is empowering for the learner to understand that even when the teacher is putting down the words, it is the author who has the final say about what message the text conveys. But since the handwritten process is very slow and relies on good penmanship, I also obtain text by transcribing the stories from a tape recording. The text is not available until the next meeting this way, but it is more readable. And that's the point. This readable material is steeped in the adult's background knowledge, uses the reader's own vocabulary and turns of phrase, and demonstrates how the writing process works.

Easily understanding the logic of how reading would help reading and writing, Madonna was eager to see if language experience would do anything for her. The theory made sense; she just didn't know if it would work for *her*.

The value of establishing a literate environment also made sense. Having children *to* read to would provide an excuse for having a supply of interesting, low-level, predictable, beautifully illustrated texts around the house that she would be able to study in the same way a child does. The books would provide the reading and writing foundation she needed. Reading the books daily, in plain view of her family, would not only start a literacy habit for herself and build her self-esteem, it would provide a literate model for her children; they would learn that adults in their family value books. I piled on additional motivation by telling her that children learn to read by being read to: I would teach her how to read and deliver books; she, in turn, by reading to baby Josephina for ten minutes every day, would provide her child with basic literacy. She wasn't sure about how well she could read to her kids. She said that before the birth of Josephina, she had been trying to read to all of them one night when Joseph (who, like many DSOs, was only minimally more literate than she) ridiculed her so badly that she became really frustrated. The more he badgered her, the worse it got. Finally, the kids fell asleep without their story. She had been too intimidated to try it again.

I explained that kids don't really know if the words are perfect until they've heard a book over and over. By that time, she'd know it, too. Then I read her *The Very Hungry Caterpillar*, explaining how it teaches counting, the names of fruits, and the days of the week in the context of its beautiful pictures. She did not try to touch the book and did not want Josephina, who was crawling everywhere and who constantly picked at my hose, to touch it either. Thinking its beauty made it look too expensive, I tried to loan her the miniature version of the same book but couldn't make an immediate sale there either. This was frustrating, since this marvelous book is nearly always an effective literature hook.

When I returned two days later, however, Madonna was ready to read *Caterpillar*. And then, after I loaned her both versions to read to herself over the weekend, she announced she was going to put books into her monthly budget. From all I could tell, she was still afraid to try reading in front of an audience. (She still had not read it to her children and kept both books in a cabinet out of children's reach.) However, she found she could use the pictures to guide her through the text successfully. By my third visit, Madonna had begun to see that she really could read and she could see how "that vocabulary thing" worked, too. Shortly thereafter, Madonna excitedly told me about reading *Caterpillar* to a sister who knew she couldn't read. Further, she had read it "like you do, you know, with sounds and stuff" and now knew that for the first time in her life she really liked reading. I knew my pair of *Caterpillars* was gone forever.

For the illiterate adult, secrets on paper are all too often secrets told. Although a visitor would normally never think of opening a reader's passport or mail or reading the notes left for and by a reader's family, that same visitor often thinks nothing of looking through an illiterate's literacy materials. I call this the zero-privacy factor. This happened to Arthur, but perhaps you excused that somewhat by thinking that people just don't recognize a child's needs. However, here you'll see it with Madonna, and you'll see it again with Danny in the next chapter.

It soon became clear that there was no place in Madonna's house where her detailed and very intimate language experience stories could be stashed without the danger that someone else would see them. The reading levels of her boyfriend and other visitors were surely minimal but were always reported to be much higher than Madonna's. (As you might guess, however, no one was available to read to her even ten minutes per day. That requires a literate value system that simply didn't exist.) Nevertheless, anyone could and did open her plastic envelope of papers, causing her tremendous stress by looking at them, however blindly. Knowing this, I realized I had to ensure that the content of this work didn't trigger domestic strife. That was frustrating, because she really plowed through her own emotionally charged stories. Even when I started to include both sides of our taped conversations in the language experience texts, she was able to read nearly all of it.

During my fourth visit, the boyfriend Joseph interrupted us frequently, needing Madonna to make him a sandwich, find a baggie, find a pan, and take care of all sorts of other "urgent" details. He even hid the remote control that Madonna used to shift channels on the soundless TV, even during our lessons. Before she had badgered him into returning it to her, she squawked that that was the only way she could tell what time it was. (You can't always tell a clock by its face.)

Finally, when I started reading a book to her, he began to creep closer and closer, not to interrupt but to listen. After he left, I asked if she wanted him included in her lessons. No! she responded emphatically of the man whose second child she was carrying. She did not want him knowing her private thoughts. Those secrets did not belong to the physical world. Madonna did not want to share her ideas, her hopes, her emotions with someone who might not handle them with care.

DSOs Destroy Self-Esteem

Madonna had managed to limit her close acquaintances to those who would make and break promises, attack her at vulnerable moments, and desert her when she needed support. A relentless trail of disempowering significant others passed through that little house.

Mama

Madonna had lost her phone service because of long-distance phone calls to her mother, who was then living in New York. Unable to write back and forth, they would use the prime-time lines to wrestle over issues like the return of Mitzi's teddy bear and the shipping of Madonna's baby bed. The mother would promise to ship things out, but nothing ever arrived. Though Madonna suspected that her father may have sold the items for alcohol money, she continued to make expensive telephoned demands for their return. When the mother did visit, she arrived empty-handed. "If this baby arrives and don't have no bed, I'm never speaking to her or my dad again," Madonna told me, angrily lamenting the loss of items gotten under another state's welfare child-care system. She couldn't go back to that state, she explained, because they would make her start either working or going to school as soon as she delivered. She wouldn't mind working, but in her opinion the things they wanted welfare mothers to do to earn their keep were not the kinds of jobs any human would really be willing to take.

Madonna had found a choice, a very nice choice, in the California "no strings" welfare system. But she did not view herself as part of the system she benefited from. When I first asked her why she thought any political system would want to keep welfare recipients under their control without any promise of change, she didn't know. She'd somehow bought into the idea that California was a free-lunch state that just liked her better than those that would put her to work immediately. But, still, as the baby's due date grew increasingly near, Madonna began to miss her mother immensely and warned me that she might move back East abruptly. "I don't know what it is. I just can't seem to get along without my mom.

I've always been a problem to her, but I need to have her around for support, y'know? I mean, she's the only family I've really got." Another time she said that the only reasons she didn't move back with the woman who'd deserted her and her children during two nervous breakdowns were because her oldest child was "getting situated" in school and because she herself was learning to read.

Ex-husband

During my first visit to the home Madonna's ex-husband stopped by to find out if Madonna would take care of their daughters for a few weeks while he and his girlfriend vacationed. This conversation took place between a rugged-looking man and a worn-out pregnant woman, each of whom clearly had a strong physical attraction to the other. Somehow, being currently involved with other official partners did not detract from a very strong connection that had led to a daughter, a marriage, a divorce and another daughter—in that order. They had agreed to disagree, but that had not ended the relationship.

Madonna told him she couldn't afford to take the kids without reimbursement; he would have to give her food money. The man then complained that Madonna did not have an address posted on her house and that she was hard to reach without a phone. (This was all couched as friendly banter, but Madonna was receiving one verbal slug after another, like a pillow that knows it is supposed to be punched. She didn't slug back: she just tried to keep herself from losing too many feathers.) In front of me—a stranger who had not even been introduced to him—her ex-husband set out to prove that Madonna was involved with a much lesser man than the one she used to have. He said more than once that the boyfriend Joseph could be working if he wanted to; there was ample employment at his own construction site. Then, he asked Madonna to write down his new phone number. When she said she didn't have a pencil (which was true— there was no paper or pencil in the house except mine) and would get his number later, he found other means to make fun of her inability to write. He was using her handicap as a mechanism for abuse.

Boyfriend Joseph

Although Joseph was reportedly a construction worker, he did not use his construction skills to make Madonna's home more comfortable. For example, a window pane in the kitchen door, broken in a struggle between Joseph and Madonna when she wanted to go to the library and was about to walk out alone, remained broken for many weeks, giving anyone access to the home—day or night. It was only after I promised Madonna that the next time I came we would drive down to the hardware store and pick up the glass and I'd teach her to replace a window that it suddenly got fixed before my return.

And although Joseph refused to drive her to the library, he also believed it was inappropriate for her to walk down the street alone where everyone could look at her. This kind of "protective" attention had been rather flattering as long as Madonna really had no place to go. The elementary school, the corner grocery store, and the laundromat were the only places she knew she could go without his taking her. And before she found out about the library, there was nowhere else she wanted to go. This is a classic example of the isolation factor and it was willingly reinforced by its victim.

Except for one living room window and one bedroom window, the home had no screens. But because Joseph believed the neighborhood was too dangerous for unprotected windows, he forbade Madonna from opening any windows except the two with screens. She begged for a fan, but Joseph never had enough cash to buy one; and although he kept promising to bring her one his mom wasn't using, he never did. For months she sat sprawled on a couch in the sweltering heat, pregnant and exhausted. Mitzi often missed school because she had been too hot to sleep the night before. Permission to sleep on the living room floor, where it was perhaps minimally cooler than on Mitzi's bed in the airtight bedroom, could only

121

be granted by the man of the house, even when he was not around. And Joseph had very strong ideas about young ladies who chose to sleep on the floor. (His own very late nights were, you may remember, spent in the comfort of his parents' home.)

Madonna was unable to read the fliers in the mail telling about the surrounding community. When I mentioned that a huge, tree-covered, well-fenced park was four blocks from her home, she was therefore quite surprised and very eager to see it. By my next visit, however, Joseph had warned her that I might be a spy and that she was to stay away from the park because it was full of Mexicans.[1] Yes, he used the word "spy," and no, I never could get her to tell me what he thought I might be spying on. At any rate, Madonna believed it was a dangerous place until I got her into my car and drove her to this neighborhood park and recreation center, complete with pool and a gym.

While Joseph's fundamentalist convictions dictated the dress and activities of the females under his control, they did not seem to apply to him. Seizing upon Madonna's self-consciousness over her weight, Joseph instructed her to be on the lookout for matched father-and-daughter swimsuits, saying he planned to take the baby to the beach to attract cute girls. And, though he regularly ridiculed Madonna's figure, Joseph forbade her from taking the mommy-and-me exercise classes at the gym. When I enrolled Mitzi in a Saturday gymnastics class—her only scheduled escape from that hot little house all summer—Joseph seemed compelled to undermine the "just for the fun of it" part. Lessons, for him, were like school; school was about struggling to reach a brass ring that no one he'd ever known could touch. He told Mitzi she wasn't taking gymnastics seriously enough.

Joseph used his truck as a tool of abuse in many ways. Mitzi reported that he enjoyed making Madonna ride in the bumpy bed when they were out driving on rough roads; he would laugh at her screams that she had to get out. There were frequent fights over his speeding and driving without a license.

He always had time (even if he had to miss work) to help his buddies haul things or to go to swap meets, but Madonna's wish to take Mitzi to Hollywood for a child-model interview was never granted. One day Madonna almost missed our lesson because he had dropped her and two children off at the laundromat and then forgot to return for them. After waiting two extra hours in the steamy laundromat, with a crying baby and no change of diapers, Madonna had pirated a cart and pushed her little caravan many blocks to her home. But Joseph had been so apologetic, she had no choice but to forgive him; after all, he'd been with his friends and just lost track of the time. To top it off, the truck was often parked in Madonna's front yard, where it turned the grass to dirt and wheel ruts.

During a brief spell of calm in her house, Madonna began to try reading ten minutes a day and found she liked it. In fact, she'd discovered bedtime reading actually helped put her to sleep in spite of her physical miseries. She announced that she was looking forward to spending more time reading. Shortly thereafter, ironically, in a burst of generosity, Joseph splurged by taking the whole family out to a Mutant Ninja Turtle movie and followed it up with a gift of an expensive Ninja video game that attached to the living room TV. Coincidence? I found myself recalling Arthur's movie-wielding Grandma. And Madonna acknowledged that just when she thinks she'd be better off dropping him completely, he does something like this that's "so sweet."

Sister

One month when Joseph was among the missing (he'd left town after deciding that Madonna's diminished sex drive meant she'd found another man), a vacationing sister, whom Madonna had previously disowned, showed up unannounced with her three children, moved in, and began wearing Madonna's clothing and eating the small cache of food that had to last the month. The two had become estranged when Madonna had grown suspicious about her sister's boyfriend's overattentiveness to Mitzi. Yet, as for Mrs. Bonadventure, the "family" label required that Madonna forgive and forget almost everything. Besides, the boyfriend wasn't with them . . . at first.

Although according to the sister her children were doing just fine in school, the report cards she showed me had consistently conflicting signals. For example, one report card showed reading level at 78% (or "real good" according to the teacher's written remarks), but comprehension at 48%; and the child had just failed the second grade. "He reads real good, any sign or word he sees," the sister recorded on my tape, "but he can't tell you what he read."

Though she didn't yet use the technical terms, Madonna understood about *parts-to-whole* versus *whole-to-parts pedagogy*. When a teacher follows the *parts-to-whole* philosophy for teaching reading, for example, he believes that you must learn the letters before the letter clusters, the letter clusters before whole words, and whole words before you can read a sentence. This approach starts with all the little parts of the text and progresses to the whole and is labeled *bottom up*. The premise is that a person must memorize many hundreds or thousands of details before having any chance of trying to read.

Whole-to-parts is just the opposite. You start with storytelling and reading aloud to the student so that he gets the *whole* idea about the text. By following along, the student may connect some important or frequent words in the story with shapes in the text. Whole words are then recognized on sight (*sight words*) and entire phrases are recognized as chunks of meaning. Being read *to* also lets the student hear multiple phonetic combinations in context. He hears that the letter *g* has different sounds when it appears in "good," "general," "beige," and "big." Seeing and hearing simultaneously allows him to learn these distinctions naturally *in process* rather than by memorizing a list of rules. Or, as Frank Smith would say, we learn to read by reading.

Parts-to-whole writing is also about learning rules and little skills related to putting print on a page, usually first looking at the capital letter *A*. Writing that is the product of a focus on rules will not be very interesting to read. Remember the spelling lesson Madonna tried to help Mitzi with? Madonna said they made their little sentences shorter and shorter as they tried to find words they could spell. *Whole-to-parts* starts with the *writer's ideas*, as is done in language experience, and creates text from those ideas. Writing that comes from the heart, mind, and spirit of the writer is empowering.

Madonna understood all that, but was too insecure around this "literate" sister to suggest that she didn't know how to interpret her children's report cards. Had she been able to, she might have caused her sister to question these entries made on a formal report card over three semesters:

1st: "Mike is a hard worker and showing much improvement."
2nd: "Mike needs to work hard on his responsibility, completing assignments and using time wisely."
3rd and final, with a failing grade: "Try to have a nice summer. Read a lot and have fun."

When I asked what the school would do differently the second time through for the failed child, the sister said he would be with a different bunch of kids. No plan for improved or even different pedagogy had been discussed with the parents. Nor had such a plan been made for her child who'd just failed kindergarten. However, the school had been "real nice" about forewarning the mother and allowing her to keep the little girl home from school on the last day so she wouldn't suffer embarrassment.

The upshot was that none of the reported "good students" in the sister's family could comprehend text. Nevertheless, this sister stood back and mocked Madonna's efforts at reading, telling her she'd never make it.

This particular episode of chaos and disempowerment ended when the sister's boyfriend moved in and soon after physically threw the very pregnant Madonna out of her own home. Although the intruders departed abruptly to avoid the police, Madonna, in a weak moment of wanting to show there were no hard feelings over *his* past transgressions, had given the tyrant who was "practically family" a key to her house, and he could therefore reenter it whenever he wanted.

Brother

Madonna had often said that her brothers, some of whom lived in New York and some of whom lived in California, had such severe tempers she would be afraid of having them near her children. That was until Madonna's mother shipped one unemployed, illiterate brother to California, without money, skills, or an ID card. The first sister he stayed with ejected him and he was then deposited on Madonna's front porch; he lived with her for the next three months, doing little except chain-smoking. Madonna was allergic to the smoke and was afraid it would damage her children, but lacked the power to set limits. Although she threatened him daily with eviction if he didn't get a job and start paying for the food he was eating, she said privately that she couldn't really do anything because, after all, "he is family." Like Henry, Madonna blindly accepted the notion that kinfolks are good folks, no matter how badly they choose to treat you.

She nagged her brother to go sign up for education assistance, complaining that "he tries to cover up by acting silly, but he can't read. He can't read at all, not even them job applications." (Neither of them could handle applications, really. On one occasion Madonna asked me to "proof" a simple form her brother had tried to fill out and she had tried to correct. The words in the few blanks they had filled in bore almost no resemblance to the information requested.) Because he couldn't read the map showing how to get to the adult education center and also claimed he couldn't follow the directions given him by someone at the employment office—it was a long though uncomplicated walk—I drove him there so he could register for job training. Later, when I returned to pick him up, I learned he'd only peeked around the corner of the reception room door and then hung out waiting for me to rescue him. I was reminded of the ghostlike faces that drifted around the gymnasium door in the ghetto, unable to lead their bodies in for help.

Madonna had just gotten her phone reconnected when the brother started begging his mom, long distance, to send him his ID card. She wouldn't do it, the expensive phone calls continued, and the phone was again disconnected. Yet Madonna felt sorry for her brother because he, like Joseph, had such a difficult time just handling day-to-day life.

From Theory to Practice

Because of the erratic home population, the extraordinary heat waves, and Madonna's own physical highs and lows, my battery of theory was presented in such a disjointed way that I questioned whether it would have the desired impact. But what I observed assuaged those doubts.

Early on I'd explained the whole language concepts and the reasons for building background knowledge. I'd read the Maurice Sendak story *Where the Wild Things Are* to Madonna and Mitzi, so when I saw a newspaper ad for a performance of a children's opera based on the story, I offered to take Mitzi to it. When Mitzi came in from school that day her mother eagerly showed her the ad and they settled in to reread the book together, Mitzi doing the reading and Madonna advising, "Try skipping over it," or asking, "What makes sense from the picture? Can you guess it?" Madonna was applying theory . . . in process. What better way to document success? I know of no standardized test on which this learner would have a chance at showing such insight.

On the day of the opera, Joseph decided to make good on his promise to take the whole family to the beach, thereby punishing Mitzi for having something to do on her own. Nevertheless, Mitzi and I dashed out the door, and I handed Madonna a copy of Munsch's *The Paper Bag Princess* as we left.

Since I couldn't drive and read a map at the same time, I asked Mitzi to serve as navigator. She examined nearly every street sign and matched it up with its designation on the map as we headed for our destination an hour away. She performed like a trooper. We did get lost a few times, but that was a characteristic of the driver, not the fault of the navigator.

Once inside the theatre, we witnessed a fashion show of little girls in long dresses and young boys in the best outfits Los Angeles had to offer. Though her simple costume was equally appropriate and the hairdo Madonna had arranged went beyond anything the competition sported, it was clear my young charge felt intimidated by the show of finery. When I bought her an oversized Wild Thing T-shirt, she decided to put it on while we were waiting for the change. Her fashion plate poses prompted a lot of other people to buy T-shirts as well! The unjust reward for her touting services was a very dull curtain raiser that I was afraid would kill live theatre for the child for all time. It was so bad, in fact, that you could feel the tension release all over the auditorium when the voice of a very small boy bellowed out, *"This is boring!"* As a diversionary tactic, I gave Mitzi my opera glasses and set her loose to do some seat hopping. After a good deal of balcony climbing, stair sitting, usher interviewing, and various other antics, she returned to ask me what all the tiny little words were on the top of the proscenium arch. It was the words to the play. The entire text was being projected above the stage. She was flabbergasted to discover by observing me that, contrary to logic, when she looked through the small end of the opera glasses, things got bigger and she could read the words. (It is so easy to take things for granted! I hadn't told her which way to turn those glasses, thereby inadvertently sending her out to look the experienced, if eccentric, theatre-goer but feel short-changed.)

At intermission, we went down to the orchestra pit where she interviewed a young musician who was reading an Avon catalogue. *Wild Things* was the second half of the program, and Mitzi enjoyed it immensely. Afterward, we went backstage to collect autographs in her program and Sendak book. With her mother's prior permission, I photographed her at the chandelier; in front of the orchestra pit; backstage; in the auditorium; with Max, the star; and with the giant props.

But the best part for Mitzi happened outside the Music Centre. The large fountain was set to run at variable speeds after children's operas, and elegantly clad little princes and princesses left a trail of shoes, socks, and finery all over the ground as they relieved their theatre stress by jumping into it. Cautious at first, Mitzi tiptoed from one water spigot to another, trying to avoid the biggest gushes; but within a very few minutes she was turning cartwheels amid a free-for-all that melted her elaborate hairdo. She emerged a soaking wet and very energized little girl.

As we drove home, she began to look over her autograph collection. When, she realized that the words that had been projected over the proscenium arch were the same as those in the book, she proceeded to read it like a storyteller. There I was, on a busy freeway, and I couldn't reach my tape recorder!

When we got back to the house, Madonna came running out to meet us with a story of her own. Mitzi chattered enthusiastically, tugging at her mother's arm, but couldn't make an impression. I felt as though I had two children on my hands. The truth was, they had tandem tales to tell.

When Madonna, Joseph, and Josephina had gotten to the beach, Madonna had been too exhausted to walk, so Joseph had taken Josephina, leaving Madonna alone with *The Paper Bag Princess*. She had started to look at it out of boredom. Then "the words just kept coming out . . . I like it and the more I liked it I just kept reading it. I didn't get tired or nothing. For once I have the courage to do it. I want to do it! It seems like it's more exciting to me than it was before." She particularly liked the ending: "And they didn't get married after all!"

It was the next week before Madonna was ready to talk about Mitzi's triumph. But when she did, she grasped the value of having the book, the performance, and the autographs as part of the literacy package. Or to put it in theoretical terms, Madonna understood the whole language philosophy. In addition, Mitzi had not yet removed the Wild Thing T-shirt; Madonna was learning to read and spell *wild thing* every time she saw her child enter the room.

Meanwhile, I had prepared a book of photographs and descriptive text documenting the *Wild Things* outing. It was written in verse, using rhyme to support some challenging vocabulary. As might be expected, the star of the story had no problem reading the text that chronicled Mitzi's adventures in theatreland. Madonna was very pleased—but not amazed—that her daughter was able to negotiate the sometimes difficult text. "That's that 'knowledge thing' you was talking about, huh?" She wasn't using technical jargon, but she clearly understood the importance of language experience and background knowledge now.

When Amy, Madonna's second daughter, came to stay for a while, she said she could read. Mitzi brought out the treasured *Caterpillar* pair to test her. Though Mitzi had missed her sister very much, her mother's obvious favoritism clearly hurt, and Mitzi tried constantly to show she was better at something. Amy was given the big *Caterpillar* and Mitzi kept the smaller one saying, "This one's a lot harder to read 'cause the words are too little."[2] Then Amy began. On the first stumble, Mitzi jumped in with a quick correction. Madonna interjected, "Patience, Mitzi. You have to give her time to think." Ah, the latency study, I thought. In 1969 Brophy and Good had discovered that teachers give more response time or "latency" to students they believe will have the right answers.[3] Madonna was applying the power of theory. A little farther, she said, "Try skipping it." And later yet, "What do you think it might be?" Madonna knew exactly how to foster good reading strategies by keeping a low affective filter.

On another day, when Madonna's sister was visiting, we got into a discussion of the importance of reading aloud to children. Madonna gave regular and informed support to whatever I said and at one point asked her sister, "Why do you think Mitzi don't know how to read?"

As I left the house one evening, Madonna said, "You know, I'm really enjoying our little visits. If you didn't come here to the house, I don't know how else this would happen." I thought to myself, "Maybe that's what I came here to learn."

At the Library

Although Madonna's children were a significant burden to her, they were also a definite way of getting her focused on literacy. Early on I began taking Mitzi and a neighbor girl to the library. Mitzi struck up a very friendly association with the gentle and energetic children's librarian, who was more than willing to help Mitzi and hold special books for her. The librarian also understood when I asked her to be on the lookout should a pregnant lady show up with the little girl. Our goal would be to make Madonna's first visit so good, there would be no stopping her.

Meanwhile, I did what I could with what I had. Mitzi, feeling secure in the house of the friendly librarian, made a gallant effort to fill out a library card application. I had to help with the street and city identification, but Mitzi did all the actual writing on the form. The person at the desk seemed a tad shocked at the mutilated paper she was proudly handed by the child who had contrived to obey as many rules as she could understand. Fortunately, the children's librarian sensed the air of resistance and facilitated the guardian signature so that Mitzi could go home with books immediately. (The neighbor child who occasionally accompanied us also attempted to get a card, but was unable to recall the spelling of her last name, her address, or her phone number. It took three separate new applications on three separate occasions before that child was able to get enough information from home to get a card.)

I never went up to the desk with the girls, but let them struggle to get meaningful dialogue going with the people in charge of serving their needs. I did stand nearby in case things got out of hand, but it seemed that too much of my "doing it for them" would further disempower these children who already were receiving daily messages reinforcing their ineptitude. Also, libraries are more hospitable to children than the world at large, and I hoped that being successful here would help them understand how to communicate with adults more accustomed to overlooking than serving youngsters.

Allowing the kids to design their own solutions also opened the path to independent decision making. And that led to one very strange little ritual: Mitzi always checked her books out and returned them at the same window, the checkout window. We read the RETURN BOOKS HERE sign each time we entered, but unless a librarian was standing right there, Mitzi did not feel secure just popping her precious stories down a chute. And it seemed inappropriate for me to squash this decision with a direct command to do otherwise. So: Mitzi and I would enter the library, walk up to the big RETURN BOOKS HERE sign, and discuss the meaning of the text and the convenience to the patron who might be in a hurry. Sometimes we would also observe the book cart that was often parked nearby, waiting to transport returned books to the shelf. Then we would go through the metal-detector archway, whereupon Mitzi would make a fast right, convert her usual sparkling smile to a look of snobbish disdain (thereby placing the personnel very much off balance), and, if necessary, wait in the checkout line to return her books . . . meticulously . . . one . . . by . . . one.

Over time, Mitzi began to read. With the help of the children's librarian, she discovered books I neither had in my personal collection nor had met yet myself. While hanging onto old, familiar books, she began to struggle through new ones. From time to time we would sit down in the children's area with her collection and I would begin to read aloud. Much in the way that Arthur had done with my first reading of *The Cat in the Hat*, Mitzi would take over the reading herself. And sometimes other children would come over to listen, silently watching as Mitzi worked her way through a book that had gripped her enough to make the effort worthwhile. At first I wondered if she knew she was being watched. Then I wondered if the little audience would embarrass her. But whatever she felt, her very cool external demeanor held and she moved ahead, neither really sharing the story nor holding it back.

She checked out larger and larger numbers of books. After one such binge, I informed Madonna that I would not be around when they needed to be returned. Understanding the consequences of late library books, Madonna said she would get Joseph to put them in the twenty-four-hour-return slot. On my next visit, however, I learned that the unemployed boyfriend had not had time. The fine was significant enough to suspend Mitzi's library privileges until it was paid. I paid it myself but informed Mitzi that getting the books back was very important; we could have bought a book with the money we wasted on fines that day. After several more visits, Mitzi suddenly lost interest in checking out any more books. Because I stayed away from the transaction desk, it was not until I tried to check out a book Madonna had requested that I found out about a new fine. A couple of books had been overlooked at home and were long overdue when they were returned. This past-due fine on her record had cut Mitzi off from further borrowing. But she hadn't felt she could report her crime, having been warned by me once already. (I did question and I still do question how much a library gains when it fines the poor. I wonder if keeping the Mitzis and the Farras away from books can possibly be that beneficial.)

One swelteringly hot day I forcefully ejected the inhabitants from Madonna's little house with its sealed windows, loaded them into my car, and then deposited them at the entrance to the library. A listless caravan of tall girl, toddler, and pregnant lady labored up the ramp to the do-it-yourself doors. The only motivation I could detect in that dejected trio was the motivation to end everything. I rushed ahead and opened a door to the foyer and the breath of cool air that came out of the building.

Madonna seemed to emerge from a trance as Mitzi dashed in to return her books at the checkout window. Josephina, usually calm and methodical in her efforts to grab my tote and tape recorder or pull at my pantyhose, was suddenly energized as well and began to run harum-scarum through the library. She also did a lot of uncharacteristic yelling. I began to relate firsthand to the feelings Pandora must have had when she opened that infamous box. I'd unleashed three individual free spirits into the cool, quiet, hallowed halls of literature.

Madonna's child-caring priorities immediately succumbed to an urge to look at home decorating magazines. Her mother was coming to visit and she needed some ideas for fixing things up. The variety on the open stacks, which she located on her own, elated Madonna. All the same, given a severe hip problem, swollen feet, and back pain that recurred with each pregnancy, she was too miserable to walk or reach up or bend over. It was no act.

This time I couldn't just stand back and let nature take its course. So I got Madonna situated at a table and delivered the goods. She couldn't exactly read the magazines, but poured over them intensely, while I chased the baby, who had discovered the new game of hide-and-seek in the labyrinth of library shelves. There was a limit to how much chasing I was up to, however, so the trip was not as long as I'd intended. (I had also forgotten what an inconvenience it is to have to change a diaper in a public restroom.) After I'd collected mother and babe, we discovered that Mitzi had not only selected an incredible heap of books, she had already checked them out and was ready to leave. Madonna also had a book she wanted to take home, and humbled herself before her daughter, clearly acknowledging that this was the person to whom she must turn if she was going to be able to. Mitzi rose to the occasion with authoritative dignity stepped up to the checkout window for the third time that day.

Soon after this library trip, Madonna announced that there was one time when Joseph was always available to drive. So she was going to start Sunday morning trips to the library. It might have worked, had the library been open on Sundays, but in that neighborhood, where public libraries are needed most, it was not. Next she announced that Joseph was just going to have to start doing some baby-sitting so she could go to the library and get some reading done in peace. That never happened either.

Although Madonna was not able to incorporate regular library visits into her life, Mitzi and, when she was around, her sister Amy continued to go to the library to check out books and tapes suggested by the children's librarian. They took home a smorgasbord of books, from which Madonna would look for anything she could get through. Lobel's *Mouse Tales* made a major hit. Madonna became such a Lobel fan that she began to ask for books just by that author. This selective interest was a major change. When I mentioned to Madonna that this was consistent with studies that show good readers often have favorite authors, she agreed that this made sense. I bought two little Lobel books to give her when she went into the hospital to have her baby.

Books on Tape

During an interview with Madonna, she said that she had bought one book for Mitzi many years before. It was the story of Bambi and had come with a cassette recording of the story. She asked if tapes were good. I said I didn't know and asked her what *she* thought. This reversal was not designed just to empower my subject; it was a legitimate effort to engage this firsthand witness in the research process. Madonna didn't think the tape had much value, because Mitzi had discarded the book and just listened to the tape. Then when the recorder batteries wore out, the tape was forgotten as well.

When, Mitzi, her neighbor friend, and Amy began to check storybooks and tapes out from the library, Madonna let them use Joseph's good tape player. *The Dark Crystal* became an institution. Then, the Bambi book (but not the tape) surfaced. Since we'd discussed the validity of taped stories, Madonna asked Mitzi to read the Bambi book. Though the book vanished again before my next visit, Madonna reported that Mitzi had read it just the way the voice on the commercial tape had—with feeling.

After that, we both began to notice parts of recorded books being recited around the house, characters' lines being chanted back and forth between the children. Quite possibly neither Madonna nor I would have noticed this phenomenon had we not been research partners.[4]

Intimations of Empowerment

Madonna had always felt she needed to let others make her decisions. She had suffered such early abuse that the idea that she could take charge of her own destiny was inconceivable. Her quasi-independent living situation began when she moved in with the man she eventually married and it continued simply because she was dumped by him far away from her mother's home. At that, she'd rallied until her mother moved in and then deserted her. Subsequently, more afraid of being alone than of being abused, she had allowed anyone who promised to keep her company to move in with her. It would be ingenuous to claim literacy development as the sole cause of Madonna's move towards empowerment, but a number of incidents indicate that she was undergoing a radical change in her attitudes about her own life, responsibility, and control.

Madonna had accepted the fact that she could not read as evidence that she was less intelligent than those who could. Once she understood that her own disempowered background made literacy a near impossibility, however, she began to study in earnest the theory that supported the notion that it is never too late. Not only did she begin to read with enthusiasm herself, she put into practice those reading strategies I'd used on *her* when *she* was teaching her own children. Madonna took charge of the reading development that she now understood was within her domain. Once empowered with theory, she engaged in intelligent, deliberate practice.

There was no question that Madonna had never wanted children. Her mother had been correct in her original diagnosis: Madonna had not yet had a childhood herself. She wanted mothering, not to be a mother. She wanted someone to watch over her, even when it came to the very serious business of birth control. She wanted to state her wishes and have someone else implement them, like placing an order with Santa Claus. Though she had asked to have her tubes tied after each pregnancy, her mother, her doctors, her husband, and her boyfriend had had the actual control over whether or not she continued to spend nine-month periods in absolute agony.

When she was without a phone, I had made preliminary inquiries about Planned Parenthood facilities for her. Madonna had been interested, but Joseph had failed to get her to her appointment on time. She blamed him for the botched effort, ignoring the fact that he didn't care if she had more babies or not. (He had explained that he couldn't get a vasectomy because (a) he might want to have more babies from some other source and (b) it would hurt too much.) Madonna had a history of waiting for service, service that was important only to her, service that was never delivered. She had the idea that the responsibility for all her needs belonged to others—disempowering . . . significant . . . others.

Then, abruptly, she took matters into her own hands. She made an appointment to find out about the necessary surgery, got herself there, and made arrangements to have her tubes tied at the time of a caesarean delivery. She had simply decided to take charge of her own reproduction. Only it really wasn't simple. She had to get herself and a toddler around to gather paperwork on her earlier hospitalizations from disorganized and seemingly disinterested agencies. The point is that once she was mentally in charge, she did it. The good news, she pointed out, was that she hadn't married Joseph, so she didn't need his permission for something his parents' church might resist.

She also got her phone reconnected. Since a major problem had been controlling the long-distance phone calls, I arranged to call her back when she called me one afternoon. She appreciated that: she wanted to discuss the rest of her life. As soon as this baby was delivered, she was planning to go back to school. I was taken aback. I never push my literacy students on that sensitive subject and had certainly not mentioned it to this young woman whom a school diagnosed as retarded. Yet on her own initiative, Madonna had used her phone to learn that there were classes available where some kind of baby-sitting was offered, though she hadn't yet gotten the particulars. Going to school was essential to her self-improvement, she told me. If she didn't go to school and start reading more, she'd just be sitting around looking at the TV and watching the kids. "That's no life," she stated.

She informed Joseph that he would have to look after the kids when she was at the library, because she now knew that she had to investigate all the things she'd discovered there when I took her. He was going to have to get used to the idea that she wasn't going to sit around the house while he went out and wasted time. He could cooperate or he could leave; there wasn't anything to discuss. For her to talk like that was an astounding change. She was willing to be alone if that was the price of literacy development.

Another sign of her radical mental change was a newfound ability to analyze conventional givens. I had been in the house when a photograph salesman had come to show her proofs of pictures taken a few weeks before. Madonna was desperate for nice photographs, and though she had stated up front that she only had $25 in her purse to spend, I watched as the salesman worked her up to a $100 order to be paid for when her welfare check came in. Though she still had a strong sentimental attachment to such items, Madonna now said she couldn't understand how door-to-door salespeople could make a living selling something so overpriced. She was never letting anybody like that in her house again.

She also announced that she planned to change the way she cared for Mitzi. For starters, she was going to take the nine-year-old child to the dentist for the first time in her life. Having lost many of her own teeth to decay, she now understood that as a mother *she* needed to prevent that disfigurement from happening to her daughter. She was going to have the baby checked out early too. These decisions about dental care were indications that she was identifying needs and taking charge of meeting them. I wanted to say, "Yea! Madonna! You've just moved your locus of control!" But I knew she was still thinking of it as "taking charge of her life."

Madonna asked if I would come visit her in the hospital when she had her baby and operation. Certainly, I would. After all, I had long before stashed away two little Lobel books for just this occasion. She said she didn't really have any other friends to call. In a neighborhood filled with women and men who were around the house more often than not, she had allowed herself to remain isolated from any associations. Also, she had managed to take her daughter to the weekly gymnastics classes for nearly three months without ever getting into a conversation with the other parents who shared the same bleachers. Joseph had warned her against talking to Mexicans, Vietnamese, or other impure people. As a result, when she was too miserable to walk the four blocks, her daughter, having no gym friends to call, had to miss class. During our phone call, Madonna said she was going to have to get to know some other mothers when she went to school. Maybe they could start to help each other. This kind of reaching out was a major change from just relying on whatever people managed to force their way into her life.

Still, no human life can be charted straight up. And the graph of Madonna's development was as full of reversals as any heartbeat pattern. The day before she was to go to the hospital, she called from a pay phone, her own phone having been once again disconnected. She had been very concerned about how dirty her kitchen floor had gotten. Joseph had pretended to mop it, but didn't sweep first or clean the mop. Then, her brother, jokingly pretending to be afraid of being evicted, had mopped it again. Not wanting to bring her new baby home to the still dirty floor, Madonna had begun a marathon cleaning, an effort that pushed her into premature labor. She had delivered the new baby three days before its caesarean delivery date. As a result, it would be eight weeks before she could have her tubes tied and she couldn't even get an appointment until she'd had a checkup.

"Does Joseph understand that he's on restriction for eight weeks?" I asked.

"It don't matter what he understands anymore," she retorted. "He is history." These were not the words of an isolated young girl afraid of being abandoned.

In the last photograph I took of Madonna, she was seated on a couch, reading nursery rhymes to her toddler. She had acquired the power of theory and knew what to do with it.

1. Bigotry is a recurring problem for the illiterate disempowered. Trapped by fear and wanting to feel better than *somebody*, they are easy prey to manipulation. Though she'd harbored no particular racial animosity or even awareness before meeting him, Madonna was quick to buy into her boyfriend's "bad Mexican" warnings, even when she saw her Hispanic neighbors out watering their lawns while her boyfriend parked his truck on hers.

2. There is long-standing research that shows that larger type—about 12 point—is easier to read than smaller type. Mitzi and Jonathan (whom you'll meet later) both make the observation outright, and Danny (in the next chapter), who was afraid to complain about anything I presented to him, consistently gravitated to the larger print. This makes an obvious case for very clear, easy-to-see print in the books bought for schools.

3. Jere Brophy and Thomas L. Good, *Teacher Dyadic Interaction: A Manual for Coding Classroom Behavior*, Report Series No. 27 (Austin, Texas: The Research and Development Center for Teacher Education, the University of Texas at Austin, December 1969).

4. After Madonna's discovery that the taped stories do have a value for readers, I began to use them with my adult students. I now make a standing offer to read any story onto an individual tape and have established a personal lending library of about fifty commercially recorded tapes of children's books. They are so popular with both my literacy and language students that there are never enough to meet the demand.

Six

Danny (and Charlie): It Runs in the Family

*T*he things we inherit go well beyond hair color or shoe size. They go beyond the sound of a voice or even turns of phrase. The ambience of literacy—or the lack of it—is also transferred from one generation to the next, like a sacred lifestyle recipe. Long before the dawn of consciousness, a child's appetites are nurtured, then cultivated and refined over a lifetime. Then the process is renewed with the succeeding generation. It is so smooth. Everyone knows what to do. But what happens when the generation in charge of passing the recipe on waits until midlife to change the formula? What happens then to the generation on the receiving end?

When I first began to work with Danny, his affable nature and willingness to reach out seemed a unique blend not likely to pass my way again. Oh, yes, Danny could not read, but this had not stopped him from moving unfettered through the formal twelve-year school system. It was a pleasure to work with him and a delight to see him starting to change, taking on the thinking patterns and responsibilities reserved for the literate man. Finally, Danny, emboldened by the power of theory, used his newfound literacy to write for a specific audience, literacy tutors, and to speak to that audience as one who'd experienced both sides of the fence. It was a simple success story, but one of a kind.

Then I met his son Charlie. Charlie, too, had gone through twelve years of schooling without benefit of what we call the

143

basics. Charlie had his father's voice, his father's smile, and his father's affable nature, and he demonstrated the same natural willingness to reach out and help others. Indeed, he reached back to help his dad, who was developing an interest in computers. But Charlie had also inherited a culture of nonreading from his father, who was now beginning the transition to literacy. Although neither father nor son was successful at traditional literacy-related activities, Charlie had the added disadvantage of having been disempowered by *technology*. You see, in spite of the fact that he'd spent years in a computer lab in his high school special education program, his computer knowledge was limited to being able to maintain the lab environment and to play games under careful supervision. The risk taking involved in literate thinking had been disallowed. Charlie's situation shows us the danger of buying into the idea that computer classes are inherently good without asking, What philosophy of education is being espoused? I didn't have a chance to work with Charlie and so couldn't give him the power of theory that was the catalyst for his father's new vision. And Charlie was already a grown man.

Can a man in middle age pass the power of theory on to a son who has already become something else—in that man's own image? I'll tell you up front, I don't know the answer. But here are their stories. See what you think.

An Author in Waiting

Affable, forty-three-year-old Danny was a graduate of a Southern California high school. He had moved through the educational system without any difficulty, his inability to read unchallenged. In fact, no one had ever actually acknowledged that he had a problem. He admitted that his teachers all seemed to like him and that there had been a tacit agreement that as long as he showed up on time, behaved politely, and caused no problems in class, he would get along just fine. Believing that he was kind of stupid, and having an extraordinary need to get along with everyone, he had never felt at liberty to ask why he wasn't being taught to read.

Because his wife was securely employed, Danny hadn't confronted the financial devastation many adult nonreaders experience. Although his illiteracy caused him to lose one minimum wage job after another, his obliging personality and well-established humility always cleared the path to more employment. In between jobs, however, his wife had pushed him to get help with his reading. So Danny had finally registered with a library literacy program, dutifully showing up on time and as scheduled, working with one tutor after another, over several years, interrupting the program only when a new job called for different hours or when home emergencies or vacations intervened. In spite of these sessions, he had been unable to demonstrate even minimum proficiency on the state library literacy exam. In fact, after his first year of tutoring he had *regressed a full grade level*, to something below the sixth month of the first grade in reading. It was that history of failure that qualified Danny for my research. Although even he could no longer recall how many people had tried to teach him, it was rumored that I was tutor number thirteen—not a lucky sign, I thought.

Some reading experts suggest that everyone in America, or at least everyone in the middle class, is exposed to so much environmental print it is impossible to grow to adulthood without minimum literacy proficiency. Having bought into this logic, I had a conflict: Danny had not exhibited this minimum proficiency on his placement tests. But he had a driver's license; didn't that show something? During our first phone conversation, I tried to establish in his mind that he *could* read *something*.

"You drive, don't you?" He admitted he did.

"Well, then, you can read a stop sign, can't you?" I pressed.

"Well, I try. I really try," was as much as he would allow.

We were to meet at the library, so I needed to know what he looked like.

"Well, I'm kind of short." That was it. He had no further details about himself to help me identify him. It was pretty clear that the low self-esteem that prevails among nonreaders was a definite barrier to his success.

Theory Is Introduced Immediately

Danny showed up right on time for our first session. After we introduced ourselves, I explained what my research was about and why it was obvious to me that he had the necessary intelligence to read and write. (After all, the business of learning a language, not only taking in words and phrases heard, but also figuring out how to use implied rules of tense and structure to express ideas in sentences not heard before, is the most complex task a human brain can address. Learning to communicate well enough verbally by the age of five to meet nearly every need is proof that the human brain is powerful enough to do anything.) We discussed the fact that his literacy perspective would shift from disempowerment to empowerment as he began to understand what it took to create literacy and how he could take charge of his own learning. I set the following ground rules:

1. I would explain the background of everything we would do together and would teach him the appropriate technical terminology, allowing us to talk about his process in professional terms.
2. I would explain why we were trying an approach and under what circumstances it had worked in the past; if a technique was experimental, I would tell him that, too.
3. He would take charge of his own lessons. If something didn't make sense, it was up to him to say so and to persist until he got the information he needed.
4. I would bring in resource materials so that he could see which studies proved what theories and would become as knowledgeable about the process as I was by the time we got through.

5. He would keep us on an effective track, telling me which methods helped and which seemed to be wasting his time. Enough time had already been wasted on things that didn't work.

6. I would record parts of our sessions so that I wouldn't need to spend a lot of time taking notes. The red light on my recorder would let him know when it was recording. I would also tell him when I was turning the recorder on. If at any time he wanted me to turn the recorder off, replay something, or erase part of a tape, I would do so.

7. We would notify each other if one or the other of us needed to cancel or reschedule a session.

8. Since I was trading tutoring for research material, I wanted his commitment not to drop out once we got started.

9. We would work together for three months.

The Filter Surfaces

The California Literacy Campaign questionnaire elicited some very interesting background information. But when I tried to get a writing sample, Danny's hand began to shake so badly, the writing looked as though it had been done by a man of ninety. His affective filter was so high around a pencil, it was clear a lot of terror was buried in his past. I decided to address that issue immediately.

He caught on to the concept of the affective filter so quickly that I presented another theory and then another. I expected him to lose interest in the details of specific studies; not only did that not happen, he proved eager to hear it all in one gulp. Everything that made sense to me seemed to make sense to Danny, and he was able to come up with personal illustrations for almost every theoretical issue we discussed. In spite of the obvious abuse and neglect he'd suffered there, he refused to say anything outwardly negative about the schools he'd gone to. He just said "they" didn't know as much back then, his teachers were too old to do much, and he suspected they were paid for student attendance rather than student learning. All this was reported with a permanent smile on his friendly face, even when tears were streaming down his cheeks.

Danny seemed determined to maintain the fiction that everything had been the way it was supposed to and that some students just don't do as well as others. It was as if denying that the system had failed him would somehow diminish the consequences. He did, later in our meeting, say it was bad when his teachers yelled at the kids, but gave no specifics. Being yelled at in school is something that surfaces over and over. Danny remembered it. Arthur mentioned it. Jonathan and Beau bring it up in the next chapter. It is not necessary to be verbally abused directly. Just the insecurity created by hearing others yelled at can leave lifelong scars.

Then, after reporting that he'd first had a really serious problem in junior high, he said, "Oh, God! It was different! I guess it was a little upsetting . . . it used to be a little frustrating, especially when the teacher wanted you to read out loud. I guess you would sink down in your seat—so you wouldn't be called on . . . you felt like hiding like under your desk . . . you feel embarrassed . . . you don't want your friends to know . . . you try to fake it, like pretend you can read, but you can't fake it." Then, again trying to forgive everyone, he added, "I guess they know more now. There's still a lot of people out there who don't know how to read."

Predictably, he'd never been read to either as a preschooler or at school. He thought his immigrant parents could read, but they had never read to him. He was sure they had done the best they could but probably just didn't know they were supposed to read to kids. When I explained that the process was never too late to start and that I read to my adult students every session, he was a little surprised. But when I asked if his wife, who he reported read romance stories, could be persuaded to read to him ten minutes a day, he couldn't say no fast enough. Though he was attending sessions at her insistence (going for reading lessons was a ritual consequence nearly every time he lost a job) he had the distinct impression he needed to take care of his own problem.

Theory Gives a Flicker of Hope

Then, as I read aloud from Krashen and Smith, he experienced something of a revelation. He appreciated both Krashen's research and Smith's taking the schools on single-handedly. The notion of club membership caused a lot of things to fall into place for Danny. Finally, he said of Smith, "Oh, he must be a good teacher! Where is he? Does he come around here?" He said he'd definitely be willing to go to Smith's class. And during the first session, he referenced the affective filter as "that thing that goes up." He didn't yet have membership in the educational jargon users club, but he understood the concept.

As we left the library, he said he could hardly wait to tell his wife about "all this" and he thought it would help his older son, Charlie, a special ed high school student, as well. He also said he planned to go to a local comic book store for reading material on the weekend. Since we both had another night free that week, we decided to meet again immediately.

It was not until I got home and began to enter my case notes into the computer that I realized the information overload I'd dumped on my poor subject. I prepared a handout that gave the key information on the affective filter, language acquisition device (LAD), input hypothesis (i + 1), boredom, background knowledge, being read to, and reading to yourself.

When we met again, I gave Danny a mechanical pencil and a blue plastic envelope with a tablet in it. He seemed very pleased, though he made no move to use the pencil. Giving him the theoretical handout, I apologized for having thrown so much information at him so fast. He again assured me that it was all very interesting, and after we had gone over the handout briefly, he was familiar with most of the material. In fact, he could almost read the handout.

He'd had a discussion with his wife and felt he needed proof to support the notions he'd apparently been unable to defend at home. He would not immediately explain what had been challenged, but as we reviewed ideas and as I prepared to read to him, he revealed that his wife claimed never to make mistakes when she reads to herself. Further, she'd told him that not being read to as a child was not relevant to their special ed son, Charlie. He had a problem simply because he was like his dad; he had a learning disability[1] and the school had a special program to take care of it. (During the time Danny and I worked together, Charlie moved from a high school LD program to a community college one.)

Since Danny had been unable to support his newfound claims of hope at home, he wanted some of those studies to show his wife. Not wanting him to get frustrated by difficult material, I suggested he just show her the handout I'd prepared. It was nice, he said, but he needed in-depth information. Clearly, his intelligence was on the line.

I reminded him of the value of *being read to* and began reading from Frank Smith's *Insult to Intelligence*. Nearly every paragraph met with enthusiastic confirmation. We had talked about miscues and the process of regression to find sense in the text when the miscues were too far off. I suggested he note when I missed a word. Sometimes I would back up to correct it, but just as often I wouldn't. He could see that not having to be perfect would lower the filter; however, since he came from a performance-oriented model, he was very interested to observe and was plainly relieved to have permission to hear that even good readers made mistakes. Then we switched to the "Power of Reading" chapter in Krashen's *Inquiries and Insights*. I reminded him that it was important that he tell me if things got boring. That wasn't likely, he assured me. This stuff was educational. He wanted to know if these books could be found in the library and looked crestfallen when I said probably not this public library, but that a university library surely would have them.

Being Read To Stirs Self-Analysis

We were on the page on which Krashen discusses how many words kids learn without being taught when Danny interrupted me. He'd suddenly realized how being read to helps you read. He said he had proof. He pointed to the long word *handicapped* in the midst of the text. Certainly he had heard it all his life, but he said he'd never known what that looked like before; now he was sure he'd never forget.

I'd been reading aloud and Danny had been following along, chiming in where he could from time to time, much the way a child will with a storybook. Only here, fortified with the theory base of a reading professional, Danny knew what was happening. He knew to be watching out for vocabulary development from context and he'd been listening to the content of the Krashen work. He had also been watching himself discover words. This was metacognition in process. It might have gone on even longer, but the owner of the office we were borrowing came in, so we had to evacuate. I offered him my copy of Frank Smith, sensing that the large print might facilitate some home dialogue. No, what he wanted was the Krashen book, the one that was solid black with small type and little tables that showed why Danny couldn't read.

I opened my mouth to argue that my personal copies have my very important marginal notes and markers in them. But he had already observed that I write in my books, and he'd seen Post-its used in offices at work: people wrote on them and stuck them all over the place. How could I say that this little $10 book was very valuable to me, when it was clearly, right then, priceless to him? A long weekend was coming up and he needed this proof that he was a worthwhile human being, even if he couldn't really read it. Before we left the office, I put Post-its on the important parts of *Inquiries and Insights*.

Then we went up to the magazine section of the library, where I read him short articles until the building closed.

Danny reiterated that he'd been very pleased to hear me read Krashen's work but wanted to go hear this man for himself. He was willing to go anywhere any day if I would just let him know when. Not wanting him to jeopardize his job, I tried to let the matter drop, but as we left the library, he reminded me to look into Krashen's speaking schedule.

Danny was right on time for our third session and carried the blue plastic envelope proudly. When I offered him a new copy of the Krashen book, he readily traded me my well-marked one. Because his wife had had a schedule conflict, he had not made it to the comic book store on Saturday; nor had he successfully defended the theories to her. He *really* needed to hear Krashen personally.

Key Words and Language Experience Start Change

We reviewed the theories we'd previously discussed, and then I moved on to Paulo Freire's work in Brazil and the concept of *generative words*. We also discussed Sylvia Ashton Warner's work using *organic words* with the Maori children of New Zealand and Septima Clark's use of *key words* among pre-civil rights blacks in the South. In each case, the *literacy-initiating words had come from the learners themselves and had been discarded when they were no longer important to the learners.* This process loses its power in classrooms where the teacher or workbook publisher decides in advance what words should be studied. We talked about the power of literacy and the value of using the learner's words.

Then, having laid the groundwork, I asked Danny if he thought the key word approach would be helpful to him. It made sense to him. Everything so far had made sense to him, so he thought he'd be crazy to pass up a chance to try something with such a well-documented success rate. I asked him for a word he would like to use. He grappled with the request as though it would make all the difference in the world. Of course, as it turned out, it did. It took about five minutes for him to decide that the most important word he could think of was *freeway*. I wrote it on a three-by-five card and handed it to him, not giving him any particular instruction, just putting the word quite literally into his hands. Then I tape-recorded his extensive monologue about the importance of freeways.

After that I began reading him Shel Silverstein's *Lafcadio* but did not finish before the library closed. The book is a humorous tale of a wild lion who learns to hunt hunters, moves to the big city, becomes more human than beast, and then suffers disillusionment with his new identity. I hoped Danny would want to borrow the book, but he had what he valued in his blue envelope. Though he couldn't really read it yet, Danny felt secure holding his little book of research studies.

For our fourth session we were able to borrow the office we'd used before. It was relatively peaceful until another tutor and student began to work next door. The tutor was given to yelling when his student failed to perform as instructed, and the failures came all too often. We ignored the noise as best we could, and I walked Danny through the language experience theory and key word concepts and reiterated why they worked and with whom they had worked in the past. Then I explained that not wanting his affective filter to go up, I had made only a half-page transcription of his lengthy recitation on the key word *freeway*. I said I was afraid that more would not only drive his filter up, it might prove to him beyond all doubt that he could not read.

I am often asked if I really expressed such concerns to Danny and, if so, how I went about it. First, if he was to take charge of what we did during his lessons, he had to understand the rationale for each technique. Second, Danny was a non-reader, not an unintelligent human being. I discussed with him—just as I do with you—in detail what I thought would be helpful and on what theory the proposed technique was based. I needed it to be crystal clear, and if it wasn't, it was not a defect in Danny. Also, I believe honesty belongs in education. When we tell the truth, we open the door to dialogue that cannot occur in environments designed to manipulate. It was critical to Danny's success that he understand he was the authority in his learning. I told him outright that I'd just transcribed part of what he knew he'd put on tape. And I told him why. That way he was in a position to decide whether or not I'd made a correct assumption. That is empowerment.

I showed him the half-page of text and asked him if he wanted to see how much of it he could identify. He took off like a bandit! He began reading as if it was old news! He got through it before I realized the recorder wasn't on. I fumbled around, at first unable to locate the normally familiar buttons; I asked him to reread it for the tape. He did, almost as well as the first time, misstarting a sentence (and not regressing) and so misreading one entire line *to make it make sense.* He made side remarks as he went along, indicating a relaxed feeling about the text. He was so flabbergasted, he could hardly believe it either.

"Oh, that's tricky," he blurted onto the tape. "Oh, that's pretty good! Oh, that works, y'know! This program really works! . . . Oh, so when you're doing your own words, you can pick it up just like that!" He snapped his fingers. "Oh, I like that! Y'know, it's just like a photograph. It just sticks with ya and you can pick it up just like that!"

"Did the word *freeway* pop out of the text?" I asked him.

"Yeah! Oh, yeah. I knew *freeway* right away." Then he wanted to know if he could have a copy to take home and show his wife. Then he said she would be "dumbfounded."

Fluidity was the big advantage in letting Danny dictate to the tape. The more typical process of having the student either write himself or dictate to the tutor would have slowed things down considerably—which is not *all* bad. Putting the words of the learner on paper as they are uttered gives an immediate sound/symbol connection lost when the tape is used. Also, the student and teacher can discuss conventions of sentence beginnings (capitalization) and endings (end punctuation) as they occur. My tape/computer process speeded up the production and increased the volume of language experience text. If the computer lab had been open then, I would have taken Danny there and possibly tried to get him started on a word processing program. (I am a strong believer in word processing programs for early literacy students.) Text production would have been much quicker—no waiting for me to take the tape home and transcribe it. Would the results have been better? I don't know. It would have meant trading fluidity for text in hand. We might have tried both. We might have stayed with the first thing that produced positive results. I am not offering a paint-by-number prescription for success. Each teacher and each student comprise a unique blend of colors that depends very much on the always changing light, so that pedagogy must be allowed to present itself anew with each meeting— like a painting in process. Just as you know a paint-by-number picture when you see it, you also know when rigid boundaries have restricted curriculum. On the other hand, real education is a living art.

After the initial buzz had worn off, he began to think out loud. "I wonder why *they* never did this? I wonder why *they* never did this in school. . . . It really works . . . This stuff really works. . . . *They* should uh done this a long time ago." Once he realized that he could and indeed had broken the code, he also seemed to understand that his stupidity wasn't the reason he had not been taught to read in school. It was the first time he'd verbalized any negative feelings towards those "nice" people who had been in charge of his disempowerment. Suddenly he was realizing that "nice" and "schoolteachers" did not necessarily connect.

However, when I tried to get him to write something, anything of what he'd had to say about freeways, he froze. Well, when he was ready, I suggested, it would be good to get him used to writing about very familiar things. He should let me know when he wanted to try. Sure, he said, but he did not seem to think it would be during this lifetime.

Success Begins Behavioral Change

So, I got out *Lafcadio* and began to read it aloud. He appreciated the story's double levels of meaning, commenting that a
child might appreciate it as a straight story on the first reading
and then later come to appreciate the allegorical implications.
This kind of thinking and dialogue about text use was new.
He was developing an awareness of audience that is essential to
successful *writing*. This *reading* observation about the writer's
audience showed up later in his *writing*, a paper about the
writing process. This is a graphic example of how authentic
literature fosters critical thinking and writing skill.[2]

He began to read some line endings aloud with me, but
was not following along with every word. I was holding the
book toward him as I read, pointing only toward the lines,
not word to word. He finally wanted me to back up to a line
that had a word he said looked like *cars* but he knew that
wasn't it. It was *ears*. (This is the same process I use with
entire classes of ESL students who are also just making sense
of our sound/symbol system.) We talked about the fact that
you can't sound out *ears*. What if, for example, you are thinking
of *ea* as in *learn* or in the past tense of *read*? Thinking you
know what *ea* sounds like will likely lead you on a merry
chase—far away from the meaning of the text. He just had
to get used to seeing *ears* as is, like in this story, in use, where
the sense makes the right word emerge. When that happened,
the way *freeway* did, reading would go much faster than if he
tried to figure out how to break up a strange word and then
sounded out the parts—which might not even be the right
parts if he'd guessed at the wrong letter clusters.

This is not to suggest that readers never learn to sound
things out. They do, unavoidably. Sounding out, or making
the sound/symbol relationship, is a side effect of reading—of
seeing and hearing many interesting words at the same time.
By reading along while being read to, new readers begin to
recognize sound/symbol relationships, just as recognizing *ears*

may give Danny a future way of reading *hears*. Of course, good readers receive this kind of low-stress, storytime reinforcement thousands of times over many years before trying to do it independently. And when Danny picks up *Lafcadio* on his own, he will be looking at *ears* while hearing my voice reading it aloud to him. But to demand that he sound out the word without first getting a tremendous amount of sound/symbol input would be like pushing a little bird out of the nest before it has feathers—simply murderous. Yet that is what happens in schools where phonics is substituted for the real thing—storytelling.

Without the storytelling foundation, a phonics focus tells the student that sounds are more important than meaning. And while missing a few sounds may not effect comprehension at all, missing meaning renders sounds useless. I had an Egyptian student in my community college elementary ESL class one semester who borrowed my copy of *Aladdin* and read the entire story to herself by our next meeting. It wasn't until we were discussing the way she'd heard the story as a child that I realized she was not pronouncing the leading man's name the same way I was. All the way through those marvelous adventures, she'd been using, of all things, an *Egyptian* pronunciation for the name Aladdin! But she got the meaning and enjoyed the book anyway. What if she'd gotten hung up on the pronunciation, as some such students do? A week of pleasure reading would have been lost and her enthusiasm with it.

Kids who enter school already fortified with thousands of books and stories back into skills-based tasks and are successful at them. *This is how the misperception that the worksheets teach can come into being.* The students are told that this is *reading instruction* when, in fact, it is a *test* to see who already know the answers because of their foundations in basic literacy. The good readers "learn" the lesson and go back to real reading. The others continue not to know what reading is supposed to be about. Little kids believe what they are told by adults. They buy into the reality they are given. So the kids who were read to at home believe they are smarter for having solved the phonics puzzle, and the kids who were never read to are shunted into drill-and-practice programs where what is called reading is not reading at all. Danny had suffered through years of "sound it out" misinstruction. But now he very quickly understood how that process impedes comprehension.

Though the hardback book was rather heavy for me to support with one hand and though Danny was normally very polite, never once during my reading of *Lafcadio* did he reach out to help hold it up. But when I finished reading there was a long pause. Then Danny slowly reached out, took the book, and turned the last page as if to see if there might be something more. He said nothing for a long time. He just stared. Perhaps, I thought, he felt a kinship with the lion who was no longer a wild beast and no longer a man.

About twenty minutes before closing time, a door slammed and the entire area went pitch dark. There was no ambient light in those basement offices originally designed to be photo darkrooms. Danny got up, eased himself out to the reception area, located the switches, and then came back to report that the loud tutor from next door had flipped the master switch as he'd exited. He went on to say that it probably wasn't an accident. That was the first offensive/defensive thing I ever heard him say about another person. It was even more significant because the person was a tutor. Then he added that he disapproved of the man's teaching style. As we left the library, Danny again brought up the obnoxious tutor and how sorry he felt for the student. Then, as though he talked theory all the time, he said, "I'll bet his filter was [gesturing toward the roof and whistling through his teeth] *way* up there!"

This was a landmark evening in Danny's empowerment. It was session four, only our third week, and he had read for the first time in his life. He was talking about text. He was involved in thinking about his own thinking and learning. He was using theory to describe the disempowerment of the student in the next office. He was entering the evaluator's club.

Authorship Continues

I took the recording of Danny's "freeway" reading and did a modified miscue analysis of it, showing it to him the following session. *Miscue analysis* is a complex process of looking at the kinds of reading errors a person makes when reading aloud and making inferences about his or her reading habits. The analysis can be used to discover how a person thinks about reading.

For example, if Danny misread the word *freeway* I could look at the kind of error and determine if he was reading for meaning or just struggling with surface issues, trying to use a word that was graphically similar but off in left field as to meaning. Take the sentence, *We were driving down the open freeway at night when a car came from the wrong direction.* A good reader might make a miscue when reading *freeway* by substituting the word *road*. Now, *road* looks nothing like *freeway*. That is to say, there is no *graphic cue* to suggest substituting one for the other. But the meaning is very similar. Good readers make this kind of miscue all the time, putting in extra words and deleting them but maintaining the integrity of the piece.

A poor reader might make a graphic miscue on the same *freeway* by putting in *finger*, a word that looks much more like freeway than *road* but that totally *misses the meaning*. Or the poor reader might struggle to sound out *fr-fr-fre-french fries* showing a concern for *phonic cues* or sounds that, again, override meaning. The formal analysis of a short piece of reading can take an hour or so, but an experienced person who understands the theory can quickly survey the kinds of miscues while the reader is reading aloud.[3]

I explained to Danny that I had not marked down every sound he had made during the reading, nor had I looked at every miscue. I had merely taken representative miscues off the tape to help me explain to him how miscue analysis works and how it can help the reader see into his or her own mind.

Danny immediately grasped the significance of good reader versus poor reader miscues. As usual, he wanted a copy of the analysis to take home to show his wife. We had to go up to the photocopy machine before any further formal pedagogy could take place.

Familiarity Breeds Self-Esteem

During our second month, Danny and I were able to go to a community college that was about to start a two- or three-day read-in and hear Krashen's opening speech, in which he urged students to go to an auditorium to read around the clock. The prospect of meeting this great man had Danny checking and double-checking how well his car was running and when and where he and I were to meet. The long drive to Los Angeles proved Danny to be an excellent driver. What he lacked in sign-reading ability, he made up for in freeway-contour memory.

During the drive I also learned that he has two sisters who he thinks must be pretty good readers, though he didn't say why. He had also asked his parents about their early nonsupport of his literacy needs. They'd told him that they were busy taking care of their own elderly parents and so didn't have time for the kids. Danny did not seem pleased about this, but it did support what he'd learned from the literature. More important, he was questioning what had happened to him at the hands of his caretakers. He had never before questioned anything authority figures had done.

Once in the auditorium, Danny began to wonder where Krashen was. Then the monarch of meaning appeared, delivered handouts, and started to speak. At first, I started to whisper the theoretical implications of what Krashen was saying, but Danny didn't need my help. During the question-and-answer period, he didn't raise his hand ("because so many other people were wanting to ask things"). He appreciated every word about the uselessness of giving people grades. And he also enjoyed the story about the Asian girl who wouldn't talk before she started reading American romance novels and then couldn't be shut up. "Oh, he's really a good teacher," he said at the end. "He really knows what to say."

We went up afterward, I introduced Danny to Krashen, and Danny got his copy of *Inquiries and Insights* autographed. As we walked away, Danny complained that he didn't think the audience fully appreciated the speaker. "They probably thought he was just some nice teacher," he mused, doubting that the uninitiated had understood much. "I mean, if they haven't been reading his books. " He shrugged and made a face as if to say there just wasn't much hope for such people. He was talking as though he'd been reading Krashen's books for years.

Problems in the Goldfish Bowl

Over time, Danny's collection of key word cards grew and showed signs of the sharing he'd done with his older son. By dictating long monologues into my tape recorder, he wrote about donuts, potlucks, and trips to the post office. Finally he started to discuss one of his problems at work. (At that point, without a formal declaration, we stopped using the key word cards.) He needed to get these problems off his chest, but he went into shock when he saw real names of real people being criticized in print in his stories. And thus I learned that Danny, like so many of the disempowered, had no sense of a personal right to privacy. Anyone at home or at work was entitled to open his blue plastic envelope and read the contents. He had never learned how to set personal boundaries. (This same zero-privacy factor had impeded the content of Madonna's language experience stories.) So we needed to set boundaries in another way if meaning-filled, unmonitored writing was to develop.

Part of my reading to him had been from Aesop's fables. We had talked about why Aesop used personification and metaphorical environments. So it was that Danny's first tell-all tale about a coworker's old car was transformed into a fable about an old mule in a circus, with Danny as the circus manager. The success of this story, both at home and at work, fueled even higher literacy ambitions.

Writing Helps Thinking

When Danny was asked to submit his circus fable to the literacy newsletter, he decided to rethink the piece. He began to edit it for a different audience—an unseen, unknown audience. He made changes in the text, tried to anticipate how things could be misunderstood, and kept revising the content.

Because we were having some trouble scheduling our sessions and the newsletter deadline was close at hand, I decided to try mailing drafts to Danny for approval. That caused considerable comment—and eventual prestige—at home. He didn't ever mail anything back, but the arrival of his manuscripts in the mail clearly identified him as an author.

In the meanwhile, I continued to bring in and read theoretical papers, including some I wrote specifically for my literacy students. I also brought in the stacks of numbered and dated drafts I had to do for papers I was writing. Danny found this very useful information, though he found it hard to believe it took me many months to finish a single paper. One of my papers on the writing process inspired Danny to write his own for the literacy newsletter. In it he outlined the importance of rereading and rewriting. Each time he read it, he grappled with the importance his words would have to a tutor who might otherwise expect a student to come up with a perfect product in the first draft. The ignorance of tutors like the one who'd turned out our lights became his personal agenda. He could see that what he knew about literacy development was something worthy of passing on to teachers and students alike.

The Learning Process Isn't Pure

Though language experience purists suggest using the exact language of the learner, I discovered that Danny was consistently confused by his own "you know" phrase, which peppered his text. When I pulled such verbal extras out, he was able to read the work much more easily. This led us to talk about the difference between spoken language and written language. The immediacy of spoken language calls for a different set of markers than does removed-by-time-and-space written text, even when the audience is oneself. He also had a working knowledge of correct subject/verb agreement that did not always carry over into his spoken language. But when he encountered these same grammatical errors in the written work, it skewed his comprehension. We discussed this phenomenon and then agreed that I should modify his dictated pieces to sound written. That netted much smoother oral reading. Understanding the process and being able to control it empowered him to modify the procedure.

Meanwhile I'd begun to retype portions of the Krashen book into my computer, thinking that since Danny felt at home reading the computer-printed, double-spaced type, he might be able to get through more difficult text in that familiar format. In addition, I prepared lengthy preview lists of words and phrases I didn't expect him to know. It worked. Still eager to know the concepts, he continued to plug away at the little book, making full use of his understanding that he was to take charge of how we spent our lesson time. But he had also caught on that overly difficult reading slowed him down, thereby exposing him to fewer words, which, in turn, slowed down his language acquisition. Over time he decided he much preferred reading his own work. It triggered no theoretical arguments at home and elicited praise from his older son, Charlie, and from his coworkers. Besides, he no longer needed to prove to himself he could read. He could read. And he was empowered to sample text.

But getting him into the habit of reading was still beyond me. Because Aesop fables are usually short and are often well illustrated, we set off in search of an edition he could check out and take home to share with Charlie. We located an appropriate one and then ran into another problem that often plagues the uninitiated users of literacy systems. Danny had a library card. He'd probably had it since his first tutor. But he had a black mark against his name (for a crime he could not recall) that prevented his using it before paying a fine. To do that he had to give up his place in the checkout line and go wait in another. Had he been alone, he might not have done it. Library rules and punishments cause a hypersensitivity about books and a negative reaction to the system that is difficult to overcome. Danny took the Aesop book home and read a few stories with his son, but felt much more comfortable with the Krashen text. Was that because he owned it outright? Was it because of the content? Was it a combination of both? I never got a handle on the answer.

Later I did get him interested in the gimmicky book *Round Trip*, which has pictures that read in two directions, right side up and upside down. He wanted to buy his own copy of it but continued to encounter family emergencies that kept him from spending any leisure time in bookstores. On another occasion, he was enormously entertained by the humorous tale of *Thomas's Snowsuit*, which he borrowed to read to Charlie. They enjoyed it together.

During a visit to his boss's home Danny had been intrigued by a computerized chess game but had had no idea how it was played. After establishing that he wanted to learn, I brought in a chess set and began to introduce the basic moves. Then I read him my paper on Vygotsky's zone of proximal development using the chess lessons as a physical illustration of how the concept of a guide to help with learning would work. It all made sense to Danny. The following week I had a conflict on our regular Wednesday meeting night, and there was an annual tutor/student award ceremony on Thursday night, so I suggested we just skip a session.

"Oh, well! If you really think that's a good idea. I mean if you really want to skip a lesson . . . I mean *skip* a lesson? I don't know. Is *that* what you want to do?" This was as assertive as I'd ever seen him. He did not want to miss a session and did not want to trade it for a ceremony. We met on Tuesday night. He might have just been hooked on chess, but then again, it might have been Vygotsky.

I also took in the Classic Comic of *The Count of Monte Cristo*. Though Danny had already seen the movie several times and claimed to like the story, and though the pictures were colorful, the simplified text was very general and the illustrations of two women were so much alike that they added to the confusion. The value of this experiment ended with the beautiful cover. We simply couldn't get interested.[4]

Empowerment Through Authority

Danny regularly checked up on my research project, implying that it was taking me a very long time to write it up. And he was always interested in my other cases, giving powerful insights into the reasons my students were having difficulty and sometimes making very useful suggestions about pedagogy. One night I had an elaborate hand puppet with me and I expected him to ask about it. He didn't. After an eternity, I finally said, "Aren't you going to ask what that is for?" He said he figured I'd talk about it when I was ready to.

I had begun work on the gang literacy project (discussed in Chapter 2) and had designed the puppet to go with the book *Tailypo*, an American folktale in which an old man chops off and eats the tail of an invading varmint, who returns to steal the man's dogs, haunt the man, and demand the return of the tail. Danny really enjoyed the story, which I presented in two forms—an illustrated children's book and a longer version with only one picture. He discussed the value of both and said he could see how the use of the puppet would lower the filter.

When I first told him about the gang project, he had strongly suggested that I avoid going into areas where I could be in physical danger. But then he surprised me. Knowing that I usually went to the housing project on Sundays, he said maybe he could help. Maybe he could come along and tell the gang members about his earlier fears and show them that he was now writing. He felt that if he explained how that happened, it might make them less afraid of trying. This was another major breakthrough. Danny was able to evaluate his own empowerment and to transfer the possibilities into the abstract world of the gang members. Do you remember how Juanita wanted to give the ghetto parents the advantages of theory? Here that same newfound power is again, manifested in a behavioral change. Literacy reaches beyond the decoding of words and marks on paper.

He also suggested that calling my gang program "Readers Theatre" might cause filters to go up. Since I was working in a gymnasium, he figured I should call it "Readers Aerobics." In addition he said the guys might feel self-conscious about having to read in front of people in a gym, so it would make sense to let them record the stories first. I would have to get a bigger tape recorder, though, so that it could be heard in the gym. Then he pondered which *Tailypo* I should present first. There were pros and cons associated with each, and he had the theoretical grounding to introduce and discuss them.

On another occasion, I read him my study of Harry (see Chapter 8), a man so traumatized over literacy that he became physically sick. Danny was really taken by Harry's story. He thought Harry was very intelligent and just needed to get the kind of help I offered. He said it was so easy, the man was sure to learn. He wouldn't even have to touch a pencil, just talk into the recorder. (Although in the beginning I'd decided not to force pencil use on Danny, I'd sort of lost track of the fact that he still wasn't doing it. This reminded me that my earlier decision may have been what caused him to stick with me.) When I said I thought having to talk into the recorder might alarm Harry, Danny reached out to the Early Bird hand puppet on the table in front of us and suggested I hide the recorder under that! "Against my religion!" I protested. My whole process is about learner empowerment. Skulking around with a hidden tape recorder would violate everything I was about. Danny understood all that. But this would just get him started, he reasoned; it would be worth it. I was shocked.

Danny had also begun another expose but this time he refused to hide any of it behind animal allegories. He called it "The Instructor Who Has a Loud Mouth." He did agree to use a pseudonym for the offensive tutor. Here is Danny's fourth draft:

The Instructor Who Has a Loud Mouth

The second night of reading, La Vergne and I were in a literacy office. The walls were pretty thick. Even so, we were constantly interrupted by a lesson in the next office. We didn't know the student's name, but we'll call him Joe. He was a quiet little guy. I kind of felt sorry for him. We'll call his instructor Herman. Every time that instructor talked, the walls shook. He was really loud like he was going to beat Joe. He needs a real soundproof room.

All of a sudden we heard a big crash and I think Joe ran out of the room.

The literacy office went completely dark. The instructor had turned off the big master switch. I had to go out in the pitch dark and find the big switch to turn the lights back on.

Then we saw Joe a second time. I think he just came down and was looking for another tutor. He was just sitting there in the lobby waiting . . . just like a little puppy dog, you know . . . lost his way.

I hope they don't keep Herman very long. He's probably scaring all these poor students away. If it was me, I'd probably do the same thing as Joe. I'd take off.

This, too, he submitted to the literacy newsletter. He wanted to get his message out as a warning to tutors who may think they are free to disempower at will. He checked up regularly on the progress of that newsletter (which was behind schedule) and felt that students really needed to start getting together to discuss the program. Previously, he'd expressed an interest in attending student meetings, but when he found that the student group had folded due to a lack of leadership, he had said he would wait until someone called him. Not so now. Faced with the frustration of a delayed newsletter, he decided to start calling students on his own to get things moving. This, my friends, is a demonstration of how the power of literacy creates the climate for a change in attitude. It is an illustration of how, given the power of the press, the once meek begin to move mountains.

Testimony of Change

As I was leaving home to meet with Danny on one of our last evenings, someone from the literacy office called asking for a testimonial from Danny about the benefits of literacy tutoring. The letter needed to be turned in the next day. I protested that there would be no time for rewrites or even review. No problem, I was assured. Time was of the essence. I ran in to my computer and printed a list of dates and key issues Danny might use as memory joggers.

Because I had a severe case of laryngitis, Danny would be on his own. I was simply unable to coach him. We weren't even going to the library that evening. I was meeting him at a bookstore. Because family-related emergencies had continued to mount, he still hadn't been able to investigate any commercial outlets where he could get the reading materials he would need to foster independent reading. No one had told him outright he couldn't buy books, it was just repeatedly made impossible for him to do it. So that night I was going to show him the book-buying ropes.

From the bookstore we walked to a coffee shop, where he used my printout to address one item and then another. Never at a loss for words, Danny took care to clarify his thoughts before talking into the tape, then dictated the following letter, which I transcribed and turned in unedited by tutor or student. It shows a newly acquired awareness of audience not present in the first draft of his freeway story. There were no "you knows" to delete.

Dear M_____,

You know I finished high school in Southern California without being able to read. In high school they never taught us to read and jobs come pretty hard when you don't know how to read that good. And my youngest one kind of teases me. He says well you're illiterate and stuff like that and you can't get a good paying job 'cause you're illiterate. My oldest, he understands. I started with my tutor La Vergne Rosow on Wednesday, _____, 199__. That seems like a long time ago. On the third lesson she had me dictate something on the tape recorder and she put it on her computer. And the next week I read it just like that, which was pretty amazing! I didn't realize it worked until that night. I didn't know about the affective filter until then. I thought it was a bunch of baloney until we started getting into it. Then you realize that that's what the whole problem is.

Then we went to a lecture at _____ College. We heard Krashen speak about the affective filter and all this stuff and how it works. He's a real good speaker. We'd been reading all his literature about the affective filter and about how teachers shouldn't give tests and how that makes your filter go up. He's a really good speaker, really interesting. He came right to the point and he joked around about it. They never told us about this in school. They didn't know anything about it.

After the lecture we stopped him and I got his autograph. He was real nice. I thought he was going to be an older gentleman, but he was real young. Then I wrote a story about a circus and a circus manager and a mule. It was pretty good. It was supposed to have been about a car, but I put it into animals. It was real interesting and kind of a cute story. But then I had to change it. After I started reading it, the thing wasn't right. After you go through it about five or six times, then you find the mistakes. Then it turned out pretty good.

Then I wrote about a teacher who was helping this one man. He was kind of loud and I wrote a story about him and I had to change the name so we wouldn't get into trouble. But that turned out pretty good. It turned out real good. I like that one. I think it's going in the newspaper, so I didn't mention his real name.

Now I'm going to give a lecture to new tutors who are starting and they'll want to know how the work is progressing. So I'll have to fill them in and let them know it's working real good. Little by little it's working. Everything falls into place.

169

Now my oldest boy, he notices the difference and my wife she knows the difference. And it's helping me in my job a lot too. And I feel better about myself and everything. It makes you feel like a different person when you know you can do it. Of course it takes time. But you can do it, you know. Of course my oldest son, he knows about it. He's really proud of me now.

I'm 43. And, the older you get it won't get any easier. But little by little it's fitting all into place. La Vergne's a good tutor too. Not like that one tutor we heard our first night. The walls shook. But it's in the newsletter. Maybe he'll pick it up and read it.

Sincerely,

Danny

From No Voice to Public Speaking

We had run a number of weeks over the initial three-month time limit and were approaching our last session when Danny and I gave our presentation to a new group of tutor trainees. Danny had accepted such an invitation some years before with disastrous results. This time he wanted to have copies of his bad-tutor essay to distribute to the audience. We found a place to rehearse in the back of an office that was piled high with boxes and debris.

After a long evening of rehearsal and some practice in the presentation room, Danny felt ready to read his paper to the audience. In fact, he felt so secure, he thought he would invite his wife, his younger son, and Charlie. On the day of the training session, Danny showed up right on time and, expecting his wife and sons to be there, looked around for his family. Not one familiar face looked back. He made his presentation, complete with humorous embellishments to the text. His delivery was so smooth that some members of the audience, who had read along with him, questioned whether he'd really had a problem to begin with. After some cross-examination, he began to wonder that, too.

I had been instructed not to lead the novices into theoretical discussions. The tutor training program only allowed enough time for methods. Much as I disagreed, I obliged.[5] No one had thought to mention this restriction to Danny, however. His writings for the literacy publication definitely reflected a change, and I had announced to anyone who would listen that this was not the same person who'd been going through tutors like candy at Christmastime, but the notion that he might have really joined the literacy club in such a short time just wasn't plausible. As soon as the future tutors in the audience began to question him, he said it was really all about the affective filter (correctly pronounced). That got everyone's attention and unloosed an avalanche of questions as the new tutors scrambled to take notes. He launched into explanations about key words and language experience and how important it is to let learning develop over time. As we exited, Danny's older son, Charlie, stood up. He must have entered during the presentation and taken a seat in the back row. Tears streaked the young man's face and he was clearly very proud.

Charlie, the Computer Whiz

After the presentation that afternoon, we took Charlie on a tour that ended in the library's literacy offices, where some long overdue computers were being installed. Though the family had no personal computer, Charlie had taken computer classes in high school for several semesters. On paper, he appeared to have access to the technology of the twenty-first century: his curriculum suggested he was in the advantaged 39 percent of the U.S. student population.[6] But appearances don't necessarily reflect what is actually going on in the schools. In Charlie's case, nothing could have been further from the truth. The young man had received no practical instruction whatever in the function of technology. However, not knowing what he didn't know, he considered himself a pro.

Seeing the new machines, he also saw an opportunity to get his hands on something familiar that he didn't have access to in his freshman program at the community college where he'd just begun classes.[7] When I mentioned that a volunteer team was being organized to run the lab, Charlie wanted to join. Serving as a library computer lab volunteer would be like visiting an old friend while at the same time returning something to the program that had proved so beneficial to his dad.

Charlie Volunteers

Charlie signed up for the computer lab training that would enable him to coach tutors like me to use the lab. Though Danny and I were officially ending our work together, I did agree to introduce Danny to computer word processing after Charlie had gotten certified and had time to train me. But still more delays caused the initial training to be postponed repeatedly. I forgot all about the lab.

One Sunday afternoon, Charlie phoned to tell me that he was certified and ready to pass his skills on to the world at large, meaning me. When I showed up the next afternoon, the lab was already open, but the only customers were Charlie and me. He gave me a cook's tour and told me his general duties as a member of the "C" team. He showed me some of the software and then demonstrated a couple of his favorite games.

The Computer as Master

I had my software with me and asked Charlie if he wanted to write a letter. He was willing to try. It would be nice to write to the woman in charge of the "C" team. When he sat down at my computer, I realized that he didn't know how to type; he had no keyboard skills. Hadn't he spent years in a high school computer lab? Yes, he had, but they had been too busy for typing and stuff like that. What had they done? Oh, lots of things, like create little programs and designs and things.

His came out almost perfect every time. Could he show me? Well, no, not without his instructor. The instructor talked them through every step so they "wouldn't get into trouble." What kind of trouble? Oh, mess up and get a bad design. But he had been in charge of setting the lab up and closing it down each time. What did that mean? Well, just what he'd told me about this lab. He'd been practically a pro walking in, he boasted. He knew how to "run" a computer lab so nothing would ever go wrong, no fires or anything like that. What he was really telling me was that he had been the victim of a teacher-dependent system that failed to give him basic user skills. He'd been taught lab maintenance, safety rules, how to obey the orders of a higher authority, and countless time-killing games, but he had not learned how to use a computer to create text. *He served the computer, and had no idea that the computer, as a tool for literacy, should be serving him.* He had been taught to exercise caution rather than take experimental risks. Charlie's years in the company of the technology of the future had been used to disempower him.

Charlie had never composed on the computer before (or anywhere else, I guessed, as we talked about his letter.) As with his dad, I had the advantage of not having to ask what he was thinking. He thought out loud. Words flowed constantly from mind to mouth. But he didn't know how to make those words come out on the screen. And my bias against hunt-and-peck typing on a computer—I find it a blatant misuse of the technology—was etched into Charlie's mind before an alternative was in gear. And anyway, his huge hands totally covered the keys, so peeking would be cumbersome, if not impossible. Once before, with Nikki, an ESL student, I'd stumbled onto a typing-teaching process that had had very quick results in teaching him to use the library's catalogue terminal. I decided to try it with Charlie.

I explained the concept of the different fingers having different letters to deal with, that the thumbs just worked the space bar, and the pinkies reached out to shift, control, and return. Then I pointed out that once you knew a few easy-to-type words, your fingers would automatically go to the correct keys. "Try *t h e*," I instructed, using letters not covered by the home finger positions. As I said the letters, I lightly touched the backs of the correct fingers. "Now try it faster." Charlie typed *the* perfectly once, twice, again.

"Hey! That's pretty tricky!" Danny's words boomed from his much larger son.

When he finally made an error, he lambasted himself as though he had committed a terrible sin. He seemed to feel the self-effacement would shield him from external ridicule. I immediately remembered the freeway ride with Danny. As we had gone up an onramp Danny had called himself stupid for not remembering to use the diamond lane when two passengers were in the car. The expressed self-disappointment, for both father and son, was much more than the simple "oh darn" one might say at a moment of self-inflicted inconvenience. They needed to let the world know they were aware of their deficiencies so that further pain would not be thrust upon them. How much humiliation, I wondered, did an authority figure have to slam down on a subordinate before that lowly creature learned to take on the task himself? But then, having suffered his typo punishment, Charlie was prepared to cheer the easy repair allowed by the word processor. He conquered *the*, *and*, *at*, *it*, *to* in minutes.

"Now, let me tell you a sentence that has all the letters of the alphabet in it. The quick sly fox jumped over the lazy brown dog. If you can type that one sentence without looking, you'll know where every letter on the keyboard is."

"Is that right." It wasn't a question; I'd heard it before from Danny.

He plunged right in as I touched his fingers as fast as I could.

To Write Is to Question

"You mean, that's it?" he asked, as he stared at row upon row of the sentence on the screen.

"It takes practice, like riding a bike," I told him.

The familial questioning came into play: "I wonder why nobody ever told me. . . ." Then Charlie typed his short letter, including some words in bold face, and, with some difficulty, we figured out how to print it out. Charlie was amazed. He'd had no idea that we (meaning people like us) would be able to do something like that! "I just don't understand why they never . . ." he thought out loud. "Are you sure that's all there is to it?" He wasn't really talking to me.

Old Habits Die Hard

The next night, making good on my promise to help launch Danny on the computer and needing a "C" team sponsor to get into the lab, I met Charlie and Danny in the new literacy computer lab. Danny was impressed that his son was chief honcho in the lab that night. Charlie was overwhelmed that his dad was so proud. I was delighted to bear witness to such mutual admiration.

Charlie logged us into the open notebook, explained the floor plan, reiterated the lab rules, and showed us where the software was impressively shelved. Then he checked the plugs, flipped master switches, and uncovered an Apple and turned it on. Wanting Danny to get used to software he could access without me, I hadn't brought mine, so we began to search for a word processing program. Though Charlie seemed to understand the request, he was of little help. He was eager to show us some of the great "literacy" programs in the lab. (In all fairness, I will say there was only one copy of our word processing program and only the computer Danny was using was connected to a printer.)

While Danny and I struggled to load and access the unfamiliar software, Charlie entered a reading game into another computer, whereupon it began making loud pops and whistles. Excitedly he kept calling us to come look at the great graphics on the color monitor. We looked and then returned to the word processing project—our own color monitor was driving us crazy as it subdivided letters into random flecks of color. We did manage to get some text generated before the library started to close. In our rush not to be locked in for the night, we ripped Charlie loose from his computer game, and he helped us get the text printed out—an imperfect product, but proof that Danny could word-process.

Unable to figure out how to save the evening's work, Danny and I asked for Charlie's help in closing shop. Oh, no! Charlie wanted to try generating his own text. So, as the final bells of the night chimed ominously, Charlie printed another message. He was astounded. Danny and I tried to rush this elated teddy bear into motion, but he had to do what he was supposed to do. Methodically, he went from plug to plug, checking everything, explaining the safety issues involved in each ritual. Finally, I understood why he'd explained that he didn't need to close up shop the day before; he hadn't wanted me to think he was neglectful. The library was quite dark as we exited.

Technology Can Empower or . . .

Our business unfinished, we met again two nights later. Again, Charlie methodically went through the lab procedures with caution and care. This time I had brought in my software, Danny had brought in something he had to write up for work, and we were eager to get into action. Danny sat at the keyboard responding easily to my touch commands. It was interesting that though he shook like a leaf when trying to manipulate a pencil, Danny was perfectly relaxed at this machine that looked more like the dashboard of his car than an instrument for literacy. Within a very short time, he had managed to edit his text and print it out. Charlie marveled at his dad's work, in print, hot off the press. However, when he saw that my program didn't print up as nicely as the lab program had, Danny decided to tackle the unfamiliar software again even though he was short of time.[8]

Meanwhile, Charlie began to try to reconcile the years of computer training he'd received with not being able to use the computer for writing purposes. He had been very fond of his high school instructor who had given him lots of praise and *never allowed him to get into trouble in the lab.* Had we worked together, Charlie would have learned about the empowerment of taking risks in the secure environment a classroom ideally provides. Now, however, needing to justify what such a good person had done with his time, Charlie had decided there had to be more to typing than I'd told him. He located the computer typing program and began to work. Before long, he had also located and photocopied a typing key from an older program and placed it at the top of the keyboard. That really helped. (This may seem a small point, but it illustrates creative problem solving not fostered in his previous computer lab experience.)

As his father continued to struggle with the new program, Charlie next tried out a reading program that ran text across the screen at a faster and faster pace until it quite literally made all of us dizzy. This kind of program is a technological version of the old slit-in-the-cardboard reading approach called single-focus manipulation. The slit limits the reader's range to one word or one line of type. It prevents the reader from sampling texts, predicting, regressing, or using any of the strategies good readers employ. It teaches through a machine what the old skills teacher taught, that you get it right on the first try and only move forward, "it" being the word or short string of words, *not* the meaning of the whole text. With that as the goal, speed is the logical measure of progress. This is the opposite philosophy from the one that looks at the reader as decision maker. This so-called pragmatic approach to reading is not required to consider the interests, emotions, or needs of the reader: stripped-down skills in neat compartments are what are being sold. Whenever I've questioned the people who sell these kinds of programs, they never have the slightest notion that a theoretical rationale is required to support practice. Nor have they even pretended that there are studies to show where and under what circumstances the program teaches reading. So, here we were, watching text fly past, faster and faster. Charlie had many such "opportunities" in high school, and had gotten the impression that it was his defective brain, not a defective program design, that was preventing success. He seemed relieved to hear that a book with large, easy-to-see print would have been a much better source of literature. On the other hand, Charlie *loved* computers and was in absolute heaven having the right to pick, choose, and use anything he decided to pull off the shelf.

Even so, when a guessing-game spelling program produced equally frustrating results, Charlie began to question the value of nice packaging. It was a difficult time for the young man, who, like his father, had always completely trusted the judgment of his authority figures. Now, simply having volunteered his time to the literacy program, he was encountering disturbing questions. I was simply unable to give any more time to either father or son. Danny had gotten a good start into literacy, but needed some kind of support to keep him going. And Charlie had spent his whole life being told he was like his dad and then making that prophesy come true. Is it possible for a pair of closely bonded people like this each in turn to help the other? I grappled with that question, feeling not a little frustration at surrendering them to their own devices. As we prepared to leave the lab together for that last time, Charlie methodically checked all the plugs, put the programs back in place, checked all switches, and made plans to return to write with his dad.

1. Unfortunately, the term "learning disabled" is applied liberally to students of average intelligence who have done poorly in school language arts activities. Though a standard definition does not exist, LD serves to place the blame on the learner for not learning to read. So far, there has not been a single adult labeled "learning disabled" whom I've taught for three or more months who has not learned to read. Three months of appropriate, focused pedagogy seems key to emerging literacy for adult learners—with or without the LD label.

2. I worry when critical thinking is treated as a sideshow, something extra tacked onto the curriculum. Recently a colleague mentioned that she was taking a class in critical thinking—a semester, it turned out, of tiny little steps to be followed sequentially when she decides to teach critical thinking to her ESL students. Within the same week, I learned that critical thinking was being added to the curriculum at a local community college. What kind of thinking, one might wonder, is going on all the rest of the time in all the rest of the classes? What will happen when, like the extra programs on self-esteem that were so hot just a few years back, critical thinking is finally dropped from the curriculum?

3. Oral reading is quite different from the silent reading a person does when no one is acting as audience. I am not suggesting that the two kinds of reading are the same. I am suggesting that miscues indicating an awareness of meaning show a different way of viewing text than miscues indicating a focus on surface issues. The Goodman, Watson, and Burke *Reading Miscue Inventory* is a book that will give the interested person more detail on the analysis procedure.

4. I have done several informal studies using both authentic and simplified versions of the same Steinbeck text. Even though the authentic text has more difficult vocabulary and longer sentences, I've found that (1) students enjoy the authentic material more and (2) comprehension and retention are much greater when the original work is used. Of course, as in all good teaching, the material has to be delivered so that it makes sense to the learner. For Danny, who could not have read *The Count* on his own in either form, the appropriate approach was for me to read it to the student, addressing difficult words as we went along.

5. As I've noted earlier, at the Third North American Conference on Adult and Adolescent Literacy in Washington, D.C., in February 1994, LVA founder Ruth Colvin

unveiled the new LVA tutor education program, which has begun to use theory.

6. According to the 1992 *Digest of Education Statistics*, only 39 percent of U.S. high school and college students use computers at school. But computers are already akin to the old movie projectors stored in back closets of yesterday's schools. Not only is the technology changing rapidly, but schools often buy them without having the funds to train teachers and staff fully in their use. A grant may set up a lab or supply hardware for many classrooms, but as problems arise and personnel changes, the computers become obsolete without being used. Proper maintenance is another expense, as it is with any machine with a huge number of users. Only yesterday I spoke with an elementary teacher who said her school's computer lab was about to close because the grant funding the lab teacher had run out and no one had been able to secure a new funding source. A computer enthusiast herself, the teacher could see that left idle, the lab would become obsolete, but if run by compter amateurs like herself, it would be destroyed.

7. Though his college did have a prestigeous computer program, it was reserved for the more academically successful students. According to the *Digest of Education Statistics*, a significant number of Americans, about 36 percent, use computers in their jobs. But the kind of use is determined by the educational level of the employee, the "more diverse applications" going to the better educated. At one company in San Diego, I observed a companywide computer system that required almost no reading and no writing skills of the employees, almost all of whom used a computer in some way. All entries were done as code numbers. One worker did complain that if a person wanted to make a suggestion or choose something not on the menu, it was just too bad. Problem solving was limited to those few who set up the computer programs.

8. For a survey of computers used in writing programs, see H. J. Schwartz, et al. After documenting an intensive, though unsuccessful, search for a defensible basic skills computer-assisted writing program, they suggest that the best use of computers in writing instruction is yet to be figured out. Yet, they observe, once students start using word processing for writing, they don't want to give it up. I believe that lowering stress related to surface issues is where computers (with simple, easy-to-comprehend word processing programs) can best serve. To a man petrified over his penmanship, a machine that will take his ideas and print them out in perfectly legible text must counterbalance a great many feelings of inadequacy. In Danny's case it is very clear that the basic word processing program was quite liberating; as a person fearful of making surface errors, a spell check program would also have made him more likely to try writing more. (Helen J. Schwartz, Thea Van Der Geest, and Marlies Smit-Kreuzen, "Computers in Writing Instruction," in *International Journal of Educational Research, Implementation of Computers in Education*, T. Plomp and J. Moonen, guest eds., Vol. 17, No.1, Chap. 3. (Oxford: Pergamon Press, 1992) 37-50.

Seven

Reynaldo, Beau, and Jonathan: Three Perspectives at Once

My plan was to focus on one high school student as a transition between my adult and child studies. Accordingly, a colleague referred me to a high school where the principal and a counselor were very willing to assist. I requested one student for a two-hour period, two days a week, and got three immediate responses. I agreed to meet with all three of these boys to see if one of them wanted to try what I had in mind. So, for our first meeting, three boys and I stuffed ourselves into a tiny, one-person office that doubled as a storage room for video machinery, file cabinets, and the public address system. The conversations from six neighboring counselling cubicles and a large bull-pen-type waiting area mingled with our own.

Though Reynaldo's first language was Spanish, I was told he could speak English well enough to attend classes held in English. Since his shyness kept him from making friends at the school, his counselor felt that working with me might give him a sense of belonging if nothing else. But he was so afraid to say anything during this first encounter, I wasn't sure what he comprehended. And he had an initial disadvantage in that his wood-shop instructor would not release him to the reading project for the first hour of the two-hour period. Although his counselor was aware of this dilemma, within the last three years her case load had increased from sixty students to five hundred, and she'd already given Reynaldo more than his fair share of her time. Reynaldo's insecurities were no doubt exacerbated by the unpredictability of both his home and school environments.

Beau had actually dropped out of the school some months before. His records indicated he was unable to do simple math and could not read or write above the elementary school level. He was a chronic truant (in part because he worked for his father in the family business) and seemed unable to learn even in the special ed classes; Beau's mother, Maureen, had therefore begged to have him released from his misery. Since it had actually been established that he was "unable to benefit" from further schooling, there were special community-based vocational programs he could have entered, but Beau hadn't yet done anything about that. Both the school authorities and his mother explained that the tall, exceptionally handsome young man was extremely shy. Earlier, over the phone, I had asked Maureen if we could set up a time for her to read to Beau just ten minutes a day. She only wished she could. Like Beau, she was a nonreader. But she was very grateful that someone from the academic world valued her son enough to give him time. He'd been twice blessed lately. He now also had a girlfriend who was eager to help him get ahead. Sure enough, it was the girlfriend who delivered him for our first session.

Then there was Jonathan, a lanky young man with a humbleness that seemed out of place in an urban environment. Jonathan always showed up for his classes and always tried to do his assignments, but he couldn't pass his tests. He had complained in a student/parent/teacher conference that his big problem was not knowing how to read. (His high school entry tests showed he had "plateaued"—that is, regardless of treatment, he was not expected to improve—at the fifth-grade reading level.) Did he have a less than average IQ? I asked. Well, test scores did indicate that; he had been in special ed for most of his school years and seemed reluctant to connect with students from regular classes. But he did catch on to things that weren't presented in print form. When teachers could be persuaded to let the special ed coordinator administer tests to Jonathan orally, the results were quite different from those he produced under conventional circumstances.

I told them that a man named Rist had discovered that children were placed in so-called ability groups based on how they looked and their parents' income. He'd also unraveled a kind of barnyard pecking order in the classroom with the teacher's favorite student picking on others and the least favored child at the bottom of the heap, unable to fight back. These classroom systems set into motion the self-fulfilling prophecies and self-perceptions that lasted a lifetime. (For those teaching papers see Appendix B.)

I began slowly explaining some of the theory behind my work. As I talked Beau focused on a felt-tip pen he was attempting to dissect. He would also yawn and stretch occasionally. Jonathan gazed around the room, whether taking inventory or seeking an escape route I wasn't sure. Reynaldo sat limply, making absolutely no sound, even when he tried to speak. Suddenly I startled everyone by asking Beau, "Are you with us here at all?"

However, Beau *had* been listening. He just wasn't buying what I'd said. "How did [Rist] work in the classroom . . . behind a one-way mirror? . . . Well, wouldn't the teacher put on an act of good behavior for him?" I'm not sure Beau bought my answer that a person could not put on an act every day for a year, nor did he seem to grasp fully that the teacher had never heard of the concept that was developing in her classroom. He vaguely accepted that the teacher was not deliberately trying to do a bad job.

Jonathan seemed to gather courage from Beau's challenging me. He wanted to know about my current study. I used a theoretical discussion about background knowledge to ferret out what things each of them was interested in. Jonathan liked science fiction and Stephen King. Beau liked sports and money and would travel if he could. Reynaldo would build a big house for his parents if he had a million dollars. I tried to draw Reynaldo out by asking what kind of house and what it would be made of. Big . . . and made of wood. Elaboration was not Reynaldo's forte. Yet when we got into a discussion of who had been where, the bigger boys were very interested in Reynaldo's having been to Mexico. They were even more impressed by his dual citizenship. After that, they were quite willing to pay attention to him, even though his responses were so quiet that I, sitting right next to him, had to strain to hear.

When I mentioned that illiterates had a history of child abuse, Jonathan stared knowingly at Beau, who picked at his pen. (At the time I didn't know that Jonathan's father had been an abusive alcoholic and his mother a passive nonparticipant in her children's lives. Nor had Beau's mother confessed her mortal fear of her husband and that she herself had been a drug addict during most of Beau's early school years.) Reynaldo said nothing. None of the boys had any memory of ever being read to.

When Beau challenged, "Do you really mean a person can get to be a reader by being read to?" I said yes, that is why I always make reading aloud part of my lessons.

"How is that supposed to work?" he wanted to know. Jonathan unfolded his arms.

I said I'd show them. I whipped out *Tailypo* (the book about an old man who eats the tail of a strange Kentucky varmint and then gets haunted by it) and read it to them. Each time my inflection changed or I used a different character voice, Beau looked at me as if to see if I was putting him on. (The poor reader has had no exposure to the powerful energy transmitted by strong reading. Dry little recitations haltingly emitted from timid little kids in round-robin groups is all they've heard, so that's what they think reading is. When they hear a genuine delivery of an authentic text, they think they are being duped.)

Tailypo was fortuitous. With no coaxing from me (I'd intended to launch again into the value of reading aloud to students), all three started to discuss their favorite parts. Then they decided they wanted to give me a chance and that they wanted me to take them on as a group. Never mind that I'd planned one-on-one individualized teaching, that the room was too small for two let alone four, and that they might influence one another's development, thereby foiling my neat research outline. This was learner empowerment and I had to practice what I preached. So I went along with the decision. Jonathan and Beau would come in for two hours twice a week; Reynaldo could come for only the second hour both days.

High-Interest Money Makes Great Bait

Sometimes history fails to repeat itself accurately. Each time I made my way to our little study room, I was so burdened by materials that I began to feel the tables had turned, that I was the one bringing gifts to these three would-be magi. Weren't *they* supposed to be bringing *me* gifts, treasured strings of data? But in retrospect, that's exactly what they did: from the first day, my efforts began to pay off.

Conscious of this group's love of money, I brought in the business section of the Sunday *LA Times*. Jonathan was a little earlier than Beau and had a chance to tell me that he had some prior exposure to the workings of the stock market through a friend, but had never dealt with it directly. Given his reluctance to take direct instruction, I waited until his cohort arrived before introducing the connection between the stories in the business section and the numbers on the back pages. Beau was sure to challenge anything that didn't make sense to him, so the stage was set. First I showed them the section's general areas, allowing Jonathan to do most of the talking and then filling in the blanks. When we began to look closely at one stock, Jonathan had a very clear explanation for the highs and lows. Beau (and Reynaldo when he arrived for the second hour) made a willing audience, asking questions and issuing challenges that indicated he was a sleeping mental giant. He was impressed that Mattel had gone from 11 to 26. "Wow, if we'da known, we coulda doubled our money!" We agreed that each of them would start with a "fund" of $100,000 and could buy stocks on any day they chose. Then we would follow the stocks till the end of school. They were to think about products or companies they liked and bring in ideas to our next meeting.

After that we looked at the business-career ads and talked about the kinds of salaries the different positions might pay. Jonathan observed that some people wouldn't know to look for those selective help-wanted ads in the business section. He was also very interested in knowing exactly what education was needed for which jobs. (It was the first of many such discussions. A kid who hasn't been seriously interested in graduating from high school has a tough time learning the names of advanced degrees.)

I was about to close the "*Times* business" part of the program down for the day, when I decided to show them the stories on the front page so they would get a strong mental picture of what that section looks like in any very large newspaper. The front page had a story on the Chapter 11 bankruptcy of Frances Ford Coppola that caught their attention, so I offered to read the first paragraph. The big-business deals, movie connections, and real estate transactions gripped all three boys' imagination. Each time I started to give it up, there were audible negatives from Jonathan and Beau, and Reynaldo stirred unhappily. We didn't get to anything else that day, and we didn't finish that article. I suggested that if they wanted me to read them anything specific, they could just bring it in. On the way home, I stopped off at a copy shop and copied the multipaged Coppola story, cut and taped three sets into a presentable text, and added them to my magi pack.

By the next session Jonathan had already written down the stocks he planned to buy and had documented his purchase price. Beau had gotten some ideas from a newspaper he'd bought on the way home from our first stock session. (Later, during a phone conversation with Maureen, I learned that Beau had decided our sessions would definitely pay off. He'd tried to discuss the market with her, but finding his mother unable to follow most of it, he'd soon gone in to talk with his dad. Their dialogue had ended quickly. "Beau is a really bad communicator," his mother explained. "He just won't try to get along with his dad or let any of his ideas in." Somehow this struck me as too blame-the-victimy, considering both Beau's parents felt his resistance to communicating with his father had started when he was a very little boy. Later still, she pointed out that his showing up regularly for class was a major behavioral change. This kind of careful observation can detect progress not measured by standardized tests.) Still, Beau's interest in the stock market had not inspired him to write anything down, so Jonathan started to help him set up his portfolio. Again I stepped back (possible only in spirit in that small space) and waited for someone to need me. Beau had fallen in love with a brand of shorts that did not seem to be publicly held. Jonathan was not able to explain the phenomenon of privately or publicly held stock until I figuratively set the two up in business in a garage, a business from which they took all the profits. The dialogue moved on to stock options and profit sharing, concepts that stayed with Jonathan when he began to look for work that summer.

I didn't distribute the Coppola article copies until hour two, so that Reynaldo would be included in the reading, but though he was on campus, he didn't show up that day, continuing his pattern of erratic participation. (There were many times when Reynaldo was unable to attend sessions at all.[1] In the lessons where I report nothing of Reynaldo, he was not present. Despite his turmoil, when he did attend he seemed to enjoy the theoretical as well as practical work we were doing. Most important, though, even during his brief encounters, he was connecting with Jonathan and Beau, if by weak threads.) Jonathan and Beau took their copies eagerly and agreed to underline any words they wanted me to talk about later. Behind our closed door, I—inadvertently at first—allowed them to violate a school rule by using colored pens!

As on the first day, great dialogue came out of my reading the Coppola story. Jonathan was following along. Beau mostly didn't look at the text, though he did seem to be keeping track of the story line and Coppola's debts. When he saw that

Jonathan was able to tally up the millions by referencing the text, he tried to follow suit. Again, we didn't finish. But by this time Jonathan and Beau were fans of the process.

Even in this very low achieving group, a hierarchy developed based on the amount of power each student had over his circumstances. Jonathan was officially enrolled in the sessions at the instigation of his primary counselor, and his special education teacher had encouraged him to participate. Beau had his former counselor's support and his mother's and girlfriend's approval, but his father distinctly disapproved. Reynaldo was participating in spite of the specific objection of a wood-shop instructor who, I learned, had him neither working with wood nor reading about people who did. Also, though very concerned about his well-being, Reynaldo's counselor just didn't have time to spend with him. According to self-fulfilling prophecies, Jonathan would have been expected to achieve; Beau would have had a fifty-fifty chance; and Reynaldo would have been doomed. But I was there to change fate. . . . wasn't I?

The Thinkers

The following session, Jonathan showed up with his own *Times* business section and was prepared to discuss a story he'd read about a luxury car designer/builder. The text was very difficult and he'd missed a lot of the detail, but he'd comprehended a lot too. In spite of the vehicle's beauty and great handling, the feature that most impressed Jonathan was its incredible safety record. He decided it had the potential to be the Lamborghini of the United States. He could see that buyers would be limited to the Beverly Hills and Palm Springs crowds, but you wouldn't need a lot of sales to have a profitable company. The big problem, as he saw it, was distribution. Still, he had some ideas about that, too. Jonathan was ready to go to work for the man. "I'm eighteen now," he said, "I can be responsible for who I work for."

I asked whether he'd ever considered going into marketing. He had. He just didn't know how to get started. We talked about ways in which he could follow up on the newspaper story. The simplest, he thought, was to call the newsroom and locate the woman who had done the interview. Though he never did this, Jonathan was intrigued at the inside perspective, the idea that a human being was at the other end of the writing, someone he could probably speak with.

Not coincidentally, one day we were looking at a full-page ad for a new car. I asked the boys to take turns trying to read the copy, telling them to stop if it got too tough. Beau was willing to go first, but didn't seem to think there was much hope. He began plugging along; then Jonathan did the same. "Well, both of you are pretty good readers, then," I said.

"Huh?" Beau asked.

"Well, you understood everything you read, right?"

"Because you're reading about a dealer and a car. You can kind of figure out the words," he allowed.

"What do you have to say about that, Jonathan?"

"You can get some idea of what's going on by the picture, and you also know it's Acura Legend and that's a car. So you've got some idea of what it's based upon," Jonathan responded.

"OK. Well those are good reader strategies. You use the pictures and all the background information that you have. You bring it to the text and then you build from there. So, you're saying that it's because you already know so much about cars . . ."

Beau interrupted, ". . . you know it's about cars, like [the] words. You know it's not going to be about a lamp or nothing. You try to fit the words with the story. And you sound it out, then you know."

I tried to make a point: "But you weren't trying to sound it out, you were going for meaning in the text, right?" However, Beau had been through years of sound-it-out pedagogy and believed it must work, even though his performance and analysis had just proven otherwise. He came back with, "And trying to sound it out, like the same thing," pointing to the text, "like *satisfactory*—that makes sense."

"So where do you start having problems?" I asked.

"When you can't read." He seemed to think that was elementary, continuing, "I don't know how to say it. Like if you read a story that you don't know nothing about, you get stuck on words."

"And you don't know what to do?"

"Yeah, 'cause you can't sound out the words that don't make sense." He grasped my point, blinked, and relaxed. Then, "So what happens when [sounding out] doesn't make sense?" We went back to the discussion of trying to skip over the occasional stump.

On the same ad, the issue of type size came up. Jonathan said that it was easier for him to read the larger type.[2] Beau, on the other hand, mumbled his way through the fine print in an effort to show that if you really want to read something, you can survive any text. To him, reading was definitely an endurance test. But he was by no means unable to follow spoken ideas.

When we talked about Vygotsky's zone of proximal development, a theory in which the Russian psychologist suggests learners need a guide to help them in their search for knowledge about something that is beyond them at the time, Beau said he thought the man's name was the most noteworthy part of the reading. He wandered off the subject, seemingly into outer space, and then regrouped, giving evidence that analysis had been going on all the time. "Well, this idea of a guide is fine, if somebody wants to help somebody. But who is gonna guide every little kid that's trying to learn?" he asked bluntly and sincerely. "I mean, there's just too many little kids. I don't know how to say it right, but where can you find a guide to help them all? And how is that supposed to work, anyway?"

"Well, you might say right now I'm your reading guide," I answered.

"Oh?" he blinked, "Oh!"

As our sessions continued, Jonathan's backpack became increasingly stuffed with newspaper stock reports. Once he came in later than Beau, slapped him on the back, and shouted, "Hey, buddy, did you see how your stock's doing? Disney is going to go up. [Dick Tracy] is a hit!"

Language Experience Supports Background Knowledge

Throughout our readings and dialogues, I documented the words that the boys could not tackle. Sometimes I just wrote the word on my tablet before starting to elaborate. When I read aloud as they followed along with duplicate copies, the boys would mark the words they didn't know. Of course, there were words they marked at first and then understood once the context had given them more information. But the first reaction was still an indication that the word was not fully familiar, so in pencil on my copy, I would mark the words I noticed they had marked: a straight underline meant all present had marked it, a starting curve up meant Jonathan, a curve down at the end meant Beau, and a hyphenated line meant Reynaldo. They didn't mark everything they couldn't read and I missed some of the words they did mark, but I did get a lot of material for my purposes through this process. The boys were never under pressure to memorize or otherwise consciously learn the words they underlined and there was seldom enough time for us to discuss every word they marked. When I noticed that my reading pace caused someone (usually Beau) to lose the place, I would slow down or stop to clear my throat.

Taking me up on my offer to read anything they brought in, Beau showed up one morning with a very large boating magazine. Since he owned a hydroplane, he turned to a section on that topic and settled down to listen to me read the captions. Despite his interest in the sport, there was a lot of vocabulary in those short passages that Beau didn't know. And because his hydroplane was a lemon, he had little operational information to give Jonathan, who was eager to swap sea stories. So, although Beau had introduced the topic, it was Jonathan who played the more vocal role as he shared the adventures of an uncle who actually enters competitions.

For the next session, I prepared a language experience story based on the boating/hydroplane dialogue, laced with words they hadn't recognized. Then I gave my traditional testimonial on the value of background knowledge, to reinforce the idea that the more the boys read, the more they would have background on, and the more they would therefore be able to read. Then I said I knew the challenge might cause Beau's filter to go up and if it did, he should just stop. I could see he was contemplating escape, but we were packed in so tight, an earthquake could not have shaken us out of the room.[3] I pushed Beau into the opening paragraph of "Ocean Tales." Through the struggle I kept reminding him of the good reader strategies (try skipping it, etc.) that we talked about regularly. He was reluctant, but began to show signs of self-amazement as he passed one benchmark after another, even *hydroplanes*. At the end of the eighth line he breathed a long sigh as I cheered and Jonathan prepared to jump in. Jonathan moved through the text like an ocean liner compared with Beau's row-boat progress. He'd been paying attention to the strategies and was enthralled at seeing his own stories coming up in the text.

When the story was finished, both boys were ripe for more hype on how *reading teaches reading*. It was up to them to go through and tell me where corrections in story line and detail had to be made. This wasn't a rereading, it was an exercise in the power to change text even after it is in print. As a result, they grabbed onto passages, grappling first with what they had said, and then with what they *should* say. I agreed to take their changes back to my computer and generate a new improved text. Here is the final edited text:

Ocean Tales

The other day Beau brought in a big boating magazine that had an article on San Diego boating sports. He showed us a picture of a lineup of hydroplanes. He has had one for about two months now. It is definitely a lemon. Beau has had so much trouble with it he doesn't even want to fool with them any more. He knows the warranty will expire soon. He plans to take it back and get an off-road vehicle instead. That is to say, now that he's gotten his feet wet, he thinks he prefers dry land.

Beau's story inspired Jonathan to tell us about some sailing adventures his uncle has had in competitions along the California coast. His uncle belongs to a racing club that competes against other clubs. Some of the men get together for the sport and a good time. Others, though, seem to take the whole matter so seriously they take the sport out of sailing.

It seems some sailors will deliberately ram a competing craft just to get it out of the race. That can lead to damage that can cause the craft to sink. Beau wanted to know why anyone would ruin a fun time like that. Jonathan said some groups do and others don't. His uncle's group is just "laid back" and out for a good time. Others don't have fun sailing. They put their value in getting a trophy. It is interesting to think that they would enjoy having a prize that was won by cheating. One would expect that the trophy would make the winners feel like prize cheats every time they looked at it.

Jonathan explained that usually the cheaters do their damage when there are no judges around to disqualify them. It might be interesting to see what their response would be to receiving an expensive trophy from someone they rammed. The trophy might read "In Recognition of the Sneakiest Little Crew in the Water." It could be presented at a banquet in front of a large group.

There are seldom trophies for acts of heroism. They also occur when there are no judges around. Jonathan's uncle was out with his crew when a storm overtook another boat. The men on his uncle's boat risked their own lives to save the crew in the troubled craft. One man was hooked onto a safety line that pinned him under his mast and under the water. The waves were too rough and it was impossible for anyone to rescue him. He drowned.

The craft of Jonathan's uncle would have floundered in the high waves had they not been protected by a big ship that happened to be in the area.

Beau asked why the Coast Guard hadn't come to the rescue. Jonathan explained that they just weren't around. The ocean is a very big place. It had been up to Jonathan's uncle and his crew to do what they could. It would have been very easy to just say there was nothing they could do. Clearly, the weather would have justified their flight. No one would have questioned them for just racing in to save themselves. But, when there was no time to contemplate whether to run away or stay and risk their own lives, they chose to make a difference. It was kind of a miracle that they were able to do as much as they did. And it was heroic.

In spite of my up-front attitude about surface errors versus substance and in spite of my reiteration that stress levels in readers and writers need to remain low, every literacy student I've ever had has exhibited a fiendish delight at discovering that the teacher has misspelled something; these boys were no exception. They had also zeroed in on some of their marked words and modified or tossed them out. I pointed out that many of the words had been on their "can't read" lists from before and that they had breezed through them in meaningful context. The sell was sailing.

When Jonathan arrived ahead of Beau one Tuesday, he asked how my weekend had been, clearly bursting to tell me where he had been the previous Friday night. On weekend midnights in a nearby coastal town, there were showings of the cult audience-participation movie *The Rocky Horror Picture Show*. Jonathan had gone from time to time over the previous couple of years and thoroughly enjoyed everything from waiting in line for hours to get in to hurling celery around the room on cue. On his first visit, he had been sold as a slave, but as a veteran, he was at liberty to take advantage of newcomers, known as "virgins." Subsequently I've been told that there are many sexual allusions in the film that Jonathan either missed or decided to spare me. Nevertheless, it was an adventure he had enjoyed talking about, so I converted it into yet another language experience/background knowledge sales pitch. I kept the entire story ambiguous, so that anyone not knowing where Jonathan had been would be unable to tell what the story was about. As usual, it was loaded with unreadable words.

The next time the four of us were together, I announced that we were about to have a demonstration of the magic of background knowledge and its importance to reading comprehension. The unsuspecting Jonathan was to give a premier oral reading for his fellows. By that time, they'd gotten used to the notion that none of my "surprises" were designed to be painful for the learner and that the concepts in Gentile and McMillan's *Stress and Reading Difficulties* were understood as well by me as instructor as they had always been by them as students. Given that, Jonathan began to read about the cult movie experience only he could completely comprehend. He tripped over some of my word plants, but usually forced the lines to come out right in meaning or backtracked to adjust. His smile grew as one episode after another showed that someone really had been listening as he'd shared his adventure.

A couple of paragraphs down, Beau asked, "Where were you?"

"Sh-h-h-h! He's demonstrating background knowledge," I intervened.

Needless to say, Jonathan was very pleased with his successful performance and was delighted to take over filling in the blanks that drove all three boys back into the text they'd marked with fury. There was editing to be done here, too. For example, I'd titled my version "Pass the *Salad*. . . ," obviously *my* background knowledge at work. Anyway, here is that particular language experience text:

Pass the Celery, etc.

The other night Jonathan became involved in a fracas that most folks would avoid like the plague. It was no ordinary street brawl; it was no organized crime. In fact, it was totally disorganized. The really amazing thing is, everybody there had waited in a long line and then had paid real money to get in. Jonathan was no virgin to the establishment. That was good. Virgins, aka people who have never been there before, get sacrificed. No, Jonathan is a veteran. He knew what he was getting into and got into it anyway. He waited in a long line for a long time. Then, at the witching hour, he got in. Then, avoiding the back row, he positioned himself very carefully. Knowing what to expect, Jonathan had his squirt bottle ready. When the time came, he drenched the beautiful girl in front of him. "She had it coming," he claimed. She'd thrown the rice ahead of schedule . . . into Jonathan's face. Or some such offense.

Jonathan had been ready for celery time. When the signal came, he joined the throng of celery missile launchers. He was very pleased with the outcome.

He was really pleased with the way the wedding went. He's gone to a lot of weddings lately. In fact, he's gone to THIS wedding a lot lately. He goes just to get in on throwing rice.

Perhaps it's the ritual Jonathan enjoys. Perhaps it's just the chance to squirt beautiful strangers behind the ears. Perhaps it just feels good to return to the mud pies and sandbox without getting muddy or sandy.

He says it's just clean fun. He says he only does this sort of thing on Friday or Saturday night. He says he never does it before midnight. In other words, he says this is under control. He may be out in search of new definitions, new ways of interpreting the language, new ways of responding to the same old commands like "pass the celery."

When the celery commotion had settled, I presented an ambiguous story, "The Trouble With Louie," that I'd recently used for an inservice of Literacy Volunteers. It had been given to me by Phil Harris, who used it in his classes at Indiana University. I explained *that* much of the history up front to build club membership. The text refers to Louie's problem of being trapped on a mat but does not give the reader any real information about his age, location, or even species. The passage is read and then the participants—individually and in writing—must identify Louie and tell where Louie is and what Louie is doing. I distributed individual copies of the large-print text and then read it aloud to the boys. I reminded them not to talk out loud or otherwise influence one another. Because knowing that an authority may look at your writing is stressful, I told them that I would not ask for their papers. After a few minutes, I called time.

Each member of my trio set up a different scenario. Beau said Louie was a wrestler pinned to a mat. Reynaldo said Louie was a prisoner afraid for his safety. Jonathan said Louie was a horse who wanted to get out of his stall. We looked at each boy's response in terms of schema theory, as it *overrides* background knowledge, which made particular sense to Jonathan, who had come to the reading session right after a class with a horse-loving teacher he couldn't stand.

The boys were sheepishly unsure whether such a powerful test should be let into the public domain, yet very slow to return their copies. Three happy campers walked out of the room that day, official owners of a large-print "Louie." Wouldn't it be wonderful if the power of theory could be packed into such small palatable packages every time?

Here is the text of the language experience story:

The Trouble with Louie

Louie is the subject of a research study in which students in a gymnasium were asked to read an ambiguous story and then tell what it was about. The experiment shows the power of schema theory and background knowledge in a person's reading comprehension.

After Reynaldo, Jonathan, and Beau heard the passage, they were then asked to write:

1. The identity of Louie.
2. Where Louie was.
3. What was happening.

They were carefully instructed not to say anything because that might influence the schema of one of the other participants.

With only three boys, three different responses came about:

• Louie was a horse trying to get out of his stall.
• Louie was a prisoner trying to escape jail because he was getting hurt.

• Louie was wrestler in a wrestling match in a situation he didn't understand.

It is not necessary to be personally related to the subject for schema to be activated around it. For example: Jonathan's second-period teacher loves horses and talks about them a lot. Jonathan had been in her class before coming to this research study. Jonathan did not have to be a horse lover to have his schema activated to the extent that he thought Louie was a horse. If Jonathan had just seen a movie about a dog, he might have been very sure that Louie was a dog trying to get out of his yard. If he had a little brother in nursery school, he might have thought Louie was a kid who didn't want to finish taking his nap. What we know and what we've been exposed to has a lot to do with how we understand text when we read it.

What might Jonathan have said if he had just been to San Francisco and had really enjoyed eating a Shrimp Louie?

Had I known that skeptical Beau was following up on this project, I would not have written the language experience story so fast. He went out boogie boarding that night and tried "Louie" out on several friends. To his surprise, they all had different impressions of who or what Louie was. This initiative clearly demonstrated a bright, curious mind, kindled by theory.

SSR Versus the Establishment

At this school, sustained silent reading (SSR) promised a radical departure from ineffective tradition. SSR, thirty minutes a day set aside for pleasure reading for everyone at the school, had been in place about six months when I arrived and was a model of effective programming. The very charismatic principal had been at the site for two years and seemed to be aware that SSR would make achievement rise all over the school. Though she didn't grasp all the theoretical underpinnings, she had set it up in a sound manner. The bad news was nobody at the school understood why it was working so well.[4]

Set up right, SSR just gives people time to establish a reading habit, something they will be able to keep up when they are out of school. It allows them to see that the school values reading for its own sake, rather than as something that will facilitate answering questions on a test. It is completely low pressure, requiring no record keeping or other accountability. Effective design differs from site to site. In some cases, the entire school reads at one time; everyone—from receptionists to custodians to principal—puts life on hold for SSR. That can create logistical problems relative to school business, and may be uncomfortable for students who are in an area unconducive to reading, such as the football field. In other schools, SSR becomes a fixed part of homeroom or some other academic environment—a block of time attached to all third-period classes, for example—to ensure that students will have reading material and that as many students as possible participate. But the key to success, the reason SSR was working at Jonathan's school during these first months, was that no pressure was placed on anyone to do anything except read for pleasure.

In the beginning, Jonathan had viewed SSR time as another waste, but a girlfriend, unaware of his problem and noting that he never had anything interesting to read, had loaned him a paperback, a science fiction story with really difficult text. By talking to him about the book, she had incidentally built up his background knowledge. Jonathan identified this himself when we began to use the theoretical language. He also could see that his English teacher was wise rather than lazy (which he'd imagined before he gained a theoretical perspective of her performance) when she expected no report on his SSR reading. That had allowed him to do what he needed to work on comprehension—read and reread passages, sometimes even going back several chapters. Once he understood this was a good reader strategy, he had no qualms about admitting how much of it he needed to do during SSR. He also agreed that the studies in the Krashen book showing that SSR programs evaluated after just a short time demonstrated very disappointing results were believable, because it had taken him quite a while to get into the system.

Jonathan was a little taken aback, however, by the 1984 Manning and Manning study showing that student interaction boosted SSR success.[5] He had not viewed his classmate's sharing and talking attention as literacy-boosting interaction—and as a teenager under the influence of a crush on a beautiful girl who "happened" to be a good student, he might have been just as content to go on not viewing it that way. Still, he was eager to discuss with me the theoretical implications of his school's project. Having the inside view of this program, he was able to think assertively about how it could work to his advantage. That understanding also gave him a different perspective when things ultimately went awry.

There are so many things that contribute to the turmoil of today's schools, it would be unfair to look at one procedure as the primary culprit. But, given the instability of families, the uncertainty of employment, and the unrest on the streets, the schools could provide a modicum of security just by avoiding arbitrary or politically motivated change. Gone are the days when a Southern California student in a moderate- or low-income school gets to become familiar with the system in the first year and with the people in charge of the school over time, or even when the student is able to attend the same school for several years. Gone are the days when a principal builds a team, hiring teachers who in one way or another fit the philosophy of the community. It has become almost a given that if a principal or other administrator is to get ahead, he or she must change schools or even districts, so the *dynamics* of an individual school *never stabilize*. Someone recognized as a troubleshooter will be moved from fire to fire, doing a little hiring here, a little there, but, with a handful of exceptions, never really getting to know the students who are supposed to be the point . . . aren't they? A poor administrator may, likewise, be moved from district to district, leaving a swath of unfinished business that impacts the lives of students never met. Some districts have an administrative policy by which each principal, regardless of competency, is automatically moved every so many years.

So it was that the very dynamic principal at Jonathan's school greeted me one morning with the wonderful news—she was moving up.

As it turned out, she had to move quickly, before her successor could be found. So rather than transition, there was a procedural shift. The new principal didn't understand why SSR works, that the main advantage of this SSR was its extraordinary flexibility that allowed each individual a chance to enjoy reading. Seeing what appeared to be fluff, a free-form fun time with books all over the school, he very pragmatically encouraged accountability—in the traditional sense of the word.

The following fall, I touched base with Jonathan, who advised me that his new English teacher was now demanding that he write a brief report on his SSR reading. Since he was barely making it through the text, this new curve was killing his drive. But, at least the power of theory allowed Jonathan to understand that the problem was not a sudden shift in his intellect. "These people don't understand what this kind of reading is supposed to be about," he explained.

This state of affairs was avoidable. Had the first principal understood the theoretical rationale for her very good practice, she could have formally or informally inserviced her faculty so that when the new principal came in, his call of accountability could have been met with informed responses. However, as it stands, this new administrator will no doubt see, among other things, a dip in the standardized test scores of the school's continuing students and a sudden drop in the ability of the new freshman class. Such a drop can, of course, be blamed on the economy, the family, or the fact that kids just don't want to learn as much as they used to. Before long, a new principal will take the reins. At that point, improperly handled, SSR will likely be hated by all concerned and will rightfully be dropped. This would bring full circle a classic example of how methods and practice, without a clearly stated philosophy, can go either very well or very badly. Methods without theory can serve or burden.

Testing Results

The readings I brought to the sessions included multiple copies of newspaper articles relating to whatever came up in earlier sessions; short teaching papers I'd written on theoretical readings and language development topics such as Smith's club membership and Krashen's comprehensible input; short papers of mine detailing studies such as Gordon Wells's *Meaning Makers* and Rist's self-fulfilling prophecies; ghost stories with regional twists, like *Tailypo*; and an endless trail of language experience stories written to reflect anything the boys had shared. In the process, I was able to modify my own writing, making it clearer while demonstrating to them that the writing process takes numerous drafts. While Beau could not believe that I'd gone to the trouble to rewrite one paper for publication twelve times by the time he saw it, Jonathan was convinced that I needed to spend a lot more time on a five-page paper perhaps inappropriately titled "Comprehension," since he found the paper confusing in many places. (There were moments when I felt a real nostalgia for the days of "teacher is right.") Though we talked about the *key word* concept of literacy introduction, we never had time to try that out. There wasn't enough time to do everything.

Though I was available to work with them through the summer, administrative and budgetary changes at the school meant our meeting room would be unavailable to us at the end of the spring term. Reynaldo's summer school and work schedule made the end of the term the official end of his participation. Beau and Jonathan expected to be part of a study-for-pay program at a local community college, but had not gotten particulars on that. Therefore, we agreed to meet at the college either before or after their classes, when we found out what their scheduling commitments were.

This uncertainty made me want some kind of evaluation on my young research partners. Their attendance and participation were obvious positives, but I designed a reading test to document their learning. Generally speaking, I explained every detail of what I was doing with them so they could participate fully. In this case, however, I did not want their affective filters raised by a reading test, so on the last day of school I instead presented a "vocabulary" test. Since it was a cold list of words in isolation, words from the "Ocean" and "Celery" language experience stories that all three had initially been unable to read, I knew they would be taking the most difficult kind of "reading" test possible. The words they knew, they would have unquestionably acquired through reading. And that was the point.

To keep their filters even lower and to reinforce the idea that words come from reading, I had copies of the two language experience stories handy, should they want to refer to them. If they did decide to look into the text for a word, however, I would delete that from my list of words successfully read in isolation. I planned to tell all before we ended our work together, but right then I needed to keep my findings as conservative as possible.

Reynaldo didn't show up at all that day. Three times that month I had hauled in an *Architectural Digest* I thought might kindle something. When he finally showed up, *wow*! He'd never seen such a magazine! His entire demeanor shifted— he seemed to come alive—but he still didn't speak. I regret that I didn't give it to him to keep then and there, because I never got another chance. The last time I saw him, he rushed up to me in the school yard to say he didn't know if he could come that day or not. His hair was newly slicked back in the style characteristic of a local gang. Having found club membership, albeit in a very high priced club, Reynaldo the Shy seemed . . . less afraid.

Jonathan had a final exam that made him late. Beau, having no other commitments, was the first to arrive. I presented him with a list of words, pointing out that he had seen them all in either the "Ocean" or "Celery" language experience stories, and asked him to say the word and then either use it in a sentence or give the definition outright. I turned on my tape recorder and began to mark words on a master list as he read them. While Beau was doing this, Jonathan came in, announcing that he would have to leave shortly to go to another final. If I wanted him to participate, it would have to be at the same time as Beau. I gave him the same instructions and then tried to separate the responses. Even though I had a tape recording of the session, sometimes I couldn't tell who had given a response first or when one of them had influenced the other. I threw out all questionable words. Of the 108 words on the list, words the boys had been unable to read when we first met, Beau plainly read 32 on his own. Of that same 108, Jonathan plainly read 41 in isolation.

They were quite pleased with the results, even though they didn't yet know the limitations I'd put on them. I suggested that at the end of the summer, we could do it again to see how much more they'd gotten from the reading they would be doing. They could see that even if all they did was just read the two little stories every day, they would be able to drive up their scores. Having collected enough data for this study, I was pretty relaxed about the future schedule arrangements. On the other hand, we did seem to me to be on a roll. I asked them if they wanted to continue meeting or if they needed a rest. Beau said that what we were doing wasn't like work at all; he wanted to keep coming. Jonathan said that this was changing his life, an observation he repeatedly made throughout our association. The school year ended on a very positive note.

Summer Reorganization

Jonathan and Beau were to call me as soon as their community college program got under way. Meanwhile, I became involved in a gang literacy project on Sundays, Tuesday mornings, and other random days. When it seemed my high school charges had forgotten that they were supposed to call me, I called Jonathan. He and Beau were planning to call me the next day, he said. The community college program had fizzled because of disorganization or poor communication, so Jonathan had been out trying to find another source of summer income. He said that he'd put down on one application that he was not available Tuesday or Thursday mornings because of his reading lessons. When I told him about the other project that took up my Tuesdays, he took the news with interest and said he could readily understand the literacy problems there. So we agreed that the three of us would meet on Thursday mornings at a local library, but that he was to call and confirm the library's hours and leave a message on my answering machine. He never did.

When I called Jonathan again to verify our next meeting, his mom answered. She confirmed his enthusiasm about "the program" and said he'd really shown a change in attitude about school since we'd begun to work together: "She makes reading seem like fun," he'd said. When I mentioned what a bright young man he was, his mother said that she knew that and thought he was just lazy. Both her children had done poorly in the early years, but the daughter had finally gotten herself turned around (meaning gainfully employed), and it was time Jonathan did the same. I tried to ease her into the idea of reading to him for ten minutes a day. This made her freeze. He didn't need babying. He needed to learn responsibility. (I heard an echo of Arthur's mother asking when he was supposed to start reading for himself. Did these mothers share a common secret?) At the end of our chat, she told me that she thought he was at Beau's house.

When I called Beau's, his father answered. I told him who I was and who I was trying to reach. The man flickered neither friendliness nor recognition, but when he yelled to Beau, he referred to me as "that reading teacher." Jonathan refused to believe I was telepathic, so I admitted his mom had put me on his trail. He said we had permission to meet at his apartment instead of the library, as long as we didn't "mess up the place." I assured Jonathan that we would try to be good.

Learning Environments

When I arrived, Beau and Jonathan were already in an animated discussion in the living room. I said I'd parked in the driveway and Jonathan took me back out and ushered me into his mother's parking spot. When we returned to the apartment, I was given Beau's spot on the couch, whereupon a large fluffy cat slithered out from somewhere and sat down about six feet in front of me and proceeded to stare at me until I left. Under normal circumstances, I'm a cat person, so I thought about using the family pet as a language experience prompt. However, after a few failed attempts at nonverbal communication with the animal, I decided to go on to the topic of freedom of speech.

A heated debate over whether flag burners should be allowed to remain in the country moved on to the censorship of a music group called 2 Live Crew and the National Endowment for the Arts' reneging on funds for a museum that showed a Christ figure in a jar of urine. Each argument called for the reading of yet another portion of the *Constitution* or the *Bill of Rights*, both of which I "just happened" to have with me, in triplicate. Their responses provided material for the two-and-a-half-page language experience story, "Two Republicans," I wrote later and mailed to them.

After these discussions, I began reading the *Kappan* article, "Arthur: A Tale of Disempowerment," which was marked by regular interruptions for questions and personal testimony. Suddenly, Beau heard a noise that had escaped Jonathan and me and ran out of the apartment. "His girlfriend must have come to pick him up," Jonathan offered. A minute later, Beau rushed in, grabbed his blue plastic envelope, and asked us not to finish "Arthur" until our next session. We agreed.

The next week we again met at Jonathan's apartment, but Beau, having neither called nor returned Jonathan's calls, didn't show. Throughout the time we spent in the apartment there was constant activity. A young man rushed back and forth between a hallway and a bathroom, though he never came out for an introduction. A teenage neighbor came over looking for company and Jonathan seemed neither to know how to tell her to go away nor what to do with her. When I asked if he wanted her to join us, Jonathan immediately said no, and she went away. (This was very much like the reaction Madonna had when I asked if she wanted her boyfriend to join us after he'd seemed drawn to my oral reading.) Several times two little boys rushed up to the screen to see if Jonathan could come out to play. And the cat maintained its sentinel position. It would be an overstatement to say the place was chaotic, but it definitely failed the tranquility test.

I got the hours and address of the local library and we agreed to meet there in the future. As neither boy drove, I offered to double as chauffeur. Jonathan called Beau and arranged for him to be ready so that we could pick him up after I picked up Jonathan. However, when we got to the house, though it seemed occupied, no one answered the door.[6] The trio had dwindled from three to two to one.

Jonathan and I went to the library. In the periodical section, there were large, well-lit tables with lots of chairs. Though there was no private space, there were, likewise, very few other people. The young man's love of history came to the fore as he discovered the magazines featuring historical stories and wonderful photographs of the Civil War era. We had located what for Jonathan would prove a reader's Mecca.

A Thirst for a Different Kind of World

Though most of what he read was officially several grade levels beyond him, Jonathan had become a regular reader of the *LA Times* business section and enjoyed exploring various sections of *Newsweek* magazine. He'd grasped the concept of text sampling and, not without some guilt, allowed himself to put things down when the going got too rough. I kept trying to convince him that he would read more if he read easier material, but with the exception of the stories I wrote for him, what interested him was only available in tough text.

We had established a routine in which he waited out on the curb before our scheduled library trips so I wouldn't have to park. One day National Public Radio (NPR) was airing person-to-person interviews with Zulus who were describing the police's ransacking of their shack village, reportedly in cooperation with Mandela supporters. Having written a literacy paper with a Fulbright scholar, a Zulu woman who hadn't written to me since her return to South Africa, I became very engrossed in the report and was many cities beyond Jonathan's before I realized I'd passed him up.

I doubled back to find him patiently waiting and absolutely nonjudgmental. Nevertheless, I explained what had happened and the concern I felt for my friend's safety. He was genuinely interested and wanted to turn the report back on while we drove to the library. I showed him where NPR was on the dial and explained that you never knew what you'd get, except that it would be much more detailed than mainstream broadcasts and would often express views commercial stations would never allow. The next time I arrived at Jonathan's curb, he was armed for a long wait, wired to a Walkman. As I drove up I played a game in my mind about the irony of a young man in pursuit of learning while popular lyrics—probably something like "Don't Worry; Be Happy"—were being pumped into his ears. Once in my car, however, Jonathan said he'd been tuned in to NPR and was prepared to discuss the rising price of crude oil.

Earning a Job

When Jonathan began looking for summer work, he had several important criteria. First and foremost, he needed to be able to schedule around his reading lessons. I assured him that we could meet late in the day or on weekends if necessary. No, he liked meeting early in the day and felt he did his best learning then. (I didn't tell him that I am a very definite night person who prefers to wake up well after lunch!) The reading lessons, he reiterated, were going to make a lifelong difference to him. A job was important for clothes and stuff like that, but in the long run, he needed to read.

Another priority was that his job be either within walking distance or on a bus line. (There seemed to be no one to look after him but himself, and he was accustomed to accepting that. When he had to go to an interview an hour after one of our sessions, I offered to come back and drive him so he wouldn't have to rush. No, he could handle it, he assured me, almost surprised at an offer of assistance.) And, remembering what we'd discussed about benefits, he always asked potential employers about stock plans and profit-sharing benefits. It wasn't essential, but he had made serious note that these benefits were important.

After he was offered a job at an amusement park, he had to go through a training program that included everything from lectures and reading to a written exam. During our lessons and on the phone he mentioned the severe pressure he felt, especially because of the reading. I offered to go over the manuals with him when we met, but he thought what we were doing was more important. He seemed to sense that authentic reading is more literacy friendly than theme park training manuals. He'd never been in the habit of studying with a friend, and when I suggested he try working with someone else who was going through training, he couldn't imagine such a bizarre activity. Nevertheless, I insisted he get help from some friendly soul; doing this alone was no way to win the game. By the next time we talked, he had taken his trainer into his confidence, explaining to her that he had difficulty reading. She told him he had to keep trying. Meanwhile, she began driving him home after the training sessions, reviewing everything as they drove. He passed the written exam even though he really hadn't thought he could do it. When he went back for a follow-up interview and learned that he'd qualified for a better job than the one he'd applied for, he saw his whole life turn around. As he described the scene to me, he cried; I did too.

The final hurdle was having to wear a theme park costume . . . in public. Most of his friends didn't have enough money to frequent the park, and he hoped he would be transferred to some low-profile place before he was discovered. But Jonathan began to realize over time that he was the authority here; even people who had traveled all over the world asked him for directions. The job was very good for his self-esteem. Nonetheless, he refused to work on Thursday mornings.

Understanding How Things Work

In an effort to help Jonathan make the reader/author connection, I brought in my little Fry Readability Scale. This was a cardboard slide-rule device based on Edward Fry's formula for measuring word size against sentence length to determine the grade level of a piece of text. I wanted him to see that after thinking about the intended audience level, an author might decide to use smaller words or longer sentences. More precisely, I hoped that if Jonathan saw how one educator had come up with a seemingly mysterious grade-level formula, he would be empowered to control his own text by thinking about these surface issues.

We decided to evaluate one of the language experience stories we had on hand. That called for some extensive syllable counting, which I did in front of him. I let him manipulate the gadget. As I called out the numbers, he slid the scale into position and determined the Fry grade level. "Wow!" He was amazed that he'd been reading such high-level material. And Jonathan had figured out how to work the scale without directions, just by knowing what it was supposed to do.

Then we manipulated the text. First, we combined sentences and substituted longer words to make the level go up; Jonathan read it. Then we reversed the process, lowering the level to second grade; he read that, too. Jonathan observed that the piece had been much better as originally written. No wonder schoolbooks are so tough to read sometimes, he suggested. "If [text authors] really believe they are helping kids with [level control], they oughta think again. . . . They oughta try this," he said. He stared at the three levels of the text and then speculated that a lot of books deliberately geared for poor readers are really harder to read because the ideas are cut up into shorter sentences. "If I were writing about sailing or something for little kids, I'd just write it so they could understand. I'd just make it make sense," he said.

"Oh? What if they didn't know some of the words?" I challenged.

"Well, you know, if the story makes sense, I mean if it's a good story, they can figure the words out," he explained.

A One-Hundred-Percent Connection

Near the end of the summer, Jonathan reread the two language experience stories my word list test had been based on. Then I readministered the test, asking him to either give the definitions or use the words in sentences. He was free to read down the list in order or skip around as he wished. There was no time limit. I just wanted to see how many of the original forty-one words read in isolation he'd retained. If he got twenty good ones, I told him, there would be cause to celebrate.

As usual we were in the library bull pen, with lots of table space. The tape recorder was near Jonathan and the language experience stories were face down, but where he could pick them up and look at them if he wanted to. He held one copy of the 108-word list and I held another. He was to mark the ones he'd identified with an X and put a long dash next to those he wanted to come back to. Quickly he began to rattle off sentences using one word after another as he bounded down the list. He got all but about five on the first pass and went back to look at the missed ones. Then he got all but one of those. His face turned red as he struggled with the last word.

"You just read it in the story; you know that word," I hinted.

Did he want to look at the story? It was fair to do that, if he thought it would help. No. He didn't want to do that, not on the last word.

"Oh, *miracle!*" It *was* a miracle and it was the last word. Jonathan had gotten through the entire list of words in isolation, the most difficult kind of word identification. He looked stunned. Then I explained that the test had been even more difficult than he thought, that the words had been originally placed on the list because all three boys had been unable to read them even in context.

"The words were put into these stories to help you understand them from the *context* . . . seeing the words in the middle of a story you already knew helped you understand and read them easily. And the more you read the story, the more of the words you knew . . . without a teacher . . . without a dictionary . . . without stress. That's how you learned all of these new words. You picked them up from reading. All of them."

"I didn't know that."

"As you were reading in the beginning, I was documenting words you couldn't get. Now you've got 'em all from just the little bit of reading you've done on these two stories . . . and, of course, whatever leisure reading you've done if these words were in it."

Jonathan was amazed and began to talk about how long, boring, and difficult the process of trying to deliberately learn lists of meaningless words had always been. "Of course that was awfully boring what we did—*and, is, a, the,*" he recited the simple words, "I wasn't even looking at it. . . . It was like [whistles]—" he laughed. "It was quite boring."

I launched into my "daily reading" lecture. "Nothing on this table has been touched," I reminded him. "I didn't help you with any of these words during the test. Even the few that gave you a problem, you went back and got on your own.

They are yours, yours to keep. And you earned them from reading. You did this yourself. The proof is on this tape. You passed the most difficult kind of test, words in isolation—*one hundred percent*. Do you realize that?"

"Slightly," he laughed nervously, "still hasn't totally hit me though." I was glad that the evidence was so neatly spread before him, the stories still face down. Jonathan was having great difficulty appreciating his own achievement. He'd never gotten a hundred percent on anything before in his life and this was absolutely his win.

As we again discussed the value that reading has for language development, Jonathan began to identify ways he could get in his daily reading. He already read about an hour at night when he wasn't working; but he worked many nights.

"I'm definitely going to have that reading program at school this year," he said, referring to sustained silent reading. "And I always get shifts with boring breaks and the lunch hour. . . ." He contemplated making the most of time at work. Still not quite ready to credit himself with success, he was very willing to plan for more.

A Special Ed Perception of School

When it was clear that Beau had dropped out of our program, I pulled out the "Arthur" article and resumed reading it to Jonathan. As before, he had many questions and comments, finding he had a great deal in common with the disempowered little boy.

As best he could remember, he too had entered special ed in the fourth grade because of his inability to read. The stigma was as humiliating for Jonathan as it had been for Arthur. "You see it was in a different classroom. Then when we'd come back the other kids would just like, you know, 'What is that class? What is that class?' That was not like cool, not . . . cool." He shook his head with a nervous little forced laugh.

"That probably made you feel terrible, huh?"

"It was like," and his voice shifted into the high pitch of a little kid, "I don't know. I don't know." Only he did know.

He remembered very little about the special reading program except that they spent most of the time filling out work sheets. But he now knew that being read to would have been more appropriate and effective. He was angry for Arthur and he was angry for himself. Because he hadn't improved in the reading program, he'd been transferred to a resource school for the mentally and physically handicapped. (Remember Madonna?) "That over there kind of made you feel stupid. When I got there I felt I didn't fit in. Those people were walking, hardly even walking around . . . I was just running around and stuff."

"Did they read you stories there?" I asked.

"Uh-uh. We did regular paperwork," he said, meaning more fill-in-the blank work sheets.

He'd also gone to a class in sign language because a lot of the kids in the school only used sign language. And twice a week he went to a Boys' Club to work on wood projects or play soccer or just run around.

After that, he moved up to another school with similar programming: endless days of trips to the Boys' Club, waiting for other people to come play ball, going out to kill time, shooting spitwads at the teacher and getting them shot back by the teacher. The basketball and baseball were fun, he admitted, and there were lots of parties, but he didn't understand what it had to do with school. Even then, he felt he was wasting his time. "It was like a baby-sitting class. It was to baby-sit us. It wasn't really work. I mean we took so many trips. I hardly did *any* work."

So little was expected of them in the classroom that Jonathan felt insulted: "She goes, 'OK, if you can do all your work and be like really good and get like the top group, the top three will go out for lunch.' "

"What did you have to do to be one of the top three?"

"You had to do all your work . . . finish what was assigned to you. That didn't seem like . . . it was something, yeah, but the people that came in late. . . ." Kids who arrived late didn't have a chance at being tops, he explained. "Beau came in late quite a bit." Jonathan had sensed the unfairness of the prize being held hostage from kids like Beau who depended on their parents to get them to class on time. Sometimes Jonathan chose not to enter the contest simply because it wasn't fair to his fellows. And for that passive resistance, he now felt he wasn't a good person. (A consistent self-perception among the nonreaders I've worked with is that they are not good . . . they are personally bad and not deserving of the better lives they see around them. You see it here as Jonathan lambasts himself. Madonna told me she deserved the abuse she got as a child. And Danny even tromped on himself for driving in a regular lane instead of a carpool lane when we drove to hear the Krashen lecture.)

In spite of the fact that his coordinator told me he was exceptionally well behaved, and not just for me, Jonathan perceived himself a bad school kid. "We were actually the trouble kids of the school. . . . During recess we thought we owned the place because we were always getting out to do anything we wanted to. . . . We actually got on the swings. I mean you're not supposed to twirl 'em. And we'd sit there and wh-i-i-i-sh! wh-i-i-i-sh! The teacher would just tell us, 'OK, come off.' About five minutes later we were back out there." It did not occur to Jonathan that this was a supervisory not a behavioral problem. Nor did he have any idea why he was not supposed to twirl the swings. He just felt guilty for doing it.

When I asked him if his mom knew what was going on, he explained, "She knew. I was like new to the program. So she didn't know exactly how the program was supposed to work. And actually the program is working how it's supposed to work . . . I mean most of my life, I haven't seen a lot of work. I've been playing a lot."

217

When he talked about the stigma of special ed in high school, he said that even his art teacher hated special ed kids. Jonathan was part of a three-member table considered the trouble group by the teacher.

"Me and this other kid, we're both special ed, and there's this other guy, he just sits back there with us, you know. And she calls us the Three Musketeers."

"I take it you don't like that," I said.

"Oh, I *hate* it! Oh, I hate her! Oh, I hate her so much!"

"Do you enjoy doing the art?"

"Oh, I enjoy doing the art. It's just when she starts griping she gets me mad! She blames me for everything that happens at that back table!"

He'd spent one period at a light table, far removed from his cronies. When the teacher announced it was cleanup time, Jonathan picked up his work from the light table and put it away. Then he went back to his regular table to wait for the bell.

"It's like I'm ready, and she points back at me and says, Jonathan, get up and clean the table you made such a mess of. You've been back there making so much noise all this period.' And I go, 'I haven't been here at all!' I was like, wow! So I just sat there and said, 'Forget you, I didn't do this.'" He expected to get an F in art for insubordination.

Reading about Arthur had unveiled in Jonathan a growing resentment for all the learning that his schools had withheld from him, learning he now knew he was very capable of.

The Chaos Connection

When I read Jonathan my paper on adult illiterates, he suddenly started to talk about home. "That one part at the front where it talks about, uh, the abuse of children, sometimes they don't read? 'Cause uh, when my dad actually lived at the house, he uh . . . he was a truck driver. He'd either come back drunk or on his way to being drunk." He told me a tragic story of a violent, drunken, drug-abusing father who would gently tell Jonathan to go to bed and then threaten to kill him when the child tried to kiss his mother good night. His older sister still keeps a little rocker, broken when her father threw it into a wall. He has no memory of his mom ever responding or moving to defend her children. Even in his home, Jonathan has always been somewhat isolated. But, interestingly, Jonathan had been able to distinguish between what people said was going on and what he sensed was the real emotional climate. Noting the disparity between conventional expectations and his own reality, he reported, "Back in [school] they blamed my problems all on my dad's leaving . . . everyone in my house was happy to get rid of my dad."

Jonathan has been told that he has a younger half-sister somewhere. He wishes he could see her, just to know she's OK, but he has no idea where to look. His mom has suggested that there may be a lot of other half-siblings "out there." The notion leaves him a little off balance.

Like other nonreaders, Jonathan was extraordinarily unfamiliar with common English idioms and expressions. His interest in the unfamiliar term "catch-22" was a perfect opening for me to begin reading him the book by the same title. I thought his love of war games and interest in history might help propel him into the world of habitual reading. It worked. He was so entertained by the book that I bought him a copy of his own. He was delighted.

When I came by to pick him up the following week, he was very unhappy. The family had had to move everything in the apartment into the middle of the rooms to prepare for a bug spraying. Afterward, he'd been unable to find a lot of his things, *Catch-22* among them. He'd also lost a book by a Japanese author whose name he couldn't recall and whom he'd discovered independently. He said, "After the house got sprayed it's hard to find things. . . . It's like my room is not full enough. I go, like, wait a second, what happened to all my stuff?"

Yet, consistent with a mindset of self-blame, he didn't see any of the disruptions as excuses for academic problems. The physical and emotional disruptions didn't feel unreasonable to him. Having few friends and no confidants, he was left to work things out on his own. It wasn't until he heard unreasonableness described in the lives of Arthur and other nonreaders that Jonathan began to recognize the inconsistencies in his own. Reading about another's chaos makes one's own chaos easier to analyze.

Empowerment Changes Attitudes

When I first encountered Jonathan he was doing poorly scholastically. Reading problems were cited as the root of his inability to succeed, and he wasn't sure if school was worth the trouble. By the end of that semester, however, he'd managed to get through enough history to earn a B in the course. That success was invaluable. He started to *like* history.

Getting a paying job was also very important to his self-esteem. And you'll recall that he held out for hours that would accommodate his reading *as scheduled*. Even when I offered to move our sessions to a different time, he steadfastly held to the hour that was most productive for him.

When I talked with Jonathan about the gang literacy project, he knew enough about the roots of reading problems to understand why the participants couldn't read. He was able to interpret theory in real-world terms. About this same time, his mother reported that he said I made reading fun. By midsummer, though he thoroughly enjoyed being read to, he had begun his own reading program. "I read a lot myself. I usually read from 9:30 to 10:30 [P.M.]. . . . This guy, I read his comic books? He also [writes] *book* books. And I'm collecting a series of his." Jonathan had begun to collect the stories that were used as the basis for the comics. Reading the comics gave him the background knowledge he needed to read the complete stories and to treat them as collector's items. Knowing that having a favorite author is a mark of a good reader allows a student to see author selection as a strategy. In other words, it affords the new reader the power of theory. Recall that Madonna, too, developed a taste for one author's work.

The previous June, Jonathan had a reading score of sixty percent at the fifth-grade level, and according to a memo from his special ed coordinator, "His academic ability levels appeared to have plateaued prior to his enrollment at [the school]." Retesting done at the school in September of the following year, after fourteen of our sixteen sessions, showed a reading score of seventy percent at the seventh-grade level. He'd moved up two grade levels in one year, after it had seemed he'd gone as far as he could go. Jonathan was not one to believe in fairy tales or expect idle dreams to come true. However, after his exposure to empowering pedagogy, he began to talk to his teachers about a more positive future. Of the math teacher with whom he'd stopped doing battle he said, "She was asking me if I'm definitely going to graduate and she was asking me how I'm doing in my classes . . . I said, 'Pretty good so far.' "

"Oh, good," I responded to this news.

"I want to really badly so I can go on to college . . . I need to go to college."

"You need to go?"

"You see, a lot a jobs now, they do require you have some type of college education and I feel it's important enough."

Decision making. Opinion drawing. Positive thinking. I began to wonder if Jonathan had moved beyond what I had to offer. It wasn't a question of *if* he could go to college or *should* go. He was simply taking for granted that he *would* go.

1. I later learned that for shop, there was a workbook Reynaldo had to fill in order to pass. As he was not allowed to take it home, he had to sit in the shop to work on his workbook five days per week. Though he claimed that far from being difficult, the workbook was quite simple and boring, the teacher was very concerned about cheating and

constantly monitored the process. (I was reminded of a quote from *Letter to a Teacher* by the School Boys of Barbiana in which a like-guarded lad wrote to his former teacher: "You are paid to help me. . . . Instead, you waste your time keeping me under guard as if I were a thief" [p.123].) Despite the fact that Reynaldo's plan had been to learn the construction trade, all his wood-shop time had been spent on the workbook; he had constructed nothing in the class.

2. The issue of type size comes up again and again. Small type, like that used in the fine print of a newspaper ad, simply slows the reader down and cuts comprehension. Easy-to-navigate type, likewise, increases speed and therefore comprehension. Remember how Mitzi made the distinction between the two Carle *Caterpillar* books? She knew the story, but told her little sister that the big book was easier to read.

3. This was prior to the earthquake of 1994.

4. It is interesting to note that university programs for education administrators often fail to acquaint their students (future principals, deans, etc.) with current learning theory. As one recent administrative credential recipient explained his program, "What we spent most of our time learning was how to play politics and how to make sure nobody got ahead of us. We didn't even talk about the kids, just how to manage their parents." Faced with a staff of teachers who, likewise, lacked theoretical foundations, he had run through tremendous amounts of special funds buying behavior-modification inservice packages that all parties, most of all his students, had begun to recognize as lists of manipulation techniques best suited to closed, lab-type environments like prisons, if even there. Though it is sometimes possible to force them into compliance, people are insulted by manipulation.

5. In Stephen Krashen, *Inquiries and Insights* (Hayward, Calif.: Alemaney Press, 1985), 91-93.

6. Eventually I did reach Maureen by phone and learned that Beau had gotten a six-day-a-week job on the docks. He'd told her he wanted to stay behind when the family moved so he could reenroll in high school and continue to work with me. I reminded her that this summer was the last time I could give the boys. She'd known it, but thought maybe something could have changed. Sunday was Beau's only day off, so I agreed to meet with him then. She thanked me in advance and said she'd have him call, but I never heard from Beau again. Like Reynaldo, I am afraid he simply didn't get enough contact time to keep going on his own. I had come in with the intention of shifting the odds for all three of my young charges. Admittedly, I had made an impact on both Beau and Reynaldo; but given just a bit more access time. . . .

# Eight

The Fugitives

Zintozonke: Unusual Odds

In the name of cooperative learning, my friend and colleague Judy Mzinyati (a Zulu woman studying in the United States as a Fulbright scholar) and I began a study that took us from the petal-strewn paths of our spacious campus to the graffiti-covered public library in crowded downtown Los Angeles. As a linguist, Judy wanted to study how spelling develops for an adult whose literacy is emerging. I was very interested in the comparative geographic and cultural aspects of illiteracy. That is to say, I wanted to know if where people are from tempers their perceptions about what literacy is and therefore affects how—or whether—they pursue it. One of the extraordinary advantages of living in Southern California is that the area is comprised of people from all over the world. With few exceptions, they're all here, exhibiting all facets of literacy, preliteracy, aliteracy, and illiteracy[1]—all of which have to do as much with perception as with ability. But, not surprisingly, people tend to cluster with those who will make life less difficult. English speakers will likely be found living among others who speak English, Spanish speakers will live where that language will be understood, and so on. But people are also bilingual and multilingual, educated and uneducated, affluent and poor. And no matter the culture of origin, there are class distinctions. Nevertheless, discovering the unexpected common denominators makes living here most interesting.

Quite by accident Judy passed a public pay phone in down-town LA and was asked by a snaggletoothed woman to help her by writing down a phone number. What a contrast they made: Judy, plain cotton dress, proud posture, short hair, scrubbed face, a Fulbright scholar; and this bejeweled woman at the phone, flamboyant theatrical costuming, elaborate ropes of hair coiled across much of her heavily made-up face. Still, Judy may have been the only black woman passing at that moment of need. And when the woman spoke, there was another overlap in their identities: both had accents tying them to South Africa. "Hey, honey," the gravel voice began, and then the woman asked Judy to listen to the party on the other end of the line and take down a phone number. The call ended, and two women from different worlds located on the same distant point on the planet had met in a way they never could have in their homelands (in this case because of culture and class rather than race). Coincidence? Most likely. Seren-dipity? No doubt about it. You see, in those brief moments Judy Mzinyati realized she'd just encountered an illiterate woman who spoke Afrikaans, a language she believed was only taught in school. Judy decided she may as well keep the woman's phone number.

Back at the university, Judy described the woman to Steve Krashen, hoping to get a clue as to how she might study this woman's unusual language development. It could not have come from reading, the most common source of vocabulary, because she could neither read nor write. "You should be talking with La Vergne," Krashen told her. We were not even enrolled in the same schools, Judy being in linguistics and I in education, and we certainly had different frames of refer-ence when it came to research, mine having moved into eth-nography and Judy's following a statistical path. Our common denominator was the Krashen class literature and the resulting willingness to believe positive things were possible, regardless of the past. After I listened to her fascinating story and she heard about some of my early cases, we decided to try an experiment. We would offer to give the woman reading and writing instruction in trade for her cooperation with our research. By phone, Judy got the woman's enthusiastic agreement to the deal and a time line was established. So it was that Judy and I designed a study from two perspectives around one subject, a woman who ultimately provided her own pseudonym—Zintozonke.

Research Without a Subject

After countless phone calls and a series of scheduled informal meetings that were foiled by one learner-generated emergency after another, Judy and I finally met with Zintozonke at a Chinese restaurant. That first interview revealed a woman who had been orphaned, kept out of school, and tortured (the elaborate coils of hair were designed to cover the scars on her face) and who had no memory of ever being read to or told stories by her stepparents or in her first two years of school, which was as far as she'd gotten in her homeland. Here in America, she had enrolled in adult education classes but hadn't completed any.

But our scheduling difficulties were far from over. We couldn't meet at Zintozonke's apartment because, although she lived alone, she was afraid someone might show up at her door during (or inquire afterward about) our unspeakable activities. (Remember the zero-privacy factor?) Because the bus ride necessary for Zintozonke to come meet us was impossibly long, I would drive to Judy's, pick her up, and then we would drive to an inner-city rendezvous with our subject.

Time after time, Zintozonke wouldn't be there . . . she was expecting company . . . she had to help a friend move . . . there was a concert . . . she didn't feel well . . . she needed to save her energy for something important later in the day. . . . Unfamiliar with my habit of chasing through three counties in pursuit of literacy, Judy would offer a battery of apologies each time "her" subject stood us up.

Nevertheless, as a result, Judy and I spent many hours in the car teaching each other about linguistics and literacy. What had begun as a parallel research study turned into a one-to-one inservice neither of us could have predicted. Even if Zintozonke had never shown up for class, her teachers would have reaped immeasurable insights that would have made the effort worthwhile. (If you think this sounds like an overt plug for cooperative learning in adult education, you think right.)

Adding Zintozonke to the equation, however, gave us an inside view of a world apart from the ones we knew. We learned how to recognize new bullet holes from old in the sides of buildings where Zintozonke said the sound of random gunfire went on nightly. We learned by experience how important it was to keep our car windows closed and doors locked even in the daytime, even when there were two of us in the car, even when we were moving at a tolerable speed. In pursuit of Zintozonke's empowerment, we drove harum-scarum through crowded streets, parked in tow-away zones, and in general bolstered each other's courage to be less conservative than either of us normally expected the other to be.

A Subject on the Run

One day when Zintozonke didn't show up on a street corner where we were to meet, Judy had a hunch that she knew where to find her. After we'd cruised several miles through a labyrinth of one-way, dead-end, and permanently-closed-for-construction thoroughfares, Judy gave a little yell. There, on the opposite side of the street, which was under construction, and halfway down the block, swayed our target population of one. Our honking did little good, joining as it did a chorus of horns similarly engaged. Even so, we thought she turned slightly, spotted us, and then moved ahead more quickly, a bright flash of color trying to meld into the crowd around her. Judy leapt out of the car and into the adjacent lane of oncoming traffic, albeit oncoming at a snail's pace. She then challenged a bus's right to turn as she dashed across two intersections and a large pit in the construction zone, whereupon I lost sight of her.

Two blocks later, there was a tap on my window and I looked around to find a panting, triumphant Judy with the dramatic Zintozonke in tow. We then went to the neighborhood library, where, once again, the trauma of filling out an application for a card reared its head. But Zintozonke did manage to find a quiet place, away from shootings, drug trafficking, and other elements of chaos, where she could look at fashion magazines and later, we hoped, other literature. She even checked out some magazines and a book to take home. But that wasn't the happy ending. There were many other close encounters and lessons lost before Judy and I officially ended our attempt to work with Zintozonke.

Naming the Phenomenon

We were trying to collect serious linguistic and literacy data on people with documented problems caused by their inability to read and write, but the nature of our research questions required us to go into the field and find our subjects. Not for us the option of running an ad in the paper calling for research volunteers who would then file into our controlled environment.

The case studies in the available books and articles on adult literacy—and there are hundreds—were limited to thumbnail investigations into the lives of people who were, in fact, moderately functional in literacy terms. The literature did not include information about, and so could not prepare us for, the level of subject we sought. What we found was both new and unnamed.

When we spread our lumpy pallet of observations and frustrations before Krashen, he accepted the possibility that a pattern was emerging, a heretofore undocumented pattern. I had many tales of people who showed up for testing at the literacy office never to return. Perhaps the mere process of being evaluated brought back too many memories of times when they were formally judged inadequate. Many of my subjects and potential subjects had enrolled in adult education

classes again and again but were unable to attend, the traditional classroom door a barrier they seemed unable to cross.
These were people who had a vested interest in learning to
read and who had, by all appearances, every opportunity. But
they'd all been so sensitized to some part of the reading/writing
process, they couldn't face any more attempts. Zintozonke,
for example, was quite literally *running away* from literacy.
This pattern of repeated flight caused Krashen to refer to them
casually as "the fugitives." They are out there in a maze of
compensations and cover-ups, able to grab just the right pas-
serby from the crowd to write down a telephone number.
They cannot be reached by traditional programs, not even by
low-key library volunteers. But, rest assured, the fugitives are
all around.

Harry: Afraid of Pencil and Paper

"There's this man . . ." said a colleague, looking around as if
to make sure no one else heard. "He's really intelligent. I
mean, nobody can tell—nobody. I've known him for years
and I just found out by accident. It was really awkward. He
wouldn't talk about it at first, even when he knew I knew. It
could cause him a lot of trouble, you know? This has to remain
just between us. I thought maybe you could do something for
him. He can pay, but it has to be absolutely confidential. I
told him I'd talk to you."

My colleague was on a mission of mercy, making it difficult
for me to say no, but if his friend was so high-profile, he was
probably not suffering the profound life problems associated
with illiteracy that I wanted to study. I wasn't interested in
a student, no matter how needy, whose primary goal was
keeping his inability to read a secret. What I needed were
research partners, research partners who would participate in
my work with theory.

But my colleague thought this might intrigue Harry. "This
guy is really intelligent," he kept stressing, "nobody can tell."
My teaching and research with adult poor readers had long

since confirmed for me that there is no correlation between illiteracy and intelligence and that illiteracy can be kept hidden from one's closest contacts. But neither I nor my colleague knew that Harry was a classic fugitive.

I met Harry in a coffee shop. My tote bag was loaded with reading and writing materials, but a glance at him kept me from even pulling out a note pad. Harry, unlike many closet illiterates, did not display props of deceit; there wasn't even a pencil in his shirt pocket. Perhaps that was an oversight, yet my experience suggested otherwise. I asked him if he knew that I was looking for research assistance and he assured me that was not only fine but he would like to participate. He was quite firm, however, about one thing: he did not want to have anything to do with reading "that puts you in a room with a bunch of people and makes you wear headphones."

He had mentioned this objection on the telephone as well. Under these machine-sensitive circumstances, I decided not to whip out my tape recorder—the right decision, I realized later, for the wrong reason. Harry wanted a private professional teacher who "knew what was going on." He had a regular girlfriend who was "pretty smart," meaning she could read, who "sort of" knew he had a problem, but he didn't want to mix business with pleasure by asking her to teach him.

I explained that my research was on learner empowerment and that my approach was to give the learner all the information necessary for him or her to continue the process independent of me. That caught his attention. He'd been on his own all his life and was not interested in a program that fostered dependence. He spoke in clear, articulate sentences; there was no doubt that he was thinking through everything before responding. To give him some background for my enthusiasm about my methods, I described Paulo Freire's work with the Brazilian peasants, work in which people believed to be incapable of learning responded to generative words and topics that related to their lives. Suspecting that the literacy problems rested with the teaching methods rather than the students,

Paulo had changed the way reading and writing were taught; the result was a literate population. Harry agreed that Paulo had been on target.

Then I described some of the reading theory and research that had come from my university classes. When I began to talk about the affective filter, a wall of feelings that goes up in the face of stress or fear and impedes memory and the learning process, I wished I could pull out my tablet and pencil to illustrate, but I was afraid he would think his cover was being blown, so I didn't.

I moved on to Krashen's input hypothesis, which promotes the idea that in order to learn to read, you must be taught in a way that makes sense to you. Then I moved to language experience using the words and ideas of the learner as a very effective way to teach reading, and on to the mass of data indicating that being read to regularly is essential to literacy development, since it leads the nonreader into literacy without correction, testing, or external stress. I mentioned Vygotsky's zone of proximal development, a zone that the learner will most likely be able to cross with the help of a more advanced person, perhaps a friend who has already figured out how to do what needs to be learned. Harry liked that: a friend wouldn't want to cause stress; stress is a bad thing. Then I told him about Gordon Wells's notion that being read to does more than develop vocabulary, spelling, and a love of reading; Wells suggests that being read to also helps to develop story grammar, a way of understanding how the language is formed by literate people in a society. Even after children know how to read for themselves, being read to is beneficial. I said that I read to my students, adults and children alike, every session, and then I reasserted why.

I asked him if he ever read anything. No, he didn't need to. He could handle everything just fine without reading, but he wanted to change careers. Not that he minded hard work. He had always worked hard and had been paid well for it. He just was able to see that his physical stamina wouldn't last forever and at middle age, it was time to start thinking about that.

Then we began talking about his early education and feelings about the literacy process. He had come from a nonreading family, but, in the industrial town in which he grew up, that was standard. People didn't need literacy to do what they did day in and day out. Though he claimed not to remember any particularly bad school experiences, I sensed a latent anguish—that he had really *disliked* being there. He got choked up, tried to pick up his coffee cup, jiggled it around, and then wiped his eyes.

I told him that every adult I've worked with has profoundly bad memories of school reading experiences. People who enter school not knowing how to read are usually treated differently and taught differently from those who do. He looked interested. I briefly described the issue of surface over substance. In writing, the surface is penmanship, spelling, and punctuation, the substance is ideas. In reading, the surface is calling out exactly the right words on the first try, substance is following the meaning and knowing it is OK to back up if things suddenly don't make sense. Then I mentioned Richard Allington's article on good and poor readers and how different their reading experiences are. Good readers read silently and to themselves; poor readers, out loud, for all to witness, word-call and sound out syllables as the teacher corrects. Though I had Gentile and McMillan's *Stress and Reading Difficulties* in my tote, it seemed premature to flash any real materials in his sensitized face. But when I began to tell him about their list of things that happen in school to humiliate readers, he began to nod furiously in agreement. That each poor reader felt stupid (because of the *treatment* their *performance* of text got in school) brought on another emotional reaction. And he very much agreed that the big correlation between IQ and reading was caused by the vocabulary that people accidently acquire by high-interest reading. He was fascinated to learn that a man could raise his IQ just by reading for pleasure.

I shared with him Ray Rist's findings on how early teacher expectations create student achievement (or failure) and told him that anyone who had learned a language had all the brain power needed to read and write. Then we talked about Smith's assertion that literacy is a social not an intellectual event and that that was why doctors run in families, mechanics run in families, and readers run in families. Smith says people do what they grow up knowing adults in their families are able to do. I said that my own work had shown that growing up illiterate in a literate world guarantees every nonreader a low sense of self-esteem, even though there is tremendous evidence that the survival skills needed to compensate require far more cognitive energy than reading or writing. Harry thought that made sense.

With no family pressure to stay in school, he had been eager to drop out of the eighth grade and start work. That had been the end of it until he entered the service. He was very proud of having qualified for missions requiring that he repeatedly jump out of a helicopter and parachute to the ground. (I began to understand his beaten physical appearance.) More than once while in the air he had seen a buddy jerk and jerk at a cord that failed to work. Once a man facing him had begun to claw at the air in panic as he realized he was falling to his certain death. Such a story! Later, I told him, we would be doing language experience. I explained the process and purpose, based on the theory we had already discussed. We would tape a conversation in which he told me something he felt strongly about. When it had been transcribed, I assured him, he would be able to read it. Based on what he'd heard, he rather thought he could.

He told me a series of stories about reading "lessons" he'd put himself through over the years. None of them had served to do anything except prove over and over that he could not learn. He knew he could learn, he said. Then he shocked me by citing the research I'd only minutes before introduced him to. He could see quite clearly that the "lessons" he had subjected himself to were not really reading. My own throat went dry: I was witnessing assimilation and application of the fastest sort. He was taking the newly acquired information, and relating it to his own experience, using it.

It was difficult to hide my enthusiasm over the prospect of having such a research partner, and that was precisely what he was expected to be if we struck a deal. Did he want to meet again, I asked? He did, but without headphones—that was critical. There was also another problem. "I don't know anyone who can read to me every day," he said, clearly needing to get the terms on the table. Again, I marveled at how he had picked up the detail. I said that I would read to him as much as possible and that we would look for materials that would be interesting and accessible to him.

I was taking exams the next week and so wasn't free, but we agreed to meet in a library the following week on the same day at the same time. He thought a library was a reasonable choice for people who were working on reading.

The interview was taking longer than I'd expected and I had to get to campus. Nevertheless, in keeping with my promise to read to him, I pulled out a copy of my article on the child Arthur, thinking the first page or so would be enough for this session. I told him that he should let me know when he'd heard enough. He agreed, reminding me that learner interest was important. But with each paragraph he became more involved with the text. In the beginning I was holding the copy between us on the table, but when I noticed he was trying to follow along (or was he trying to *look like* he was following along?), I turned it farther and farther in his direction until I was holding the copy almost upside down to myself and following along the margin with my finger. From time to time I would back up and point to a word to be sure he had the place, and he would nod. The notion that Arthur's mother couldn't read struck home for Harry. It made sense in terms of what we'd already discussed. The family's ownership of expensive toys but no children's books also moved him to comment. When we got to the language experience discussion, I started to remind Harry of what that meant, but he already knew. Each time I thought I'd stop reading, he seemed eager to go on, saying nothing, but refusing to look away from the page. I felt like the mythical leprechaun whose captor was afraid of looking away for fear of losing the pot of gold. But to Harry, this text was far more than a pot of gold. He had lived several chapters of Arthur's story in an earlier decade. The part in which Arthur mentions an ominous character in one of his pictures as being a real person in his neighborhood drew a knowing gasp from Harry. He grew remorseful at the revelation that no one in Arthur's extended family could spare even the critical ten minutes a day to share a storybook with him.

Power, child abuse, neglect—word after word, phrase after phrase, section after section, Arthur's story filled him with a sense of familiarity. I wanted to take the time to discuss each line, but I needed to leave and it didn't seem possible to do so without finishing the entire piece. When I did, I wondered whether or not to offer the copy to him. Because the text was difficult and the narrow columns cut many words in half, I was afraid he might get frustrated and discouraged trying to read it alone. Then I saw he already had it in both his hands. No matter that I'd been afraid to pull out my tape recorder, it could never have captured that scene anyway. Nor the next.

The iron was so hot, class or no class, it seemed right to ask him if he wanted to talk about some episode. I could write it down now, put it in my computer and print it out for him to read at our next session. "Oh, no!" he blurted as he simultaneously looked down at his wrist (though he wasn't wearing a watch) and started to jump up. "I can't now!" His entire face looked rushed and troubled. Then, just as quickly, he said, "That was it! Did you see it? That was my filter, just then!" More application . . . what a find!

"It went up when you said . . ." He was unable to repeat my suggestion that we get him involved in the writing process. He looked calm again, but when he tried to pick up his coffee cup, it made loud banging noises on the saucer before he let it go and forced both hands into his lap.

"You've jumped out of helicopters!" I wanted to yell, "yet, you're afraid of a pencil. That's not reasonable!" But I knew it was reasonable, perfectly reasonable. He'd suffered a few broken bones and had faced death a hundred times jumping out of helicopters. He'd been shot at, too. But none of that gave him the deep, sickening agony that he'd suffered over not being able to write. His fear was perfectly reasonable, all things considered. So I said, "When you're ready, you've got some great stories to tell, interesting stories."

Two hours before what would have been our next meeting, the phone rang. It had been snowing in the mountains and Harry was calling to say he couldn't get to the road. He needed to cancel. No problem, I assured him, we'd just meet the next Friday.

The next Friday, about two hours before the time we were to meet, the phone rang. If he hadn't identified himself, I wouldn't have known it was Harry. He was desperately sick and had to cancel. I didn't reschedule another session—I don't condone killing people in the name of research. It was a frustrating feeling; here almost within my grasp was a chance to reclaim a genius, and he was hiding from the pain that he'd been taught came with literacy. Cognitively he'd grasped every reason not to be afraid, but he *was* afraid. I've seen this fear before; it is common among the many who are mishandled in school. They often enroll in adult classes and then never show up again: the process itself is traumatizing. The courage to keep trying has to come from within. An outsider can't manufacture motivation strong enough to counterbalance the burden on the mind. There is no magic catapult to keep them coming back; they must boost themselves over the wall of terror. Some never make it.

Three weeks after his sick call, I called Harry's home. His girlfriend answered and said she'd have him call. He never did. He was hiding out and running away from the everpresent dragnet of literacy. Harry was a fugitive.

Maureen: Poised for Flight

Even over the telephone, there was something very likable, very sweet, about Maureen. It was not just her expressions of gratitude for the help I was giving her son Beau or the obvious empathy she felt for all of her children; Maureen had the spirit of a proud fawn, trying to take a stand while poised to run away in the same moment. During our first phone conversation, she decided to stay, long enough, at least, to try to find out how to spare her children more of the agony of academic disaster.

Beau was her primary concern. He was so like her, she said, so wary of unproven claims, and—she appreciated my having already observed—so bright and inquisitive. We talked in generalities for some time about the problems of illiteracy and the ways it could be prevented before she confirmed that Beau's was a stereotypical case. Like Harry, Maureen was quickly able to convert theory to anecdote, particularly ones about Beau. He had been abused by his father and neglected by her and she regretted it. She'd been seriously using drugs when he was little and just didn't look after him or his sister. Both older children had been damaged in the early years and had very low self-esteem. But now she was eager to set things right.

Her own goal was to work as a drug counselor. Indeed, she had started to enroll in a local program, but, confronted with the mass of reading required, had retreated before beginning. She just didn't want the embarrassment of having to face people who could tell she couldn't read.

"Can't read?" I queried. "What kinds of things *can* you read?"

Maureen was not accustomed to thinking in terms of could dos. Her talk was laced with inabilities. But after some prompting, I discovered she was really a low-level literate, knowing the alphabet, street signs, and store names, not much else. She didn't correspond with anyone and was completely under the control of a domineering husband who was very willing both to ridicule her incompetencies and to make her pursuit of self-improvement almost impossible. This portrait of an oppressive figure maintaining control of his family through intimidation confirmed the presence of a disempowering significant other for both the illiterate mother and her son. As she described the present unsettled situation (their home was on the market), I recalled Beau's inability to commit to any long-term activity because he might be moving away. Since the realtors could show the house at any time, Maureen had to be sure it was always in order. She didn't like housekeeping, but her husband would become enraged if anything was out of place. He was afraid that prospective buyers might be dissuaded if the house wasn't immaculate. Given the recession, a sale could be lost over the slightest hitch. Indeed, although there had been a couple of earlier full-price offers that had fallen through for reasons her husband wouldn't discuss with her, Maureen said the listing agent had recently suggested they lower the price. How soon did they need to move? Well, that was kind of hard to say, but having the house on the market did keep Maureen within its walls. Though she seemed to welcome *any* deterrent to competitive situations, I began to wonder if the threat of moving wasn't just an effective way to manipulate both Maureen and her son, who had just begun to read. After all, the house had been on the market for nearly three years.

Some years before, Maureen had been hired by a small company and had worked her way up to manager. The paperwork terrified her, but she discovered that if she got off by herself where no one could watch her, she could manage. Yes, she'd never thought of it that way before, but she had had some success. Unfortunately, the company had closed and Maureen was afraid to try anything else.

Her teenage daughter was a poor reader too, but Maureen felt the girl read better than her mom. But related self-esteem problems manifested themselves in overeating and a fear of meeting strangers. Maureen wanted to help her but didn't know how. I explained that I had a very full schedule, but was willing to do what I could in a couple of visits. We talked about theory and strategies, and Maureen seemed relieved to find she might still be able to help her daughter.

There were also three younger boys. They, as might be expected, were also nonreaders, but Maureen was quick to

point out that at least she wasn't on drugs any more and
she knew that was having a major impact—she could see the
difference between the two sets of children. Beau was particularly attached to his five-year-old brother and tried to protect
him from their dad as much as possible. That was really good
news. We discussed the possibility of getting some good, low-
level books that Beau could read to the five-year-old and that
Maureen could eventually read to the younger children.
Knowing that the family didn't have book funds in the budget,
I offered to visit some used-book stores and see what I could
find. In the process, I would search for a sampling of early-
teen books mother and daughter might share. Maureen was
elated.

It was several weeks before I found some appropriate books,
but when I called Maureen to say that I'd found some good,
inexpensive material that she was welcome to use as long as
she wished, she was eager for me to come right over. On the
next available date, I did.

When I got to the house, no one answered for quite some
time. When the door was finally opened a crack, it was by a
very chubby young girl whom I'd obviously just awakened,
even though it was midmorning on a school day. I handed
her my card and asked for her mom. Maureen wasn't there,
and the girl didn't know when she would be back. I left a
message for her to call me when she came in.

The following Saturday I called again, reaching Maureen's
husband, the man who had handled an earlier call of mine quite
oddly when I'd tried to reach Beau for summer scheduling. He
said Maureen was in the shower and to call back in ten minutes. When I called back, there was no answer at all.

Two weeks later, I called one last time. Maureen was sorry
she had not been at home when I had come; there had been
a family emergency. I said that I still had the books in my
trunk, but when she didn't invite me over, I didn't press. She
was trying to figure out what to do with her little boys that
afternoon, and when I mentioned that her local library had a
story hour, she sounded genuinely grateful. She never went

to the library, she said. She had to take her daughter for schoolwork sometimes, but always waited outside. On second thought, she *had* been to a library once a long time ago. Though the details escaped her, she vaguely recalled not having a very good time and never went back.[2]

But for now she seemed willing to enter one for the sake of her children, if she had something safe to do and no other risks to take. A story hour. And she could just watch how they did it. Yes. That sounded like a very good idea. She would do it. Later, when she was free, she could call and I'd bring her the books I'd selected specifically for her and her children. I saw no advantage in trying to push any harder than that. She was a fragile human being struggling against tremendous odds to protect her children from their father and illiteracy. It was easy to see how she'd fallen into substance abuse and why it was so difficult to change. She deserved credit for just thinking about it.

We never talked again. If she didn't call me, I doubt she called anyone else about literacy help. By all indications, like Zintozonke and Harry, Maureen is a fugitive too.

Postscript

I never met Maureen face to face. Harry and I met only once. Because Zintozonke met with Judy and me several times over an extended period, you might be tempted to hope that she was different. But literacy is a frame of mind, reflecting a value system that is ingrained in the literate person's lifestyle.

It is reflected not just in the fact that a person *has* books—you and I knew that after a trip to Arthur's book-filled home. It is reflected in the interaction of the individual with reading and writing—how the person thinks about the process of using or making text. Though she complained of relentless boredom and went to great lengths to look literate around friends who could read, Zintozonke was almost uncatchable at lesson time and she never returned to the public library. Nor did she return the book and magazines she borrowed. It was not that she held these materials in low regard, quite the contrary: she held them in very high regard. Like the books in Arthur's living room or the ones safeguarded by Madonna, Zintozonke's book and magazines were placed in a very visible, very safe, inaccessible place, on the display shelf of her glass-topped coffee table in her living room. There, small corpses of unfulfilled hope, they rest in unread peace, just out of Zintozonke's reach.

The big difference between fugitives and other adult non-readers (who do complete programs of one kind or another) is that fugitives are so afraid, they physically flee the scene. Intellectually they know to ask for help—by registering for classes, by hiring a tutor, by purchasing a box of programmed learning materials, by pleading for a literacy volunteer. But when the actual lesson looms, the fugitive has a limitless repertoire of escape tactics. Conscious? Subconscious? That doesn't matter. What does matter is that the fugitive may be impossible to reach.

Theory, by itself, is not sufficient to lure the fugitives out of hiding. All three of these adults fully understood not only why they'd failed but also that they had the potential to succeed. I find their understanding a clear indication that something went horribly awry in their early schooling. The quality of education provided each and every student demands accountability. But rather than holding the *student* accountable for an insensitive standard or a set of items on a checklist, it seems most reasonable for our educational *providers* to be accountable to the one who best knows whether things are or are not working—the student. That's where the power of theory will be most valuable.

1. Although I've used the term *preliteracy* earlier to describe children not yet associated with text, I'm using it here to describe adults who have not yet acquired literacy but are expected to acquire it. *Aliteracy* describes a person who can negotiate text to some degree but chooses not to engage in text use.

2. Bad library experiences in connection with poor readers come up again and again. They were a major issue regarding access to reading materials in the gang literacy project. The child Farra had been condemned to failure in the first grade over library books. I had watched Danny's enthusiasm get swatted down over some kind of library card problem, and Mitzi had nearly stopped checking out books because of a fine. Zintozonke was nearly shut out of the system while trying to get a card when a clerk disapproved of how crudely Zintozonke wrote on the application. Maureen's was one in a long line of negative reactions to public libraries.

Nine

The Power of Theory

Poor- and nonreading adults can take charge of their own learning and achieve literacy, and the resulting empowerment can affect all other areas of their lives. For this to happen, however, they need to know what we know; they need empowering theoretical frameworks. Then, as before-and-after experts in inappropriate and then appropriate pedagogy as well as firsthand witnesses of what has been possible in their own lives and the lives of their children, these new literates have a vantage point that cannot be rivaled by the external observer; they have the inside view.

It takes courage for educators to explain to their students what they are doing and why. Such an approach calls upon the person of unquestioned authority to risk self-analysis and to be willing to change *in process*. Part of the change I am suggesting here is to allow the subject the right and responsibility of informed decision making. Empowering educators design solutions that make sense to individual learners at particular times. Empowering pedagogy is a fluid way of being and working that has discovery as everyone's goal. It requires an ongoing recognition that the truths of today may be the falsehoods of tomorrow and that what is obviously right here and now may be assuredly wrong in a different time and place. Even the theory I'm espousing here must be constantly questioned. If it stands up to the fierce scrutiny of those who use it, well and good. If it proves faulty, it must make way for more effective theories.

When the power of theory is placed into forsaken hands, amazing things can happen. But not overnight. And not without ongoing support. True, empowering pedagogy has very quick, very obvious results. But understanding a theoretical connection in the moment and applying it to the past does not ensure long-term success. Long-established patterns of behavior and ways of thinking not only need time to be displaced by new ones, they need support—far more support than if the desired patterns had been fostered in the first place; old prophecies die hard. Though Danny began to read during his fourth session, remember that he needed his little blue book of studies just to defend his arguments at home, arguments for which his own ability to read served as undeniable evidence. And although sixteen to twenty-two weekly or biweekly sessions proved to be the magic number in which my efforts began to effect behavioral changes, none of these participants were ready to grab a book and walk off into the sunset of literacy. They all needed more focused, individualized attention.

How that attention might be packaged should be the subject of considerable experimentation. Adult education programs, community colleges, libraries, and community centers are obvious headquarters for continuing literacy education. House calls and distance education (teleconferences, two-way video communication, etc.) are also appropriate delivery systems in some cases. But this is the place to stretch, not limit, the possibilities. Lest we yield to the temptation to find fast fixes (like the training programs Henry went through) or easy-to-market, attractively packaged programs without benefit of theory or even field testing (like the computer reading program Charlie tried), it is critical that we focus on learning and the learner, engaging the learner in informed, empowered decision making. To that end, we can follow some very basic guidelines.

Tell the truth. And don't lie.

If we vow to tell the truth, we are free to back off when we are wrong. If we hide behind a cloak of mystery, using the old "Trust me" or "Because I said so" instead of reason, we are forced to carry a very heavy burden of guilt each time we fail.

You'll get a better job if you do better in school is simply not true if there are no jobs where you live. Jobs are about supply and demand; only when there are jobs will any qualifications count.[1] The truth might be *You'll have a better life if you enjoy reading* or *You'll have a more interesting life if you understand more about the world* or *Writers have more power than nonwriters do.* Recall that Madonna found reading before bed made her more relaxed. Jonathan (who did get a job) began to explore the *American History* magazines he'd never seen before. And Danny discovered that through the newsletter he could inform the world of injustices a tutor with "a loud mouth" had made against a student. When students discover they have been told the truth, they can deal with the related realities . . . realistically.

Let me give an example of a categorical lie: If you'd tried *harder*, you would have learned better. Nearly every subject had been accused of failing to try, failing to go the extra mile in some distant classroom. How unreasonable! In the real world learning is a natural consequence of being engrossed in meaningful work. How silly it would be to tell an engineer that he would have designed a better bridge if he'd gotten more gray hair in the process or an architect that you can tell by the absence of crow's feet that her buildings aren't timeless. Such observations reflect no reflection, yet they are made by alleged educators day after day. Sure, the eyes may burn from reading relentlessly and the back may grow stiff from sitting too long at the computer, but if the task is intriguing, important, and achievable, there is no need to command misery into the equation. The work will drive itself. People want to learn. The prospect of discovery pulls them across oceans and into outer space. We didn't go to the moon because of hard work, we went because we needed to know what was there. Jonathan struggled to read his girlfriend's science fiction book because it was interesting *to him*; Madonna investigated the adult school programs around her because *she* needed to; Danny drove to a lecture in Los Angeles because *he* had to hear it. Learning is a powerful motivator. And that's the truth.

Don't call it reading if it's something else.

Reading is the process of using text as a jumping off place for thought. It is a thinking, decision-making process. It is about using text in meaning-filled ways to expand the reader's mental universe. Activities that do otherwise may have a purpose, but they must be called whatever they are. Calling something that is *not* reading *reading* spreads misinformation and leads to learning disorders.

In 100 percent of the cases discussed here, the students had been involved in school "reading lessons" that had failed to show what reading was about at all! One hundred percent of the time there had been no story reading to students, no sharing of good books, no discussion of authorship or audience or purpose. Nothing suggested that reading was pleasurable and that pleasure reading was good. Nothing suggested that reader interest was essential to comprehension. Nothing allowed that some people prefer this and others that. No one had ever engaged these nonreaders in discussions about beautiful pictures or about questions they might have regarding what the author had reported. Yet, with all that missing, 100 percent of the time they had been forced to engage in activities that *masqueraded* as reading. One hundred percent of the time they were the victims of a terrible lie and the joys of reading had been hidden from them—in the very schools that called *them* failures!

Yet each of these documented, total failures was able to understand that one of the fundamental features of developing literacy is *being read to for pleasure*. Hearing that being read *to* for pleasure is the first step in the literate home—that it is the means by which story forms and writing style and a love of good books are developed—these people not only agreed to be read to, they enjoyed it. And perhaps as important, they were able to discuss many ways in which they could see their own literacy emerging as a result. Being read to initiates the joy of reading.

If we have a sound reason for having children stand up and bark sounds so their classmates can laugh and ridicule, let's at least tell them it's "bark and ridicule" time. Perhaps when we all understand exactly what it is we're doing and use the correct and commonly understood words to describe it, we'll be able to discuss how much what we are doing leads to what we say we want to accomplish.

Having to read aloud was a source of pain and agony reportedly inflicted in school on every nonreader here. It began in the early years and continued into high school unless, of course, he or she dropped out. But it often also manifests itself throughout life as adults are afraid to speak up in private conversations or speak out in public places. A call to speak can drive the filter up in seconds; for some, just the thought of performance instills terror.

Jonathan reported that all of his high school teachers would confirm that he hated reading. When confronted with round-robin reading, he told me he would glare at the offending teacher and pretend to refuse (the real problem, of course, being that he was unable). In an early reading class in which his teacher had students use a microphone for oral reading practice, Jonathan got a D because he would not go up to the mike. He *acted* hostile because he was scared to death. As Beau discussed how oral reading in high school made him feel, the young dropout said he "wanted to go out for a drink of water and never come back." Is this surprising? How many students are pushed out of school by teachers who press for immediate performance? Theoretically speaking, such practice is calling for *output* before sufficient *input* has been provided.

The book *Stress and Reading Difficulties* helped all my research partners understand that theirs was an affective issue. Forced public performance drives up the affective filter and impedes learning . . . in public classrooms at all grade levels every day across America. Theory helps to define inappropriate practice.

Beware of overgrouping and labeling.

Labels and overgrouping stigmatize for life. They are responsible for the missing-joy factor in school. No one would challenge the notion that advanced calculus students and basic numeracy students need different kinds of exposure to math. But to divide a group of students based on whether they could make correct change for a dollar bill when some had never actually held a dollar or a dime would be silly to anyone. The basic feel for making change would best be fostered by letting those who could and those who could not make change work together—with real change. How long would it take you to show me that there are ten dimes in a dollar?

Yet those who have touched books are quickly removed from those who have not, when both might gain a lot through interaction. Instead of connecting with the literate society at school, the nonreaders are labeled as intellectual outcasts in need of different basics from those who come from literate homes. The stigma of ability grouping makes people feel bad.

It must be acknowledged that individual teachers effectively counteract overgrouping all the time. About five years ago I heard two teachers discuss how they'd gotten some poor sixth-grade readers to visit a second-grade classroom in the same school. Each week the older kids read stories they'd been practicing to the younger ones one-on-one, without the threat of ridicule. The result was better reading and self-esteem for the older kids and a sense of security for the younger ones, who suddenly had big friends on the playground. The ideas of prophecies, filters, risk taking, and club membership were all demonstrated in this refreshing experiment. When I encountered one of the teachers at a conference recently, I asked her if she had ever gotten around to writing about it. She hadn't and wasn't doing the matching anymore. Complaints about the noise level from all that reading had dampened her and her colleague's enthusiasm, and anyway the other teacher had now left the profession. The young woman said that special ed kids get a bad rap, noting that she felt it was *who* was making the noise rather than *how much* noise was made that had really been the issue.

Jonathan, Madonna, and Arthur specifically addressed the stigma of ability grouping. Jonathan said that in order to avoid explaining what his "special" fourth-grade reading class was for, he lied, answering "I don't know. I don't know." Nevertheless his classmates began to look at him differently. And the stigma was honored later on, and not only by his schoolmates. He reported that his high school art teacher "hates special ed kids."

Madonna, though she felt she couldn't learn to read, was mortified over being in a class for the retarded, and begged her mother to get her out of it. Though she hated being pregnant, it was a welcome relief compared with her "special" status at school.

And Arthur, after being moved to a special reading room, sensed that everyone was watching him go in there and said, "They all know I'm stupid." He didn't say *think* he said *know*. Before students are labeled in any way, it would be wise to consider the self-fulfilling prophecy.

Don't call it writing if it's penmanship.

All of these informants totally confused handwriting with the ability to document ideas. "I'm not a good writer" was used interchangeably to mean "My penmanship is unlovely" and "I can't get my ideas from my head to my paper." Arthur complained to his illiterate mom about the severe boredom of his handwriting lessons. But she had been taught that if you can't get the right answers, the least you can do is make "it" look nice, so she ignored his complaints, saying that that was how school was and he might as well get used to it. Handwriting practice was being used to waste Arthur's time. Eventually it may be used to push him out of school. According to the Educational Testing Service's 1992 survey of student attitudes toward writing, in 1990, 62 percent of the fourth graders believed they were good writers, but only 44 percent of the eleventh graders felt that way. After all those intervening years of schooling, shouldn't it have been the other way around? And the 1992 *Condition of Education* said that "in 1990, male eighth graders produced writing proficiency scores similar to female fourth graders." Is it possible that little boys are so intimidated about handwriting over the years that their writing fails to develop? Arthur was being told to focus on form, not ideas, in the fourth grade.

Even though Danny was incapable of handwriting (remember how he trembled like a palsied old man?), he proved he was capable of generating written text using simple word processing on the computer. Fortified with that success, Danny suggested that Harry (one of the fugitives) could easily have learned had he also been taught with recorded language experience. Those sensitized to pencils by early misteaching must be taught the writing process without them. In the process they may be able to unravel what has caused their disabling fear of risk taking.

Don't call it homework if it can't be done at home.

Impossible assignments disempower. Farra, who was about to fail the first grade, was given library books to take into her chaotic home even though her teacher had no idea whether anyone there knew what to do with them. Was an illiterate mom supposed to read to her? Her teacher's impossible expectations taught Farra that she was inept.

Mitzi, who had already failed the first grade, was given "spelling" homework that required she write sentences using a list of words neither she nor her mother could read. In what way was this spelling if she didn't even know what the words were? And there wasn't a teacher in her home to assist her. What was she to do?

Arthur, in danger of failing the fourth grade, had consistently failed to do parent-centered homework assignments with parents who neither could nor wanted to do homework.

What was the goal of those assignments? What was the theoretical rationale for their design? If Arthur had been able to ask those questions, he might not have ended up saying, "They all know I'm stupid."

These children had no way of evaluating the appropriateness of the school's requirements. How different life might have been had their teachers first explained that in order to do homework, there needed to be a home with some very specific features, features that are also the essence of an effective classroom:

- A quiet, well-lit study area.
- A safe place in which to leave books and papers.
- Comfortable furniture.
- A library.
- Reference books.
- A full belly and a rested body.
- A caring, capable teacher.

How different might life have been had it been the teacher's responsibility to ensure that home teachers were available before saddling these children with tasks they were otherwise guaranteed to fail?

Replace the boring with the important.

When we care about what we're doing, we're not likely to be bored. This is a big deal when you consider that everyone whose story I tell in this book found school a boring place. School that isn't interesting to the students fails them. Were he setting up a school, Jonathan said he would make sure it was interesting for every student so they would want to stay there.

The theoretical discussions about boredom I had with Jonathan and my other research partners caused me to clarify my own thoughts on the topic. Some years back I attended my first conference of the Comparative and International Education Society, a gathering of people from all levels and walks of life and from all over the globe. What struck me as extraordinary about this particular group was that it was the responsibility of the individual participants to get the most they could from the conference. People felt free to get up and walk out in the middle of a presentation in order to go hear something else. If you were bored at a CIES meeting, you were at fault for not changing things. There wasn't time to pretend. The purpose of the conference was to learn.

How different school would have been for these students had they been free to seek out the interesting. What if someone had been available to discuss the stock market daily with Beau? What if Jonathan had been exposed to National Public Radio instead of swing-twisting rules? What if Reynaldo had been introduced to Frank Lloyd Wright? What if Madonna had worked in her school library and had gotten to select storytellers? What if Danny had spent his years in school writing about issues of social importance? What if Henry had started writing a book about life as a migrant child? Mightn't this world be a different place if someone had cared enough to show these folks that they were smart enough to do anything they wanted to do? Boredom is not a sign of stupidity but a sign of a brain in need of something to learn. Understanding that, Beau was able to look at his own daydreaming as a positive rather than a negative. And Jonathan was able to see the boredom he felt during lunch and breaks at work as a sign his very able mind needed to read.

Boredom is a way of wasting time in place, and wasting time is unforgivable. "Busy work" is a sick practice that figured much too largely in the academic lives of all these nonreaders. In his initial interviews, under the misbelief that he was a defective student, Danny suggested that teachers just hadn't known much back when he went to school. But the evening he began to read, he immediately grasped the implications of the years he had wasted in disempowering classrooms. "Why didn't *they* do this?" he began to ask out loud. And his son Charlie, who had had a very friendly relationship with his high school computer lab instructor, initially was equally un-willing to think anything negative about his schooling. But when he suddenly realized how simple making his own words come out of a machine could be, his lament echoed his father's verbatim: "Why didn't *they* do this?"

Jonathan grew increasingly intolerant of the nice folks who had been paid to educate him but who had chosen instead to run what he termed a "baby-sitting" service. He resented the lost years he might have spent being read to and reading to himself. Madonna and Henry had each spent *eight years* in the formal system. Danny had spent *twelve years* in school and had an excellent attendance record. The same for Charlie. Jonathan had spent *eleven years* in school. Beau had spent *eleven years* in school, though his attendance had been erratic. Henry had spent about *ten years* in the formal system and had "success-fully completed" countless training programs. What *in the world was going on in all those classrooms for all those YEARS???*

Danny, Madonna, Jonathan, Beau, and Henry all cited specific school efforts to waste their precious time. Once they understood what might have been done instead, they also understood how the system had disempowered them. How valuable the power of theory would have been early on!

Don't use external rewards and punishments to manipulate.

When what is going on in the classroom grips the imaginations of the people there, artificial motivators are a silly waste of resources. People instinctively need to learn; in fact they can-not help it. Why invent "rewards" that insult the intelligence?

Jonathan found being taken out to lunch as a reward for finishing an assignment meaningless and degrading. When Madonna won a Special Olympics trophy in a race in against her retarded classmates, she was humiliated and tried to hide the trophy as she crept home. Inequity makes everyone a loser.

Empowered with theory, Jonathan and Madonna under-stood that this school-fostered manipulation violates all that is written about critical thinking—these kinds of controls are part and parcel with those used to force rats through mazes and dogs to salivate at the sounds of bells. Understanding behaviorism, Jonathan and Madonna identified school tests and capricious homework assignments as tools used to disem-power those the school has failed to serve.

Grades are the most insidiously effective external devices because they are misrepresented as academic success or failure. No one cares enough to tell the truth. Students in advantaged schools know the secret—that academic success is what hap-pens when an unexpected tumble of discoveries occurs in the life of the learner. Academic success is when the lights go on. Academic success is when a person suddenly realizes that she or he can't get enough information about a given topic. Academic success is when the learner realizes that she or he knows a great deal about something very interesting. Aca-demic success is that consuming experience of not being able to stop thinking about whatever it may be that is vitally inter-esting to the learner—even if it is not in the curriculum. *There had not been one flicker of academic success in all the years of all the lives of all the learners in this study.*

From the time they were little children, all these learners had been instructed to work for grades. Therefore they weren't able to see grades as external negative motivators, behaviorist rewards for doing something a person is not naturally drawn toward. Good grades had been accepted as proof of intellectual ability by every person I interviewed; all had *wanted* good grades in school. To varying degrees all had *worked hard* to get them. Yet none had achieved high marks. Grades serve to undermine those not taught in school; grades perpetuate artificial stratification; grades identify the underclass; grades undermine the disempowered; grades teach the oppressed that they are worth less and so should expect less of society's pie.

When I told my subjects about behaviorism and what that meant in terms of success and decision making, they were able to see that their negative reactions to irrelevant tests were intelligent, not deviant. (Can you imagine attending a conference and then taking a test and then getting a grade? It is we who evaluate the conference, not the reverse. And it is the speakers, not the door prizes, that get us to attend. Come to think of it, door prizes are used to coax people to stay when the event is boring.) External motivators are designed to manipulate movements, not stimulate thinking. Unearned lunch "prizes" or the failure to "win" them, meaningless trophies, tests, grades, school buzzers, labels, and dress codes are ways of training the masses to become obedient soldiers (less necessary in a peaceful world), rote assembly-line workers (jobs now being done by robots), and model prisoners. How much more of this does our society require? And how should we decide who participates—who invests that irreplaceable commodity, time—who forfeits his or her human potential? Perhaps it is time to discuss these matters with the clientele.

When in doubt, ask the authority.

To be sure, students cannot know what they don't know, so asking for closed-end goals up front would be foolishly limiting. But students can identify needs *in process* that those responsible for setting things up may have completely overlooked. It is so easy to replicate the familiar. All too frequently we decide what the intellectual and behavioral outcomes of a curriculum should be, without regard to the possibility that some learning is unpredictable. And given the preponderance of yes-butters and naysayers within the traditional channels of control, ideas from those unaware of perceived impossibilities might provide heretofore unimagined solutions. That is to say, we can introduce the philosophy of critical thinking into the day-to-day practice of our schools. Besides, if we want to serve the consumer in a way that will truly foster club membership, we must encourage the student to assume the responsibility for identifying specific improvements. And then we must allow new, informed solutions to evolve . . . a kind of ongoing field test of what's working and what would work even better.

One day I asked Jonathan what he would change if he had the power to make things better at school. As he tried to be heard above the noise of the relentless public address system and painfully loud buzzers that occasionally drowned out his voice on my tape, Jonathan said he would definitely change the furniture. The desks for the students seemed to him deliberately uncomfortable. The teachers get to sit in nice chairs with padding, he observed, while students are stuck in hard wood or plastic that never fits the body. It struck him as a class distinction, a deliberate affront, every time he tried to cross his legs or turn around. Physical comfort, Jonathan pointed out, was an elementary part of Maslow's hierarchy of needs. But then he went on to say that caring counts.

Schools need ways to show the individual students that they are cared about. Though most of the people I had worked with reported having "gotten away with" rule violations, most sensed that no one fully understood what they needed or cared about their satisfaction with school. To remedy that situation, Jonathan said he would have someone "actually help out . . . come around and say, 'Well, do you have any questions?' or 'Anything I can do to help you?' It would be a whole lot better. You'd make the other person *feel* a little better . . . someone saying, 'Yeah, there's actually someone here to help you.' "[2]

The library legacy must be for everyone.

Right now, our school and public libraries are monuments to our societal inequities. For a quick overview of who we've appointed to be the literate elite and who the disposable and voiceless labor force, check your local hours and holdings.

A colleague of mine recently called to share the good news that he'd been engaged to participate in a special grant program to study the effects of increased self-esteem on an identified group of minority students in a low-income elementary school where test scores had been declining. Getting the special treatment was expected to cause test scores to rise among these students. The one-year pilot program would be continued if the kids did as well as expected. The principal at the school had made it clear to my colleague that he was eager to do anything possible to help the kids in his school improve their test scores.

"Well, tell him to open his school library and to make sure it's open before and after school and during lunch and breaks so kids can get at the books they want," I suggested.

"What do you mean, open it?" he asked.

"If it's a poor school where the scores are low for all the kids, you can bet the library's closed and reading has taken a back seat to budgeting," I explained. A closed library sends a loud, clear message that literacy is not part of the curriculum. Since my colleague is a statistician with an insatiable need for numbers, I knew he'd take me up on my next suggestion. "Go to the principal and explain that you're interested in finding out about the leisure reading habits of his kids," I said. "Then get him to take you to the library so you can see how things are laid out. Find out how many books per student this library holds. Also find out how many kids per week go through the library. That should take you about thirty minutes. After that, go to the most affluent school in the area and do the same. I'll bet you'll find a powerful correlation between the child/book ratio, the library use/hours available and the school's test scores across the curriculum."

According to the National Center for Education Statistics, by 1985 almost 94 percent of all public schools had libraries or media centers and the average number of book volumes was 7,668.[3] But what the stats don't show are how many of those school libraries are actually open, how they are staffed, by whom, for how much time, or who actually uses them. Though in general terms we can see that small schools usually have fewer library books than large ones—in itself suggesting a variety of questions in terms of choices—the formally reported figures don't reveal the quality or condition of the holdings.

Nor do they tell us that in one elementary school library hours depend on the availability of a community volunteer while in another the librarian hauls in new books from conferences and promotes them to any reader she can find. Such differences show up only if you go and look and wait in the hall with the child who must return a book to avoid a fine that might wipe out bus fare or lunch money, perhaps on the day of a standardized test . . . or any day. I've been in those halls and listened to those kids.

My colleague was intrigued with the notion that access to libraries might influence scores, and two weeks later he called again. There was, he said, no need for phase two, the affluent-school part of the assignment. His project school's library had long since been closed. And the principal had no idea how many books were in his closed library. "How did you know?" he asked me, "How did you know that library was closed?"

"It's the rule," I told him. "When the library is out of service, test scores go down. In poor schools where the parents are not expected to make literacy demands, the library is closed. That's the rule." When my bowl is full and yours is empty, we don't need a statistician to tell us who's going hungry.

Which is not to say, of course, that every open library really functions as a source of literacy. We found that out when we saw Farra being put through the motions of checking out a library book but never being taught what that meant. She was indoctrinated very early into the punitive world of fines and the consequences of trying to act like a library user when she hadn't been taught library procedures at home.

Nor is class distinction in school libraries an exclusively American matter. Last summer while visiting schools in New Zealand, I had a chance to go to a Maori school, one that prides itself on a bilingual program that has caused a marked improvement in the learning levels of its students. But the library in this school had far fewer authentic bilingual story books than I'd seen in an affluent New Zealand school, and the teacher who was the half-time librarian explained that I would be one of the last people to visit it. That very week, because of budget cuts, the Maori school library was officially closing its doors.

We can turn this situation around. First, we must teach the *literacy basics* in a way easy for both students and teacher. That means *having a well-stocked library* of teacher-selected titles *in each classroom*.[4] This accomplishes four things:

1. Students can browse leisurely rather than feel pressured to grab a book and run.
2. A child unfamiliar with the process is able to ask a knowledgeable adult for help in finding a first book or a next book.
3. An atmosphere of camaraderie is fostered in which students learn to make recommendations to one another.
4. Students learn how to check out books and how to find reference information.

This classroom library system encourages library users club membership.

Then, we need to integrate school library use into the curriculum and make sure the hours and facilities can and do accommodate every student. Closed libraries fail those least able to buy books, the poor and members of illiterate value systems. Such discrimination must be stopped. As for public libraries, the population of this study faced incredible barriers.

When Danny finally found something to check out of the library, he had to stand in a different line to pay off a long-forgotten fine. Had he been alone or in a hurry, he would probably have left without his book. And even though he did overcome that particular hurdle, he chose not to go after more library books. A smidgen of salt makes an open wound sting.

And remember Jonsey, the great big gang member who was brought to tears when I tried to press him to enter the bookmobile? What had happened to him? And remember Maureen, who had to drive her daughter to the library to do school assignments from time to time? Some distant, forgotten library experience had been so bad she waited for her daughter outside. How many Maureens have such terrible though buried memories of libraries that even when they drive up to the door, they can't go in? How many children do those Maureens have? Fines, rules, lines, and restrictions too often serve to sift the marginally literate and laboring classes out of the library system.[5]

And what about access? When Madonna wanted to march her tribe into the library on Sunday mornings, the only day she was assured transportation, her library was closed. And when Henry was ready to take his son by bus on Saturdays after work, there was no library open for them either. The libraries in their neighborhoods did not set their hours to serve blue-collar people, the bus riders, the folks without telephones, the people who need public libraries most.

The costs of *not* letting Mitzi, Danny, Jonsey, Maureen, and Henry feel comfortable about books and libraries are far greater than the fines not collected and the extra or replacement copies not bought. We need a library community outreach beyond the bookmobile. We need librarians who go into neighborhoods, knock on doors, and read to anyone who is at home. And then, when our nonreaders are ready to make the transition into regular libraries, those libraries must be open in *all* neighborhoods *every day*. Libraries are repositories of the joy of literacy; they must be the legacy of all.

Educate equitably.

There was a great deal of comment about President Clinton's decision to send his daughter, Chelsea, to a very expensive private school. The tab, it is said, was $8,000 a year, compared with the $5,237 spent to educate a public school pupil in a moderate-income district (it's $3,100 for the poorest districts).[6] In addition, it was presumed that the President would want to make sure Chelsea got to school and back safely and so would have her picked up and delivered. To that I say: More power to him! He should look after his child. And he was being very honest about what he considered a good school, meaning he had begun to notice that not only are all schools not created equal but there are public schools in the United States to which he would not even have *considered* sending his child. It's about time we had a President who admitted that. After all, the education he gave this child would determine whether she would rise to the occasions of the next century with strength and courage or would grovel in the pit of social discards.[7] Like each valued child in America, she must be nurtured in an environment that will let her be the best she can be. I believe our President should have gone even further. He should have found out exactly what it is that made this school so good. Fortified with information that no other President has had the motivation to get, he would be able to set standards for *every* school serving *each* child in the land. As President, he should value and care for each child as though she were his own.

Consider how much better the future will be when the president cares enough about Farra to make her classroom as good as the one he chose for Chelsea. The school libraries will of course be equal as well. And since the streets of Farra's ghetto are no safer than the one on which Chelsea could not safely walk, both children could be given rides to school. And both will be well fed. When every Farra follows the educational model set by Chelsea, the issues of drug abuse, random violence, and gang membership will be archaic notions from a time well past. The money we spend on education like this will give more predictably positive results, but with a promise beyond imagination. Can we afford *not* to make this the education we choose to buy?

What about funding?

From time to time there are suggestions that volunteer literacy programs like Literacy Volunteers of America can handle the relentless avalanche of adult learners. These organizations have never been consistently endowed with public funds and are hard pressed to cover operating expenses through fund-raising efforts. Such irregular money sources preclude the long-term planning that would make maximum use of volunteer energy. Meanwhile, ironically, the costs of responding to crimes strongly linked to poverty and illiteracy use up money that otherwise might well be spent on literacy programs. "I wish we could have gotten our hands on just part of the money spent recently on that big drug war party," said Linda Light, director of the Huntington Valley Literacy Volunteers affiliate, after then-drug czar William Bennett had conducted a major PR campaign at a remote resort in Southern California. "The money they spent on helicopters and other exotic transportation gimmicks could have bought a lot of books."[8]

Light spends about a third of her time writing grant proposals and following through with the related reports. Nearly every day a new proposal form lands on her desk. Sometimes the requirements are too restrictive or the time lines too short. Often private and governmental funders are interested in new, creative programming rather than in maintaining current programs. And since volunteers who have gone through the eighteen-hour basic training quickly meet their fifty-hour or six-month commitment, the tutor education program is ongoing.[9] Under the current system of funding, volunteer literacy systems cannot offer the incentives that might foster long-term retention of literacy volunteers. So, literacy education, like all other public education, is by and large the domain of reliably funded agencies.

The educational legacy I advocate—and that is essential, not optional—of course depends on our tax dollars. The current funding base for our schools gets 46 percent of its money from local sources, 48 percent from the state and only 6 percent from the federal government.[10] This of necessity creates a narrowing spiral for schools in areas where the tax base is diminishing, and that in turn means an ever greater underclass from which fewer and fewer families will ever emerge. It means the rich get richer, the poor get poorer, and the middle class gets vacuumed out of existence. And that signals the decline and fall of the great American experiment. To those who—for whatever reason—ask rhetorically, *How can we pay for education when the world's economy is in a tailspin?* I respond: *We already do.* Our only decisions are *which* education to buy and *how* to make the payments.

Our quick participation in the extraordinarily expensive war in the Middle East gives a clear message to the American people that when there is a very high priority, there are ample funds. We have also chosen to send tanks, guns, and personnel to Somalia to protect their food supply. Despite the underlying humanitarianism and the peace-keeping assurances, most of us sense that tanks and guns in any language suggest aggression. (Had a superpower moved into Southern California to keep peace during the LA riots, the most peaceful of us might have risen with whatever rocks and bottles we could find.) But as we watch warring tribes of heavily armed men kill one another, anyone who gets in between, and outsiders who try to shift the balance of power, we see that it's not too different from gangs in America, killing off one another's members, any innocents in between, and the police. *The desperate and uneducated will use the only power they have—the power to create anarchy.* And they will fight to the death to keep that power. *People with nothing to lose can be dangerous indeed.* We have paid dearly for this lesson. Has it taught us anything? As a society we have a pressing need to reorder our priorities.

Pragmatists may want to consider this: According to the U.S. Department of Justice, the ratio of convicted criminals in local jails to paid staff looking after them is 3.4:1. That's one staff person for every 3.4 criminals.[11] (Compare this ratio to the class size for urban school children—reportedly 17:1. That's one adult to every seventeen children. And many classrooms have far more children per adult than that.[12]) A very large percentage of the public housing population I worked with had spent at least some time in jail, and Henry had been there numerous times. Mightn't it be more cost effective to provide quality education—to everyone, in whatever ways we can—than to cage, care for, and feed criminals at random intervals for life? And for the adults who have missed learner-centered attention, isn't today a very good day to turn things around?

1. While literacy will not produce jobs, illiteracy can certainly make getting one more difficult. Though the inability to read will not necessarily prevent graduation from high school or even college, it is a big factor in the academic failure that ultimately leads to dropouts. In the ghetto housing project, high school graduates were so rare that in almost a year's time, I never met one. According to the U.S. Department of Education, unemployment is more likely among those with lower levels of education than those with higher. In 1991, 14.8 percent of the unemployed had only one to three years of high school, while only 7 percent of the high school graduates were unemployed, and only 3 percent of those with four or more years college (U.S. Department of Education. 1992. *Digest of Education Statistics*, 383. Washington, D.C.). Understand too that the term "unemployment," because it relates to people currently in the documented job search market, excludes many of the people who would like to have a regular job but who do undocumented day labor, casual labor, or work for friends and relatives on an occasional basis. It also excludes those who have given up the search—or never started it. To be in the labor force means you are documented either as working or actively looking for work. And in 1989–90, only 69 percent of the nation's formal dropouts were in the work force and only 32 percent of those were employed. These figures don't begin to cover the people who have not been documented as dropouts because they left the system in the early years. Any number of Madonna's children, for example, could be overlooked in such a census. And, as has been historically the case, regardless of years of education, women fare significantly worse in earned income than do men (U.S. Department of Education. 1994. *Digest of Education Statistics*, 392. Washington, D.C.).

2. These were Jonathan's insider perceptions. Lacking access to class-size statistics or their impact on education, he had no way of knowing that growing numbers have limited his opportunity to get individual help at school. Nor could he guess that even less help is available to mainstream students.

3. National Center for Education Statistics. *1992 Digest of Education Statistics*. Washington, D.C.; U.S. Department of Education.

4. Joyce Ragsdale, a kindergarten teacher in Long Beach, California, who runs one of the most holistic programs I've ever seen, reads to her children many times each day. She then leaves the newly introduced books standing in the chalk trough for anyone to get at. The books are often borrowed, sometimes lost, and loved to the point that they wear out very quickly. But her kindergarteners, who come from both affluent and very poor homes, all love to read. Ragsdale spends over $2,000 annually to supply her classroom library. (And that donation to education is no longer tax deductible.) Her colleague Gayle Miller, whose first-grade classroom is a science laboratory all year round, has books on all kinds of environmental issues and up-to-the minute experiments. Miller says her out-of-pocket classroom expenses are over $3,000 a year, not counting things like baggies and foil, which she buys along with her own groceries. During the time that I worked with Madonna, I let her keep any books she seemed likely to enjoy or share with her children. I probably invested over $150 on those books. Literacy requires literature.

5. The public library, community college, and university librarians I have interviewed all report that fine collection is not profitable and may discourage library use by the very poor, who cannot risk fines. They also agree that across the board, those patrons who can afford to pay keep the books until they are finished with them. I submit that it is time to rethink procedures, perhaps conducting expected

impact studies on issues involving the service area patrons—all of them.

6. *The Condition of Education*, U.S. Department of Education, 1992. The highest spent in K–12 schools is $8,000 per pupil per year.

7. You may find this an extreme either-or. But I think the possibility of a middle ground is becoming less and less. There are the students guided to apply to West Point, Harvard, MIT, Smith (you know the names), and there are the students who are encouraged to take vocational education classes. It is true that in California there is an enormous state university system available to process huge numbers of middle-class students—new citizen and adult reentry included. And there is the model community college system that offers whatever the local community members want—including opportunities to transfer to the state or other university systems. There is no denying the models of equal opportunity those systems were designed to be. The reality is that the state system is so underfunded that whole departments are closing down (including teacher education programs), students are often unable to get the courses they need to graduate, and entry is by no means guaranteed every citizen who qualifies. Tuition and fees are always on the rise—blocking access to more and more single parents and those in low-income brackets. The community college system also keeps increasing tuition, blocking access to the working poor and those who just want to explore a liberal education. Classes are cut annually, often in areas of great need. (There were 114 people on the waiting list for one of my English-as-a-second-language classes this spring. And people who don't learn English will learn to survive without it.) For more on the community college crisis see Rosow, "The Working Poor and the Community College," *Phi Delta Kappan* (June 1994): 797–801. Sure, there are still chances to overcome unequal access to education. And certainly some of the privileged

will squander their tax-supported gifts. But they are the exceptions—not an entire class of people. Education remains key to middle-class success. And as we remove opportunities to remain in or enter the middle class, we have less and less middle ground. The silent majority of the Nixon era is preparing to become the volatile majority of the twenty-first century's underclass. Through school equity, we can still make a difference. But time is short.

8. Linda Light's office is staffed by two and occasionally three people who share two part-time positions. Grant writing, tutor and student recruiting, tutor training, book and material acquisition, public relations, political participation, and student interviews and evaluation all require professional attention, just as they would at any fully funded agency.

9. The great majority of LVA volunteers do move in and out of the program, having designated a certain amount of time for it and then meeting that goal or simply getting frustrated from dealing with this unreliable population. And a few people volunteer just to get the free training. Not enough volunteers remain in the program for a period of years to make a significant dent in the ever-growing need.

10. *The Condition of Education*, 1992.

11. *Bureau of Justice Statistics Source Book*, 1991; U.S. Department of Justice, Bureau of Justice Statistics, Census of Local Jails, 1988.

12. As I've mentioned, I get into quite a few classrooms a year and really do notice when there are not enough places for all the children to sit and that sort of thing. So I was rather shocked to read that the formally stated pupil/teacher ratio in the U.S. elementary classroom is 17.2:1. Only in a specially funded special education program have I ever seen such a small class. But, to check up on my memory and ability to count, I called veteran elementary teacher Gayle Miller. In her Long Beach classroom,

though she's taught various levels over the years, she's never been scheduled for fewer than thirty kids. There may be a week or so between the drop of one and the arrival of a replacement, making her number as low as twenty-nine, but, like all the classrooms I've seen in Southern California, there are thirty—quite often thirty-two or thirty-three—and sometimes more in the class-room with one teacher and no other adult in the room. She said the times when chicken pox or some other such fast-moving epidemic hits her school, dropping her class size to twenty or even eighteen, she is amazed at how much more she can get done with the kids. "I'd really like to find out how much learning could go on with that size of class for a full year. But I can only guess. I've never had the pleasure of trying it." Miller suggested that sometimes credentialed teachers who are actually assigned to non-classroom jobs are included in the averaging. It's possible that's how the statistics say 17.2 when the actual bodies are upwards from thirty.

Closing Thoughts

*T*he people involved in this study are admittedly the negative products of public education. There is no denying that all across America very effective teachers are doing a great deal with very little. I have been in many of those classrooms and have come away heartened by the tenacity of the gifted teacher in the face of adversity. But there is too much adversity. And education is not supposed to be an *in spite of* activity. It is time to make *every* classroom a place where *every* teacher would want to go *every* day. That would give the students a powerfully positive message during the many hours they are required to be there.

Would National Standards Cause Positive Change?

We are fortunate that the myth of a single instrument to measure anything to do with student language arts performance is finally under fire. The issues of validity (does it measure what it says it measures?) and reliability (are the results obtained over time and over populations consistent?) are key. Though empirical evidence has argued against the use of so-called broad-based tests for generations, the allure of cheap bulk processing—even when it isn't accurate—is tough to resist. Such tests can be administered to huge numbers of people by someone who doesn't know them at all and they can be scored by a machine; this makes them cheaper and faster and ensures their profitability to marketers and administrators. Unfortunately, cheaper and faster is not necessarily good for human beings.

A series of national standards for public school students is currently being developed. This new program is based on what teachers know about how to measure results. Though one might wonder why teachers aren't trusted to measure student success as a matter of course, the heartening part of these standards is that they recommend multiple measures and a variety of efforts over time. This suggests portfolios and narrative reporting will enter general use.

We must watch with interest to see whether the process remains under the control of the teacher, who knows the student, or suddenly shifts to a set of external goals that teacher and student must either rush to accommodate or ignore with full knowledge that doing so will mean "failure" from a national perspective.

Empowerment is key.

Our national priorities must shift toward a literate, empowered population. If we continue to train people to obey like sheep, we will continue to get people who think like sheep. Creative thinking and decision making are mind sets, not isolated events produced when externally summoned. Idea-rich environments give people who have ideas a free rein. We must empower learners with all that we know today so they may create more than we can imagine tomorrow.

Empowerment is not bred in a vacuum. It lives and breathes in an unrestrictive environment that recognizes and respects that the human brain must think to grow. That environment can be kept secure if all participants understand what creates it. If our general population of learners understands literacy theory, it will be impossible for them to be inadvertently disempowered. And those who would willingly limit power once again to a select few at everyone's expense will find the unreceptive audience they deserve to find.

Self-assessment is empowering.

While many experimental processes have been successful in self-evaluation, there is now a process-oriented instrument that has been field-tested among thousands of adult learners over several years. Al Bennett, California State Library Literacy Specialist, has spearheaded a movement to move completely away from the external evaluation of adult learners. The California Literacy Campaign learner inventory (see Appendix C) is a self-evaluation process facilitated by the adult learner's tutor. Though Bennett is cautious not to suggest that it would be appropriate for children (as I predict it would be), he is very pleased that the instrument has been developed and continues to evolve as the direct result of literacy students' and their tutors' input. The version in Appendix C is an early edition (the one I used) and will be replaced by a newer one soon. This self-inventory process is very much in line with the kinds of empowering theory discussed throughout this book. Whatever the current trends in education, we still need to know how education is doing. In a program of learner empowerment, it is the learner who should make that evaluation.

Theory is empowering.

While working on the final edits of this book, I attended the Third North American Conference on Adult and Adolescent Literacy in Washington, D.C. Ruth Colvin, founder of Literacy Volunteers of American—my literacy godmother—was there and royally intimidated me by promising to attend and then showing up at my session, one in which I presented the experimental adult literacy program I'm designing in Beaumont, California. One of the advantages of a California Literacy Campaign program is that the design is left entirely to the local people. Each CLC program is unique, reflecting the needs of the community in which it operates. Having had a year to experiment with the power of theory on a larger scale than my self-funded research has allowed, I had a hefty collection of anecdotes in my brag bag. The program introduction had included, of course, my literacy roots—LVA—and my complaint that this organization's tutor education does not provide the tutors with theory. After my presentation, Ruth invited me to her session that Sunday in which she was presenting the new LVA tutor education program. "I think you'll be pleasantly surprised," she said. I was. It is with extreme delight that I announce to you that the new LVA tutor program includes theory.

Recommendations in a Nutshell

It may seem simplistic to offer seven little solutions to the massive problem of adult illiteracy. However, a philosophical shift is by no means simplistic. The steps that follow are the means by which a transfer of power can take place within the existing framework of public education. Less than this will require dramatically more radical shifts in educational organization.

1. Put theory into the hands of all citizens of all ages.
2. Eliminate anything in the learning environment that does not promote learner empowerment.
3. Put the responsibility for teaching in the schools, where that activity is officially funded—*and fund it.*
4. Fund education as the leading national priority.
5. Put a quality, leisure-reading library in every classroom.
6. Make public literacy (in libraries and through other programs) available to all people, even if they work long hours. Libraries must be open seven days a week, especially in the ghetto.
7. Make empowering pedagogy the standard for all adult education (adult basic education, nongovernmental organizations, schools of continuing education, library literacy programs, prison literacy programs, training programs, etc.)

I know that some of my critics will point out shining examples of people who have managed to survive oppressive homes, shabby schooling, and the very worst society has to offer, who have risen above all kinds of attempts to hold them down. They have learned without being taught and they have gained insights into worlds never heard of. They have thrived on adversity, and they have done so without theory. I offer these people my congratulations and I rejoice in their success. But I think my critics are as well aware as I am that these people are exceptions, not the rule. And I would also ask what these extraordinary people might have become if they'd been on a level playing field—what did we lose without knowing it? Further, I would suggest that if we decide to treat each student as though he or she were our own child, we would have a bumper crop of success stories, so many perhaps that success would become the norm. And I would finally suggest that to do anything less is to provide a foundation of inequity—that very fertile ground for social revolution.

It is empowering for students to understand what is going on in their lives and how they can take charge of the outcomes. It is empowering for students to understand that no teacher has the omnipotent right to make demands "because I say so." Probably none of us has gone through the school system free of inexplicable frustrations that caused us to question our own quality as human beings. But such frustrations occurring day in and day out, over generations, perpetuate the cycle of disempowerment. If the power of theory has made such significant differences when placed in the forsaken hands shown here, think what it might do on a grand scale. Think what it might have done for you.

La Vergne Rosow's Annotated List of Good Books (for adults and children, for themselves, and for gifts)

Dear Book Person,

This is *not* a list of *every good book* I know. It is a representative sampling that I've devised because so many people have asked me how to find good books. I've included notations on what I think makes a particular book special. It is of course impossible to list all the right reasons for buying a book. Take, for example, two Shel Silverstein books, *The Missing Piece* and *The Missing Piece Meets the Big O*.

- I enjoy them myself. They are fun to read. The pictures are nice to look at. The ideas are clear.
- I can read them to a child and the child will enjoy them just as much as I do.
- They are philosophical, having tremendous underlying messages that entertain during the reading and tease the brain long afterward.
- They can be enjoyed by adult ESL students.
- They make wonderful gifts. (I gave the pair of them to friends for a wedding anniversary. I give one or the other to people of all ages for all kinds of occasions and no occasion at all.)

If you're unsure about when to use a book as a gift, let me offer a little help. Books are great gifts for weddings, showers, new babies, old kids, adults, children, birthdays, graduations, going away, wish you were here, welcome back, congratulations, anniversaries, vacations, retirement, new jobs, promotions, or just when you want to say "I care."

And a word about "children's" books. I used to think I had to have a child with me when I went into that special section of the bookstore or at least know a child with a birthday approaching. Then I began telling salespeople I was a teacher, but that got a tad awkward when the inquisitive wanted to know who and where and I answered "engineers at XYZ Corporation." So, now I just tell the truth. I love children's books and want to buy myself a new one, but if I see something that would suit some little kid I know or somebody I know who's not a kid or if there's a gift drive for people I don't know, I may buy an extra book, and if I don't just slip it into my library without thinking, I may actually give it away.

You see why there isn't time for me to say all this and more about every item on my list. But I'm so fond of *Aesop's Fables* that I have a separate section just for them.

Read on!

La Vergne Rosow

Poetry

Where the Sidewalk Ends. Shel Silverstein. New York: Harper and Row, 1974. Humorous, well-illustrated poetry. Good for all ages. Simple language, heavy thoughts; high-spirited spoofs. (The grammar, punctuation, and vocabulary make this a wonderful ESL class text, which is how I've used it several times. Adults love learning these poems and sharing them.)
The New Kid on the Block. Jack Prelutsky, drawings by James Stevenson. New York: Greenwillow, 1984. Prelutsky is the

latter-day Silverstein. These poems have funny twists and truisms.

The Headless Horseman Rides Tonight: More Poems to Trouble Your Sleep. Jack Prelutsky, illustrated by Arnold Lobel. New York: Greenwillow, 1980.

Eric Carle's Animals Animals. Anthologized by Laura Whipple, illustrated by Eric Carle. New York: Philomel, 1989. This book has short poems by authors from around the globe, all with beautiful, imaginitive Carle illustrations.

Seasons. Warabe Aska, with additional poetry selected by Alberto Manguel. New York: Doubleday, 1990. Thought provoking, with beautiful pictures. A wonderful coffee-table book.

Animalia. Graeme Base. New York: Harry N. Abrams, 1986. Large, hardcover picture book, appropriate for all ages. At first blush it looks like an alphabet book, but it will hold all audiences for hours with its inventive alliteration and detailed drawings. It is a gift book and a keep book.

Storybooks

The Giving Tree. Shel Silverstein. New York: Harper & Row, 1964. A very touching story of a boy and a tree who loved him. This story is simple enough for preschoolers but can provoke thoughtful dialogue among those who celebrate symbolism.

Lafcadio: The Lion Who Shot Back. Shel Silverstein. Harper & Row, 1963. This book is about bigotry. The double entendres allow the adult to enjoy one book while reading another aloud to the child.

Babushka Baaba Yaga. Patricia Polacco. New York: Philomel, 1993. This imaginatively illustrated retelling of a Russian folktale teaches a lesson about face value versus heart. Superstition and gossip unfairly influence the life of old Baaba Yaga.

Stellaluna. Janell Cannon. San Diego: Harcourt Brace, 1993. What comes naturally to the young bat Stellaluna makes her a misfit in her adoptive family. She hates the food and the long daylight hours. And she's a negative influence on the good little birds she teaches to hang upside down outside the nest. She is an anthropomorphism of every teacher's most dreaded nonconformist. This book, while appropriate for pre-schoolers, is enchanting to teens and offers an opportunity to empathize to the adult trying to adapt to a strange new culture. Like the Polacco and Silverstein books above, *Stellaluna* faces social issues in a very direct, yet palatable, style.

The Polar Express. Chris Van Allsburg. Boston: Houghton Mifflin, 1985. This book is beautifully illustrated, and is some-times packaged with a recording. It is a touching story about imagination.

The Dark Way: Stories from the Spirit World. Virginia Hamilton, illustrated by Lambert Davis. San Diego: Harcourt Brace Jo-vanovich, 1990. These international myths/folktales are myste-riously written. There is a brief historical accounting of the phenomena at the end of each tale. If you don't know where the cry of the banshee comes from, you need this book. A very fine gift book.

Hershel and the Hanukkah Goblins. Eric Kimmel. New York: Holiday House, 1985. Beautiful illustrations and an eerie story make this a good parent/child read-together book. The last page gives a historical accounting of Hanukkah.

Thirty Chilling Tales: Short and Shivery. Retold by Robert D. San Souci, illustrated by Katherine Coville. New York: Dou-bleday, 1987. These are nice, short, and very well-told folk-tales from around the globe. Good for preteens, teens, adults, and classes.

The Four Million and Other Stories. O. Henry. New York: Air-mont, 1963. These well-written stories for adults have poten-tial for present-day comparisons.

History

How Many Days to America? A Thanksgiving Story. Eve Bunting, illustrated by Beth Peck. New York: Clarion, 1988. This gripping description of a family being driven from their beloved home by soldiers, escaping into the night, and arriving by small boat on American shores connects with refugee students from everywhere. Fine pastel illustrations.

The Star-Spangled Banner. Illustrated by Peter Spier. New York: Doubleday, 1973. This beautifully illustrated book of the text of our national anthem also has historical documentation and a wonderful set of early American flag illustrations. Every American home should have one.

Shh! We're Writing the Constitution. Jean Fritz, illustrated by Tomie dePaola. New York: G. P. Putnam's Sons, 1987. A clearly written and illustrated chronicle of the agonizing and humorous process of writing the Constitution. A copy of the final document (but not the Bill of Rights) is included. A good supplement for any student of U.S. government or history, but too difficult for *very* basic ESL students.

Letters from the Past. The Highgate Collection. Virginia Henkel, illustrated by Bruce Luxford. Petone, New Zealand: Nelson Price Milburn, 1989. In her grandmother's attic a child finds a bundle of old letters written between her grandmother who was living in New Zealand and her grandmother's pen pal, a child living in London from 1910 to 1912. The correspondence ends with the sinking of the Titanic. The beautifully handled story teaches history in the language of ten-year-olds.

The Titanic Lost and Found. Step into Reading Series. Judy Donnelly, New York: Random House, 1987. This book's very clear illustrations and large type relate the story of the ship that was not unsinkable. After he read *Letters from the Past* and this book, a workplace ESL student of mine who had never read for pleasure in any language eagerly moved on to a *National Geographic* story about the Titanic.

Tut's Mummy Lost . . . and Found, Step into Reading Series. Judy Donnelly, illustrated by James Watling; includes photographs. New York: Random House, 1988. An adult ESL student from Egypt recommended it for entry-level ESL. But she *was* exceptional and *did* have some background knowledge. When I reminded her of those two things, she amended her recommendaton to advanced beginner.

(Because many of the Random House Step into Reading books have grade-level indicators on the cover and letters to parents just inside the front cover, they may appear to have been written exclusively for children. I explain to my adult students that this is incorrect, that anyone who enjoys the books should read them. They are high-interest, easy reading for new-reader adults and adult ESL students, and provide a very useful foundation of history. My students agree.)

A Wall of Names: The Story of the Vietnam Veterans Memorial. Step into Reading Series. Judy Donnelly. New York: Random House, 1991. It is impossible to read this with dry eyes. For Americans who are too young to remember, for those who do remember, for ESL students who heard the story very differently, and for Vietnamese students, in particular, this is a powerful little history loaded with universal human issues.

Pompeii . . . Buried Alive! Step into Reading Series. Edith Kunhardt. New York: Random House, 1987. This well-illus-trated large-print story puts the reader at the site of the vol-cano.

Who Shot the President? The Death of John F. Kennedy. Step into Reading Series. Judy Donnelly. New York: Random House, 1988. Large type and historical photographs make this one a winner with adult students of all types.

Witch Hunt: It Happened in Salem Village. Step into Reading Series. Stephen Krensky, illustrated by James Watling. New York: Random House, 1989. High intrigue, large print.

Meet Abraham Lincoln. Step-up Paperback Books. Barbara Cary. New York: Random House, 1989. There is a series of these books, by different authors. They are written in a sim-ple, interesting narrative style with numerous black-and-white illustrations. Others in the series are: *Meet Benjamin Franklin* (Maggi Scarf, 1989), *Meet Thomas Jefferson* (Marvin Barrett, 1989), and *Meet George Washington* (Joan Heilbroner, 1989).

Martin Luther King Day. Linda Lowery. Minnesota: Carolrhoda, 1987. Has large-type, easy-to-read text.

Harriet Tubman. The Great American Series. Kathie Billingslea Smith, illustrated by James Seward. New York: Simon & Schuster, Little Simon, 1988. This booklet is well illustrated with a combination of colored drawings and photographic reproductions from the National Archives.

Go Free or Die: A Story about Harriet Tubman. Jeri Ferris, illustrations by Karen Ritz. Minneapolis: Carolrhoda, 1988. This booklet and the one above led a young black volunteer literacy student into the world of her roots, a world she'd never encountered in school. She began an intense, academic research study that continues to this day.

Young Albert Einstein. Laurence Santrey, illustrated by Ellen Beier. Mahwah, N.J.: Troll, 1990.

Gandhi. Longman American Structural Readers. Lewis Jones. White Plains, N.Y.: Longman, 1985. This booklet has clear, comic book-like illustrations and includes a 500-word vocabulary list. The text is clearly written and the story is well told.

Classics

Grimm's Fairy Tales. Illustrated in color by Noel Pocock. New York: Children's Classics, 1988. The typeface is a little hard on the eyes, but this is a fine collection of the old stories, making it good bedtime reading.

Giovanni's Room. James Baldwin. New York: Dell, 1977. Though very difficult reading for ESL students, when I put it into a historical context and showed a video on Baldwin's life, this proved an extremely motivating book. It is borrowed continually from my personal lending library.

Go Tell It on the Mountain. James Baldwin, New York: Dell, 1970.

Of Mice and Men. John Steinbeck. New York: Penguin, 1993. An ethical dilemma that can lead to thoughtful dialogue.

The Winter of Our Discontent. John Steinbeck. New York: Penguin, 1986.

Black Boy. Richard Wright. New York: Harper & Row, 1989. Powerful, honest storytelling.

Beautiful Pictures / Novelty

The Very Hungry Caterpillar. Eric Carle. New York: Philomel, 1969, 1987. Available as a large book or in a tiny-book version. The caterpillar eats his way through the days of the week, numbers, and a grand assortment of foods. (There are many good Eric Carle books in print. Some are only in hardcover; others are also available in paperback.)

The Very Busy Spider. Eric Carle. New York: Philomel, 1989. The tactile surface of the spider's web grows on each page. Letting either the young child or the adult new reader connect with the book through the sense of touch can be the beginning of a connection with literacy in general.

The Mixed-up Chameleon. Eric Carle. New York: Harper & Row, 1984. This great introduction-to-colors book also deals with too many wishes coming true.

Round Trip. Ann Jonas. New York: Scholastic, 1983. There is very little text per page, but once you get to the last page rightside up, you must turn the book upside down and continue reading!

The Little Drummer Boy. Ezra Jack Keats. New York: Macmillan, 1987. Keats is an author/ illustrator. Any of his work is worthwhile. This book puts each line of the song on a different page and includes beautiful illustrations.

The Weaving of a Dream. Marilee Heyer. New York: Puffin, 1989. This enchantingly illustrated retelling of a Chinese folktale has large blocks of text, making it a good bedtime storybook for one caregiver and one child.

Oh My, a Fly! Jan Pienkowski. Los Angeles: Price, Stern, Sloan, 1989. This pop-up book tells the story of the little old lady who swallowed a fly and many other creatures.

A Book of Boxes. Books for Young Readers. Laura Mason. New York: Simon and Schuster, 1989. Each two-page spread has a surprise of a different kind in a different kind of box. This book won't last long but will be fun while it does.

The Eleventh Hour: A Curious Mystery. Graeme Base. New York: Harry N. Abrams, 1988. Available in heavy cardcover through Scholastic. This is *the* book to buy for the eleventh birthday of anyone you know. Base wrote it specifically for that usually overlooked year. The elaborate and detailed illustrations lead the reader through a you-solve-it birthday mystery. But if you can't figure it out, you can break the seal at the back of the book to see the answer Base thinks is correct.

Easy Reading

Old Devil Wind. Bill Martin, Jr., illustrated by Barry Root. New York: Harcourt Brace, 1993. Text © 1971 by Holt, Rinehart and Winston, Inc. Each two-page spread of this inventive, predictable text is an understated work of Halloween intrigue. A great read in itself, I've found it makes marvelous readers' theatre fare.

The Five Chinese Brothers. Claire Huchet Bishop and Kurt Wiese. New York: Sandcastle, 1989.

Do You Want to Be My Friend? Eric Carle. New York: Philomel, 1988. The simple question is repeated throughout the book. There is only one line of type on each page. The powerful illustrations provide a surprise ending.

Have You Seen My Cat? Eric Carle. Saxonville, Mass.: Picture Book Studio, 1987. The sixteen-word vocabulary will allow even the earliest reader a chance to enjoy a *whole* book.

The Very Quiet Cricket. Eric Carle. New York: Philomel, 1990. A beautifully illustrated book with very little text, but the text that's there is predictable. It is ideal for the young child who has zero reading experience. When the last page is turned, you hear a cricket chirp!

Mouse Soup. Arnold Lobel. New York: Harper & Row, 1977. Large, easy-to-read type; funny stories. Introduces the new reader to use of quotation marks and other conversational punctuation forms. Gives the ESL student of any age good, conversational English in an easy-to-read context supported by simple drawings.

Mouse Tales. Arnold Lobel. New York: Harper & Row, 1972. See above.

George Shrinks. William Joyce. New York: Harper & Row, 1985. Only one line of text per well-illustrated page.

The Pied Piper of Hamelin. Deborah Hautzig. New York: Random House, 1989. Good illustrations, easy-to-read type, good story. Shel Silverstein has written a poem response to this story, so I present the story and then the poem to foster the idea that the reader becomes a writer and that reading gives you ideas.

One Fine Day. Nonny Hogrogian. New York: Aladdin, 1971. Predictable text and a fun-to-read story.

Stone Soup. Retold by Ann McGovern, pictures by Winslow Pinney Pels. New York: Scholastic, 1986. (A dramatization on cassette is also available.) Predictable text and more comes with this old folktale with funny, funny illustrations.

The Mystery of the Missing Red Mitten. A Pied Piper Book. Steven Kellogg. New York: Dial, 1979.

The Mysterious Tadpole. A Pied Piper Book. Steven Kellogg. New York: Puffin, 1992. This is the story of a nice little pet tadpole that becomes a huge dinosaurlike creature belonging to a very little boy.

The Story of Ferdinand. Munro Leaf. New York: Puffin, 1964. This excellent message is well delivered by a bull who would rather smell flowers than fight.

Fredrick. Leo Lionni. New York: Alfred A.Knopf, Dragonfly, 1967. This, like other Lionni books, has a universal message. It values Frederick, a different kind of mouse, who collects stories for the winter instead of nuts.

Alexander and the Wind-Up Mouse. Leo Lionni. New York: Pantheon, 1969. A strong message about loneliness and not being liked all the time.

The Paper Bag Princess. Robert Munsch. Toronto: Annick, 1980. This is a spoof on chivalry, feminism, folklore, and other sacred cows. A good gift for females of any age who have just broken up with a mate or who seem overly concerned about finding one. (Robert Munsch has many other excellent books on the market. They are well-illustrated and fun to read.)

The Alphabet Tree. Leo Lionni. New York: Alfred A. Knopf, Dragonfly, 1968. The social message here is peace.

Regards to the Man in the Moon. Ezra Jack Keats. New York: Macmillan, 1981. Minimal text per page, great illustrations.

A Giraffe and a Half. Shel Silverstein. New York: Harper & Row, 1964. This predictable text has great black-and-white illustrations and is a wonderful read-aloud treat for children. (It's also a hit at stuffy meetings.) It does more than lead you through an incredible vocabulary adventure; the progression of the text also fosters fraction awareness. An excellent choice for your favorite math teacher's birthday.

The Missing Piece. Shel Silverstein. New York: Harper & Row, 1976. This simple story has only one or two lines of text on each page, so it is great for children. But it carries a double message, so it is also great for the very sophisticated adult.

The Missing Piece Meets the Big O. Shel Silverstein. New York: Harper & Row, 1981. A companion piece to *The Missing Piece.*

More Text, Fewer Pictures

Coyote & Native American Folktales. Retold by Joe Hayes, illustrations by Lucy Jelinek. Santa Fe, N.M.: Mariposa, 1985.

The Stories Julian Tells. Ann Cameron, illustrated by Ann Strugnell. New York: Alfred A. Knopf, Bullseye, 1981. Humorous stories, large print, detailed black-and-white illustrations.

Are You There God? It's Me, Margaret. A Dell Yearling Book. Judy Blume. New York: Dell, 1979. This sensitive coming-of-age book has long been popular with young teens, so I gave it to a teenaged Amerasian, who shared it with a Columbian, who turned it over to an Asian general, who shared it with a young Iranian, who really got hooked on Judy Blume.

Timeless Tales. Retold by Tana Reiff. Syracuse, N.Y.: New Readers Press, 1991. A series of four books written for new readers: *Myths, Fables, Legends,* and *Folk Tales.* The text is large and the illustrations are well done. Although the books do come with cassettes, the reader does not model good storytelling and the cassettes serve to discourage rather than encourage further use among fluent speakers of English. Some beginning ESL students, however, appreciate being able to hear each word pronounced separately and distinctly.

Adults Only

Uncle Shelby's ABZ Book. Shel Silverstein. New York: Simon & Schuster, 1961. Suggests things little children might be tempted to try—like how to get the fire truck to come to your house.

The House That Crack Built. Clark Taylor, illustrated by Jan Thompson Dicks. San Francisco: Chronicle, 1992. This haunting, predictable text follows the meter of the famous children's rhyme *This Is the House that Jack Built* as it chronicles the impact of cocane from the drug baron to the farmer to the baby of the addict. I first introduce the original rhyme and then this book. Language and literacy levels make no difference as the primitive illustrations and methodical text pound out a universally disturbing commentary. It is not a gift book, but everyone who sees it wants a copy to keep.

Pairs of Books

When I give my nephews books that are available in two sizes, I buy both. That way, my sister will cherish and care for the big version and the kids can carry their little ones around at will.

There are large and small versions of the following Eric Carle predictable book titles:

The Very Hungry Caterpillar
Do You Want to Be My Friend?
Have You Seen My Cat?
The Very Busy Spider.
The Little Engine That Could. The Complete Original Edition. Watty Piper. New York: Platt & Munk, 1989. There is a new, improved "simplified" book by the same title that is very easy to confuse with the authentic story. The "easy reader" is more difficult to understand in some places and lacks much of the spirit of the original. Make sure to get the original text.

English and Spanish

For the monolingual teacher or tutor or one whose other languages do not include Spanish, having easy-to-read books available in both English and Spanish imparts some of the bilingual advantage to students whose native language is Spanish. As a side effect, the English speaker may start to pick up elementary Spanish vocabulary. This is empowering to the student, who may not be able to read well but who can certainly take the professional role regarding the Spanish pronunciation.

Perro Grande . . . Perro Pequeno/Big Dog . . . Little Dog. A Randomhouse Pictureback. P.D. Eastman. New York: Random House, 1982. This has bilingual text on each page.
El Bebe de los osos Berenstain/The Berenstain Bears' New Baby. A Randomhouse Pictureback. Stan and Jan Berenstain. New York: Random House, 1982. This has bilingual text on each page.
Alexander, que era rico el domingo pasado/Alexander, Who Used to Be Rich Last Sunday. Judith Viorst. New York: Macmillan,

Alladin, 1978. This problem is humorous in any language. All of the Alexander series are popular.

Donde Viven los Monstruos/Where the Wild Things Are. Maurice Sendak. New York: Harper & Row, 1963. Madrid: Alfacuara,1989. This is a wonderful read-aloud book.

La Oruga Muy Hamrienta/The Very Hungry Caterpillar. Eric Carle. New York: Philomel, 1989. The preliterate Spanish-speaking mother can learn to read as she reads this story in Spanish. Later, having built up background knowledge, mother and child can convert to the English version with ease.

La Pequena Locomotora Que Si Pudo. Version Origian Completa/ *The Little Engine That Could.* The Complete Original Edition. Watty Piper. New York: Platt & Munk, 1989, 1992. In several cases when I've had adult students using the English copy as a translation dictionary, the students reverse it midway on the first pass and start using the Spanish book as the translation dictionary. This story has just enough predictability to make it work for low-level or new readers or ESL students.

More Advanced Bilingual Options

Dover Publications, Inc., New York, has a Dual-Language Book series that offers classic short stories in the original Spanish, Italian, or French, with the English translation on the opposite page. This allows students studying either language to attempt quality reading in the target language while having the convenience of idiomatic translations immediately accessible.

Planet-Friendly Books

Rain forests, oceans, animals, and other natural gifts have a universal quality. Though not all of my students arrive caring about any of that stuff, the fact that I'm willing to haul in the research material contrasts sharply with the kinds of things they must dig out of the archives for themselves just to write a paper for class. Over time, the consciousness is raised and occasionally zealots develop.

The Rainforest Book. Scott Lewis, with a foreword by Robert Redford. Venice, Calif.: Living Planet, 1990. This book has very brief, single-topic focus items within its long chapters, so a focus item can be used to whet the appetite for the longer reading. It covers a wide range of issues and provides addresses of places to write for more information.

Rain Forest Secrets. Written and illustrated by Arthur Dorros. New York: Scholastic, 1990. This children's book presents a lot of scientific information in a palatable form. My adult students often ask to borrow it.

The Great Kapok Tree: A Tale of the Amazon Rain Forest. Lynne Cherry. San Diego: Harcourt Brace Jovanovich, Gulliver, 1990. The illustrations in this book are of actual Amazonian flora and fauna. Inside the front and back covers are two-page spreads locating existing and formerly existing rain forests around the world. The world map has a border of rain forest animals. In the story, a variety of animals come down out of a rain forest tree to whisper in the ear of a sleeping logger and ask him to spare the great kapok tree, their home. The book is dedicated to the memory of Chico Mendes, a rubber farmer killed because of his efforts to prevent logging in the rain forests of Brazil. Occasionally I use it to introduce the two-page Chico Mendes story in *The Rainforest Book*. This beautiful book is a wonderful gift for adults and children.

The Sign of the Seahorse: A Tale of Greed and High Adventure in Two Acts. Written and illustrated by Graeme Base. New York: Harry N. Abrams, 1992. With traditionally detailed and colorful illustrations, Base leads the reader into an epic poem that progresses from a seahorse hangout, teeming with life, to the destruction of a coral reef. Appropriate for all ages.

50 Simple Things You Can Do to Save the Earth. Berkeley: Earth Works, 1989. This little paperback is chockfull of one-and two-page essays on how to save the earth. It includes a multitude of places to write for more information.

15 Simple Things Californians Can Do to Recycle. Berkeley: Earth Works, 1991. The same idea as above, only localized.

Heron Street. Ann Turner, paintings by Lisa Disimini. New York: Scholastic, 1989. The paintings throughout the book give it an eerie mood as the story leads us from a wildlife-filled American shore where herons live, hearing only the sounds of the grass, to the arrival of pilgrims, soldiers, children, and homes. One home has a dog that barks at the single heron who flies over a now tamed land. This story and its pictures speak profoundly.

Four Against the Odds. Stephen Krensky. New York: Scholastic, 1992. Four biographies of environmentalists serve to open the eyes and whet the appetite for a better world.

Aesop's Fables

It is good to see the same story told in different ways:

- For the good reader, it is very interesting to see how the same tales have been modified to reflect the morals of the time. And different selections are more popular during different political climates. The thing about Aesop is, he's got something for everyone.
- For the new reader coming across a familiar story with a lot of new text, the comfortable sense of security that comes with background knowledge encourages the skipping strategy when an individual word is impossible to read.
- For the ESL student from a storytelling home, Aesop's tales have often been heard in the native language, again providing background knowledge.

However, because the texts have been getting retold for almost three thousand years now, there are some wonderful collections with some very old English (and not just English, I'll bet). And some collections include selections from various sources, with no attempt made to standardize the writing. So before getting too taken by the typically interesting illustrations, read several random fables to get a taste of what's in store for the reader. A case in point is the first one on my list, a reissue of a 1600s text including that spelling, and decorated by line drawings by the famous Alexander Calder. I give copies of it to artists, historians, English teachers, and linguists, but never to computer-science majors!

Fables of Aesop According to Sir Roger L'Estrange, with Fifty Drawings by Alexander Calder. New York: Dover, 1967. This is not a book for children; nor is it for new users of English. It uses much of the English vocabulary and spelling of the 1600s. It is a wonderful gift book for the literate art lover. Adults only.

Aesop's Fables Illustrated in Color by Charles Santore. New York: Jelly Bean, 1988. This large, hardcover book has only one fable per page and beautiful illustrations. The text is large and the stories are well written. It is appropriate for any age. There is a three-page foldout picture of the race between the tortoise and the hare. It is a conversation piece!

Aesop's Fables. Retold by Anne Gatti, illustrated by Safaya Salter. Orlando: Harcourt Brace Jovanovich,1992. Many of the illustrations in this book are suitable for framing, and the text is written in clear language with clean type, making it a charming gift book, if you can bring yourself to give it away.

The Lion and the Mouse. A Pop-up Book. New York: Ottenheimer, Derrydale, 1988. This is one of a series of Aesop stories in pop-up form.

Aesop's Fables. New York: Exeter, 1987. This has clearly written text with just a few color illustrations. It spends two to three pages per fable and so is not appropriate for the very new reader.

The Fables of Aesop with Drawings by Frank Riccio. Chicago: Calico, 1988. One fable occupies a page or a page and a half, with simple illustrations. Good for intermediate readers and all Aesop lovers. It may have gone out of print!

Aesop's Fables Illustrated by Arthur Rackham. New York: Avenel. A facsimile of the 1912 edition. These are very short little fables, two or three per page with clusters around one moral. It has nice line drawings and a few colored illustrations.

Aesop's Fables with Drawings by Fritz Kredel. New York: Grosset & Dunlap, (1947) 1988. This edition has many clear line drawings and a few color plates. Well written, clear language.

Aesop's Fables Retold by Graeme Kent. Illustrated by Tessa Hamilton. Newmarket, U.K.: Brimax, 1991. There is only one illustrated fable per page. However, in addition to the modern color plates, tiny reproductions of woodcuts from around 1800 are inset here and there. The book is a visual delight and the fables are well written.

The Aesop for Children with Pictures by Milo Winter. New York: Checkerboard, (1919) 1947. A fourteen-by-twelve-inch trim, heavy cardboard cover, large print, colorful illustrations on nearly every page. This one has a plain moral stated at the end of each fable—1919 style.

Aesop's Fables: A Classic Illustrated Edition. Compiled by Russell Ash and Bernard Higton. San Francisco: Chronicle, 1990. These fables are written in modern English, with traditional morals after each. The illustrations (at least one for each fable) are collected from Aesop editions from the 1850s to the present day, from Randolph Caldecott to Alexander Calder. This is a book to be read and looked at or revered and preserved. It is appropriate for any age and any audience. An art lover's delight.

Aesop's Fables Illustrated by Fluvio Testa. Hauppauge, N.Y.: Barron's Educational Series, 1989. Translated from an Italian publication, this version does not state the moral anywhere. The text is easy on the eyes and is well written. There is one fable per page, with a full-page illustration opposite. It is a joy to view.

Aesop's Fables. Illustrated by Nora Fry. New York: Children's Classics, 1989. Hardcover with newsprintlike pages, a few color plates, a few line drawings. The print is large enough to read easily, but stories may be broken up over several pages. The introduction says it contains some old spellings and punctuation, though I haven't located them . . . but the way I spell, a lot can look normal that isn't. There are traditional

idiom messages at the ends of all the fables, some of which I
have not found elsewhere.

Aesop's Fables. Illustrated by Lisbeth Zwerger. Saxonville,
Mass.: Picture Book Studio, 1989. Clear, modern language
tells the fable and spells out the moral on one page, while
fresh watercolor illustrations are on the opposite page.

Aesop's Fables. Retold by Ann McGovern, illustrations by A.
J. McClaskey. New York: Scholastic, 1963. Cheap paperback
with newsprint-quality pages. About seventy fables written
in modern English, each with a moral fed into the last line.
My teaching favorite!

Aesop's Fables Retold by Steven Zorn. Philadelphia: Running Press, 1990. A miniature hardback with fourteen fables.
Considering the small size of the book, the text is quite large.
The messages are vignetted in a nice frame at the end of
each.

Aesop's Fables. Reset in new typeface from editions in the public
domain, illustrated by Walt Sturrock. Morris Plains, N.J.:
Unicorn, 1988. With a full-page color illustration on the left
and a fable set in an elegant border on the right, this book is
a delight to behold. But, much of the wording is stiff, reflecting
the older texts from which it is drawn (for example, "Cease
your blows" is used instead of "Stop hitting him!") This is no
problem for the good reader, but can confound an ESL or
new reader. So, the moral is: consider the audience before
you buy the gift.

Aesop's Fables. Retold by Blanche Winder, introduction by
Earle Toppings. New York: Airmont, 1965. Easy-to-read English. There are no messages at the end.

Aesop's Fables. Introduced by Isaac Bashevis Singer, based on
the translations of George Flyer Townsend, illustrated by
Murray Tinkelman. New York: Doubleday, 1968. Clear language. Clean little ink illustrations here and there.

Aesop's Fables. Retold by Fiona Black, illustrated by Richard
Bernal. Kansas City, Mo.: Andrews and McMeel, Ariel, 1991.
A small thirty-two-page book, six-by-five-inch trim. The print

is easy to read and the English is modern and well written. This is a nice giftbook.

Aesop's Fables Selected and Illustrated by Michael Hague. New York: Henry Holt, 1985. Ten-by-twelve-inch trim, twenty-seven very nicely illustrated pages. The print is large and the English is clear modern prose.

Fables of Aesop. Translated by S. A. Handford, illustrations by Brian Robb. New York: Penguin, 1954. This is a huge collection of seldom seen and familiar fables. It is of interest to the collector. WARNING: *This is not classroom appropriate.* Bigoted and racist messages are incorporated right in with up-to-date ones.

Not Aesop, But

Fables for Our Time. James Thurber. New York: Harper and Row, Perennial Library, 1983. Thurber makes fun of all that is precious and American, including, but certainly not limited to, Little Red Riding Hood, Ben Franklin, Abe Lincoln, and even Aesop!

Reference Books

There are numerous fine reference books on the market. The following comments are just indicators of how to select student-appropriate ones.

Webster's New Collegiate Dictionary. A Merriam-Webster. A great deal of information about writing, grammar, and punctuation. Better than buying a grammar book.

Webster's Collegiate Thesaurus. A Merriam-Webster. Has alphabetical leaf markers, clear text, easy to read.

The New Roget's Thesaurus in Dictionary Form. Edited by Norman Lewis. Newsprint paper but a clear, easy-to-read text.

Longman Dictionary of American English. White Plains, N.Y.: Longman, 1983. A dictionary for learners of English. Written for nonnative speakers of English, this book gives basic grammatical information, a few full-page illustrations identifying all items in a room or store, and other very helpful hints that assist the person unaccustomed to using the dictionary. For example, at the bottom of a page of words starting with f, there is a boxed message: SPELLING NOTE, words with the sound /f/ may be spelled **ph-**, like **photograph**.

The New Oxford Picture Dictionary. English/Spanish Edition. Edited by E. C. Parnwell, translated by Sergio Gaitan. New York: Oxford University Press, 1989. Adults appreciate the clear, colorful, number-coded pictures on every page. There is a one-word-to-one-word Spanish/English representation for each item pictured on the page. In the back of the book there are some easy reference charts for the days of the week, months of the year, basic colors, and numbers. The English/Spanish version is one of a growing series of bilingual dictionaries. I have found that many ESL adults enjoy having them to support their children's first language literacy.

Dictionary for Children. Newly Revised Edition. Edited by Judith S. Levey. New York: Macmillan Publishing Company, 1989. This dictionary has a clear, easy-to-read typeface and uses the selected words in sentences.

Appendix A

The Affective Filter and Learning Problems

*I*t is common knowledge that when we are under stress, we are able to do far less than when we are relaxed and comfortable. However, most stress and learning research has to do with *output* (or what the learner can *do*—write, speak, recite, read aloud) rather than *input* (or what the learner can take in—hearing, seeing, feeling). But three researchers, Dulay, Burt, and Krashen, have come up with a term that accounts for many learning problems relating to *input*. They call it the "affective filter."

The filter, as they explain it, is a wall of feelings that is very low when the child is born. Babies learn tremendous amounts of information during their first few days and weeks of life: faces, feelings, friends, how to get food. According to Frank Smith learning is what the brain is designed to do. Real learning occurs naturally and effortlessly. Therefore, just as the stomach craves food for the body that a hungry person must supply, so does the brain crave information that an inquisitive mind must discover—unless external forces disturb the process. As babies begin to have negative experiences, their affective filters begin to rise, making it more difficult for new information to enter the brain. During times that the young are happy and comfortable, the filters will lower, but never again to point *zero*. Young children, however, still manage to learn tremendous amounts every day. When they are relaxed and happy, they easily and automatically process *life*.

But, let us suppose that they are in a stressful situation. Let us suppose they are in a home where big people yell a lot or hit the smaller ones. The young children will experience stress that will cause the affective filter to go up—like a shield against unfriendly energy. They have no control over it— indeed, perhaps it is there to keep them from processing so much bad information they lose the will to live.

So, the person who is yelled at or hit at home—or who witnesses such violence—may have such a high filter that he or she arrives at school a disabled learner. Such a learner may want very much to do well, but will have the echo of yelling or memory of abuse overpowering everything else. If the student is very lucky, she or he may get a teacher who will comprehend the filter's barrier to learning and who will work to lower it at least for the school hours. As often as not, however, the child will be confronted with performance demands that call for *output* when, indeed, no *input* has served as a foundation. For example, the child may be forced to answer questions when he or she just doesn't know the answers, or will be commanded to read aloud when he or she doesn't know the words. Under such circumstances, the child may begin to get a high filter from simply walking into the classroom—or *any* classroom. Over time, the child will learn to believe that he or she is too stupid to learn. This opinion can last a lifetime. And people who *believe* they *can't* learn will make that prophesy come true.

The implications of the affective filter extend across all age groups, across subjects, and to both first and second language learners. Adult students who find themselves in high stress situations—such as a death in the family, an automobile accident, or loss of a job—need to understand that their learning level will be reduced. Knowing that, they need to either put themselves into situations that will support learning, or give themselves time off when things are too stressful. Adult learners who understand the affective filter have both the wisdom to expect the reasonable of themselves and the power to control their own learning environments.

References:

Stephen D. Krashen, *Inquiries and Insights* (Hayward, Calif.: Alemany Press, 1985) 10–11.

Frank Smith, *Insult to Intelligence* (Portsmouth, N.H.: Heinemann, 1985).

————, *To Think* (New York: Teachers College Press, 1990).

Ray Rist, "Student Social class and teacher expectations: The Self-fulfilling prophecy in Ghetto Education," *Harvard Educational Review* 40(3) (August 1970): 411–51.

————, "Social Distance and Social Inequality in a Ghetto Kindergarten Classroom," *Urban Education* 7 (October 1972): 241–60.

Appendix B

Summarizing Ray C. Rist

"Student Social Class and Teacher Expectations: The Self-fulfilling Prophecy in Ghetto Education," and Its Implications for Adult Learners

Rist found that teacher expectations not only led teachers to treat expected low achievers differently, the teacher's behavior set up a classroom pecking order that was never reversed.

There was a study done in 1970 by a man named Ray Rist who had decided to spend time in a New York ghetto classroom. He agreed not to write which classroom or which school it was or the names of any of the students in the classroom because he was not trying to embarrass anyone. He just wanted to find out why the ghetto children were not achieving as well as the children in other schools. So, he ended up studying the same group of kids for three years, first observing them in kindergarten, then in first grade, and then in the second grade.

During the time that Rist was in the classroom he kept track of who said what. He kept track of how many times the teacher called on each child. He kept track of which kids got to do special tasks in the classroom—like lead in the Pledge of Allegiance. Rist also interviewed each of the three teachers the children had during the years he was observing them.

He discovered that the kids who the teachers *thought would not do well* were the same ones the teacher *did not call on for fun activities* in the classroom. He also discovered that those same children were *called on for answers much less often* than the kids the teacher had first thought were "smart." He also observed that the children who were *expected to do badly were corrected or ridiculed* for their classroom behavior *much more often* than the kids the teachers expected would do well.

And he documented another very interesting classroom phenomena. The kids the teacher picked on were picked on by other, higher achieving students in the class. In fact, there was a kind of barnyard pecking order that established itself in the classroom. And the children who were expected to do well in their lessons picked on the slower students. BUT THE PROCESS WAS NEVER REVERSED! The poor students never spoke up to defend themselves against the teacher or the higher students in the classroom. Likewise, the low achieving students accepted the level of achievement the teacher expected of them.

This process is called the self-fulfilling prophecy because kids learn very quickly to behave the way teachers expect them to behave. The kids fulfill the prophecy that is given to them. That is to say they will act smart or they will act stupid because they trust that what adults say is true. That means there are big differences in school performance even though all students who have learned to speak a language by the age of five have proven their brains are as sophisticated as a brain needs to be. A person who can speak one language *can* learn *anything*. Yet *learning* depends on self-perception.

One obvious implication adult learners can take from this study is that environmentally imposed learning restrictions were placed on them in ignorance. When the adult decides to break a disempowering prophecy, incredible things can happen. Adults who suddenly *believe* they can learn, CAN LEARN. Informed adults have the power destroy disabling myths of the past . . . to change their own prophecies.

Reference: Ray C. Rist, "Student social class and teacher expectations: The Self-fulfilling Prophecy in Ghetto

Education," *Harvard Educational Review* 40(3) (August 1970): 411–51.

"Social Distance and Social Inequality in a Ghetto Kindergarten Classroom" and Its Implications for Adult Learners

In 1972 Ray Rist conducted a one-year study in a kindergarten classroom. Early in the year, the teacher placed the children into three *ability groups: high, medium, and low.* The groups indicated what kinds of students the children were. It is important to remember that this was the first time any of these kids had ever been to school. So, they had no academic records for the teacher to check.

When Rist began to question *how the children were assigned to their groups*, he found that it had to do with *what the children looked like* and *how much money their parents made.*

Rist's earlier study had shown that what the teacher expected was what the teacher got in terms of classroom performance. The 1972 study showed that the expectations had nothing to do with what the kids were willing or able to do. This is a very important finding because it helps to explain why kids from poorer or less educated families tend to do more poorly in many schools. The teachers did not understand that they were making this kind of difference to the students and the students thought that they were born to be in some particular academic level. The Rist study starts to explain why poor students run in families. Because of this and other studies, adult students can begin to look at ways of controlling their own intellectual achievement.

Reference: Ray Rist, "Social Distance and Social Inequality in a Ghetto Kindergarten Classroom," *Urban Education* 7 (October 1972): 241–60.

Appendix C

California Literacy Campaign
Adult Learner Questionnaire

This form, which was the one I used when working with the cases documented in this book, is reprinted here with the permission of California State Librarian Gary Strong, who reminds you that the form is under constant revision as a result of suggestions from adult learners and tutors in the CLC programs. A new edition is in press now. In addition, State Literacy Specialist Al Bennett wants me to clarify that the form is part of a "process" and is used by the learner-tutor team to self-assess achievement and identify goals.

Readers who wish more information should address their inquiries to:

Literacy Specialist
Library Development Services
California State Library
Post Office Box 942837
Sacramento, California 94237-0001

Because the California Adult Learner Progress Evaluation Process (CALPEP) form was designed from input of CLC adult learners and their tutors all over the state, it reflects a variety of philosophies of education at once. The sections I have crossed out are ones I chose not to use. They reflect a bottom-up, parts-to-whole philosophy that has been phased out of the newer versions of the questionnaire.

It may be interesting to note a few points regarding perceptions about reading and writing reflected in the sections that adult learners and their tutors have chosen to discard:

• Reading   *R–Readiness recognizes letters and numbers* suggests these little parts must be recognized before a unit of letters like one's own name or the word STOP. The adults involved in this process discovered that this sequence was backwards. *A–Application to new situation.* Even though they could not

---

CALIFORNIA STATE LIBRARY
California Adult Learner
Progress Evaluation Process

REQUIRED INFORMATION

WHERE WE STARTED
(Please discuss all the following questions with the adult learner by the end of the third tutoring session.)

Adult Learner's name: _____

Tutor's name: _____

(1) **Date:** ___ ___ ___
　　　　　　Mo.　Day　Yr.

(2) **Reading habits:**

Here is a list of some things that people often read. How often do you read these things *outside the tutoring session?*

Of those you do read, which are easy for you to read; which are hard?

	Not at all	Sometimes (once or twice a week)	Regularly (almost every day)	Easy to Read	A Little Hard	Very Hard
Street/traffic signs	☐	☐	☐	○	○	○
Menus	☐	☐	☐	○	○	○
Mail/bills/letters	☐	☐	☐	○	○	○
Labels/instructions	☐	☐	☐	○	○	○
Notes from school	☐	☐	☐	○	○	○
Bank machines, etc.	☐	☐	☐	○	○	○
Comics	☐	☐	☐	○	○	○
Reading books to child	☐	☐	☐	○	○	○
T.V. guides	☐	☐	☐	○	○	○
Newspapers	☐	☐	☐	○	○	○
Magazines	☐	☐	☐	○	○	○
Religious materials	☐	☐	☐	○	○	○
Work materials	☐	☐	☐	○	○	○
Books	☐	☐	☐	○	○	○
Other _____	☐	☐	☐	○	○	○

have read the studies on the self-fulfilling prophecy (Appendix B) and the affective filter (Appendix A), all of the learners in this book were able to apply the concepts to incidents in their own lives and to project application of those ideas in situations beyond their own lives. This recognizes that humans can think abstractly even if they have not had a chance to learn the alphabet.

CALIFORNIA STATE LIBRARY - *California Adult Learner Progress Evaluation Process*

---

(3) Writing habits:

Here is a list of some things that people often write. How often do you write these things *outside the tutoring session?*

Of those you do write, which are easy for you to write; which are hard?

	Not at all	Sometimes (once or twice a week)	Regularly (almost every day)	Easy to Write	A Little Hard	Very Hard
Checks	☐	☐	☐	○	○	○
Notes/memos	☐	☐	☐	○	○	○
Orders	☐	☐	☐	○	○	○
Recipes	☐	☐	☐	○	○	○
Forms/applications	☐	☐	☐	○	○	○
Reports	☐	☐	☐	○	○	○
Letters	☐	☐	☐	○	○	○
Stories/poems	☐	☐	☐	○	○	○
Articles	☐	☐	☐	○	○	○
Greeting cards	☐	☐	☐	○	○	○
Crossword puzzles	☐	☐	☐	○	○	○
Other _____	☐	☐	☐	○	○	○

(4) Outside the tutoring session, approximately how much time do you read during a typical week?

☐ Not at all
☐ A few minutes
☐ About an hour
☐ Two to three hours
☐ Four or more hours

(5) Outside the tutoring session, approximately how much time do you write during a typical week?

☐ Not at all
☐ A few minutes
☐ About an hour
☐ Two to three hours
☐ Four or more hours

(6) Reading Goals:
The adult learner wants to improve his/her reading so he/she can . . .

Indicate CLC Start Level

	R	W	S	P	A
Goal: _____	☐	☐	☐	☐	☐
Goal: _____	☐	☐	☐	☐	☐
Goal: _____	☐	☐	☐	☐	☐
Goal: _____	☐	☐	☐	☐	☐

- Writing   *R–Readiness—write letter and numbers* at the top and *Application for different purposes* at the bottom reflects an early confusion between penmanship and authorship. Even though he was miserable trying to use a pencil, Danny was able to write all kinds of essays, using his tutor as a secretary. Computer word processing programs promise to make a significant contribution to the writing performance of all authors.

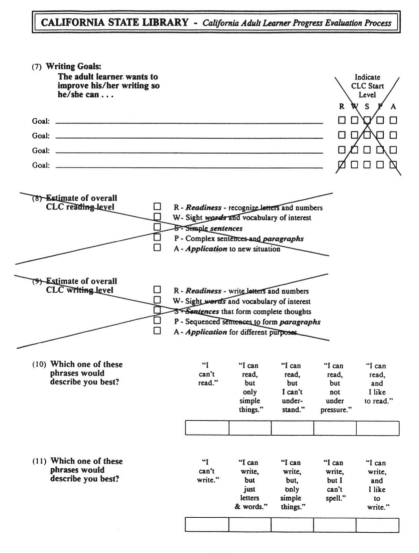

```
╔══════════════════════════════════════════════════════════════╗
║ CALIFORNIA STATE LIBRARY - California Adult Learner Progress Evaluation Process ║
╚══════════════════════════════════════════════════════════════╝
```

(7) **Writing Goals:**
The adult learner. wants to improve his/her writing so he/she can . . .

Indicate CLC Start Level

R W S P A

Goal: _____   □ □ □ □ □
Goal: _____   □ □ □ □ □
Goal: _____   □ □ □ □ □
Goal: _____   □ □ □ □ □

(8) **Estimate of overall CLC reading level**

□ R - *Readiness* - recognize letters and numbers
□ W- Sight *words* and vocabulary of interest
□ S - *Simple sentences*
□ P - Complex sentences and *paragraphs*
□ A - *Application* to new situation

(9) **Estimate of overall CLC writing level**

□ R - *Readiness* - write letters and numbers
□ W- Sight *words* and vocabulary of interest
□ S - *Sentences* that form complete thoughts
□ P - Sequenced sentences to form *paragraphs*
□ A - *Application* for different purposes

(10) **Which one of these phrases would describe you best?**

"I can't read."	"I can read, but only simple things."	"I can read, but I can't understand."	"I can read, but not under pressure."	"I can read, and I like to read."

(11) **Which one of these phrases would describe you best?**

"I can't write."	"I can write, but just letters & words."	"I can write, but, only simple things."	"I can write, but I can't spell."	"I can write, and I like to write."

Appendix D

Reading Aloud to Your Children

*F*ollowing is an excerpt from a letter to a young mother who was just learning to read to her preschoolers. She wanted to help other young mothers understand the value of reading aloud to their children, so I offered her some of the theoretical notions I've learned.

Dear Rona,

Because your children are still quite young, there are some very simple books I want to share with you. But simple doesn't mean boring. Even the very first children's books should be selected with attention to the pictures and the story. And then there is a magical way of knowing when the book is no longer appropriate—the child loses interest. Interest is key to learning to love reading and it is critical for the avid reader. You can neither love nor passionately pursue something that makes you yawn. Reading attitudes predict all other academic success. So, when you understand reading development, you also understand what kinds of things to look for and the kinds of questions to ask as you visit your kids' schools.

There is a great deal of research that shows you will learn spelling, vocabulary, grammar, syntax, punctuation, and writing style just from reading for pleasure. This applies from the cradle to the grave. And for the very young, sitting in the parent's lap, that is where all this stuff starts.

(One of my class requirements is that students read for pleasure a minimum of 10 minutes every day. It doesn't sound like much, but it is really 300 minutes per month! Of course, more is even better. And it is equally important to have things to read that are not too difficult. When people are busy opening and closing the dictionary, they are losing precious leisure reading time. So, it is better to read a lot of easy material than a little bit of difficult material. The more you read, the easier it will get and the faster you will go.)

There are some wonderful children's stories that parents who are just developing literacy can read to themselves first and then read again and again to their children. Even our school library has begun to order from La Vergne's good reading list. I try to help adults with young children locate their local libraries. If it has a good children's book section, they are fortunate. If it doesn't, they need to know to ask the librarian where the best local children's collection is. What is important is that the parents understand what makes a good book so that they don't waste precious reading time and scarce funds on junk.

One of my favorite authors is Eric Carle. He has written and illustrated many marvelous children's books. Quite a few of them are published in both a big book version and in a tiny book edition. The little ones are cute and easy for youngsters to carry around, but the big ones are really easier for children and adults to read because the print is larger and much easier to see. When I send gifts to my nephews, I send the little ones to the kids and a big copy to my sister. That way she can read to them and they have their inexpensive little ones to look at all the time. But your local library should have many Eric Carle books for you to try out on your children. Then, on birthdays or at other gift-giving times, give them their favorites—or *your* favorites—ones *you'll* be glad to read again and again.

The Very Busy Spider is one of Carle's best pairs. It has a busy spider busily spinning a web you can actually feel grow as the story progresses. (What wonderful conversation

312

material for parent and child! It fosters the notion of talking ABOUT the book DURING the reading. It creates an expanded universe of language and ideas that springs from text and moves beyond.) And on every other page it repeats the lines, "The spider didn't answer. She was too busy spinning her web."

For young, new readers, there is something called "predictable text." It is pretty simple and works like this. There is something in the story that has to be repeated over and over. As you read the book out loud to a child, she or he will start to be able to guess what will be coming next. Before long, the child will begin to say the predictable part out loud as you read along. You just read slowly and let them chime in when they want to.

Several things happen when a mother (or father) does that.

1. The child learns that books are fun. This kind of activity goes on six to ten times a day in good kindergarten, first, second, and third grade classrooms.
2. The child starts to get some of the words from the book into her or his mind without even trying. This gets much better results than the old flash card memorization and it is not just painless, it is pleasurable.
3. Then, later, left alone with the book, the child will be able to "read" part of it without any help. Some people call this prereading. To me, it *is* reading.
4. Part of being a good reader is called "risk taking." It is taking a guess at what is coming next. It happens when you are about to turn a page and you guess what the word at the top of the next page will be. Maybe you're right, maybe you're wrong. If it makes sense, you keep reading; if it doesn't make sense, you back up and reread. Good readers do this all the time. Poor readers think they have to be perfect on the first try. Fearing failure, they don't take risks. Predictable text teaches risk taking.
5. Hearing the parent read aloud, make a wrong guess—one that confuses the reader, and then hearing the parent back

up to make things make sense, teaches the child that reading is about MEANING rather than PERFORMANCE. If the parent is willing to make a mistake, the child will learn that mistakes are just part of the process. If the parent is a risk taker, the child will be, too. On the other hand, if the parent can only perform when perfection is guaranteed, so little reading will be done, literacy will never become a family priority. Ideas about risk taking can carry over— into writing and into life in general.

6. Being free to chime in with the parts they predict, as you read along, teaches children that they are supposed to be ACTIVE in the reading process. It teaches them they are supposed to PARTICIPATE. This is very different from what happens when the teacher tells all the kids to be quiet and won't let anyone react as the teacher reads a book. You want to get kids to comment and question. It is very good to stop to respond to their remarks as you go along. The point is not to rush through the reading assignment; the point is to ENJOY interacting with the book. It also demonstrates that books are starting places for thought. If the thinking goes completely away from the text, that's OK. There isn't any rule that says the author is in charge of the reader's mind.

> *Text, regarded as thought provoker, empowers. It gives the reader a place to start independent thinking.*

Is this making sense? I've been in classrooms where a child would be punished for shouting, "Wow!" Such classrooms produce failures. They disempower. They destroy self-esteem.

7. There is something else that is probably more valuable than any of the other stuff. When the little girl is sitting in her mother's lap, listening to good stories, she is building memories that will last forever. Reading will become a comfortable and natural thing for her. And when she does it years later with her little girl, she'll remember Mama.

Being read to is very powerful. I always read to my students. There are questions they think of, as they hear me read, that don't come up when they are reading alone. Age doesn't matter. *Literate people read to each other...often. Illiterate people never do.*

Cheers!
La Vergne Rosow

Index

The theories and theoretical concepts presented to the learners in these case histories are shown here in bold type. Because they are occasionally implied, rather than explicitly named, you may find a reference to a theory that is discussed, but not otherwise identified on a page indicated. And you will notice that some theories or methods are limited to one chapter. Though I used a full pallet of possibilities with each case, in the interest of space, I detailed different features of the process within each study. For example, the use of *key words* is spelled out in detail only in Danny's story. But notice that *key words* is cross-referenced with *organic words* and *generative words*, because those are terms also applied to this *learner-centered process*. Yet, because the entire book is about the power of theory, some references have not been indexed at all. There is also the possibility of human error. Consistent with the philosophy of empowerment through the writing process, and cognitive development through dialogue, I do invite you to send me your notes about needed additions, changes or clarifications for inclusion in future editions.

Further, if you or your adult learners have anecdotes that you feel significantly support, enlarge or challenge the material in this book, I would love to see them.

We're all in this together.

La Vergne Rosow